'I was taken all the way back to the early sixties and The Railway Hotel in my hometown of Harrow, north-west London, where aged 15 I heard the blues played live for the first time. Those days, deeply influenced by Bob Dylan, are captured here magnificently by Tudor Jones.'

> —*Tony O'Malley*, *Co-founder of British soul pioneers Kokomo*
> *www.kokomo.band and a member of 10cc in the seventies.*
> *He also played on Dylan's 'Desire' album.*

'Tudor Jones has brought into focus the importance of 1960s Britain to the formation and consolidation of the emblematic and enigmatic Bob Dylan, from his early appearance in the BBC play "Madhouse on Castle Street" when he was still absorbing all the musical genres he could, including the melodies and rhythms of English Folk Music from Martin Carthy, to the fully formed icon, the "Great White Wonder" of the Isle of Wight Festival in 1969. This is a fascinating book for all those interested in the politics and culture of 1960s Britain as well as for Dylan aficionados.'

> —*David Boucher*, *Cardiff University and University of Johannesburg.*

'In this well-written book Tudor explores Dylan's relationship with the Britain of the 1960s. The upshot is that we find out a lot more about Dylan and 1960s music in Britain. It's a great read.'

> —*Gary Browning*, *author of The Political Art of Bob Dylan.*

BOB DYLAN AND THE BRITISH SIXTIES

Britain played a key role in Bob Dylan's career in the 1960s. He visited Britain on several occasions and performed across the country both as an acoustic folk singer and as an electric-rock musician. His tours of Britain in the mid-1960s feature heavily in documentary films such as D.A. Pennebaker's *Don't Look Back* and Martin Scorsese's *No Direction Home* and the concerts contain some of his most acclaimed ever live performances. Dylan influenced British rock musicians such as The Beatles, The Animals, and many others; they, in turn, influenced him.

Yet this key period in Dylan's artistic development is still under-represented in the extensive literature on Dylan. Tudor Jones rectifies that glaring gap with this deeply researched, yet highly readable, account of Dylan and the British Sixties. He explores the profound impact of Dylan on British popular musicians as well as his intense, and at times fraught, relationship with his UK fan base. He also provides much interesting historical context – cultural, social, and political – to give the reader a far greater understanding of a defining period of Dylan's hugely varied career. This is essential reading for all Dylan fans, as well as for readers interested in the tumultuous social and cultural history of the 1960s.

Dr Tudor Jones is a political historian and is Hon. Research Fellow in History of Political Thought at Coventry University, UK. He is the author of *The Revival of British Liberalism: From Grimond to Clegg* (2011), *Modern Political Thinkers and Ideas* (Routledge, 2002) and *Remaking the Labour Party: From Gaitskell to Blair* (Routledge, 1996). He is also a lifelong admirer of Bob Dylan.

BOB DYLAN AND THE BRITISH SIXTIES

A Cultural History

Tudor Jones

Routledge
Taylor & Francis Group

LONDON AND NEW YORK

First published 2019
by Routledge
2 Park Square, Milton Park, Abingdon, Oxon OX14 4RN

and by Routledge
52 Vanderbilt Avenue, New York, NY 10017

Routledge is an imprint of the Taylor & Francis Group, an informa business

© 2019 Tudor Jones

British Library Cataloguing-in-Publication Data
A catalogue record for this book is available from the British Library

Library of Congress Cataloging-in-Publication Data
A catalog record has been requested for this book

ISBN: 978-1-138-34040-4 (hbk)
ISBN: 978-1-138-34129-6 (pbk)
ISBN: 978-0-429-43560-7 (ebk)

Typeset in Bembo
by Out of House Publishing

Printed and bound in Great Britain by
TJ International Ltd, Padstow, Cornwall

To the memory of my parents, Brynmor and Eilonwy.
In memory, too, of my lifelong friend Richard Evans, who also
admired the music and lyrics of Bob Dylan.

CONTENTS

ACKNOWLEDGEMENTS

With regard to the initial source of encouragement to write this book, I should like to express my gratitude to Craig Fowlie, Global Editorial Director, Social and Political Sciences at Routledge, to whom I mentioned over lunch in a very pleasant restaurant in central London over 15 years ago my desire to write a study of Bob Dylan's impact on popular music and culture in Britain during the 1960s. Craig responded at the time in a favourable manner to my suggestion. Looking back even further in time, to the British Sixties, I would like to record with fond memory my many conversations about the music and lyrics of Bob Dylan, often quoting and dissecting at length the latter, that were held with my friends Richard Evans, Roger Griffin, Andrew Haynes, Kerry Renshaw, and Tom Woodman, when we were all undergraduates at the University of Oxford in the mid-to-late 1960s.

For assistance in researching this book I would like to thank Frank Underwood, to whom I spoke about Dylan's first visit to London in the winter of 1962–63, and also Ray Foulk, co-organiser of the 1969 Isle of Wight Festival, which Dylan headlined, performing before an audience of about 150,000 people. I should also like to thank Rivers Gambrell, Ollie Richards, Leah Wilson, Ingrid Crossland, and Joanna Zang, who typed parts of the text of my book, and Neda So who helped with the editing.

With regard to the practical completion of the book, I'd like to thank Craig Fowlie for his forbearance, patience, and advice throughout the lengthy course of the entire project, and, during the final stage of production, his Editorial Assistant Rebecca McPhee.

My thanks are offered, too, to the staff of the Upper Reading Room in the Bodleian Library in Oxford, where I spent many hours of study, and in particular to Ellen Hauser and Paul Sullivan there, as well as to Octavia Cox and Katie Kele at Rewley House, all of whom consistently expressed interest in the book as its preparation developed.

   Finally, I'd like to thank my friends David and Laura Farrant, Alex Kazamias, Francis Leneghan, Ken and Angie Reid, Andi Reiss, Dani Rivers, Kerry Renshaw, Cristina Stefan, and Myriam Ugarte for their continued interest and encouragement while I was researching and writing the book. In a lighter vein, I owe my thanks, too, to the staff of Al-Andalus, the Dewdrop Inn, Joe's, Pierre Victoire, Quod, the Rose and Crown, Xian, and my other favourite haunts in Oxford, as well as to those at familiar places in my native city of London, including Anastasia, Gabriella, and Isabella, and, at the George IV next to the London School of Economics, Simon Coady, who, while discussing the fortunes of Tottenham Hotspur FC, also expressed regular interest in *Bob Dylan and the British Sixties*, as the preparation of the book evolved, as did Olga, too, who worked there for most of that period. All of them alleviated the solitary routines of research and writing with refreshment, sustenance, and good company.

INTRODUCTION

This book seeks to provide a cultural-historical study of the impact of Bob Dylan as a singer-songwriter and musician upon British popular music and culture during the 1960s, a period of great and sustained musical and cultural creativity and energy in Britain. The book will address the question of Dylan's influence across a wide range of particular genres within British popular music during that decade, including traditional folk music, contemporary acoustic music, rock, folk-rock or electric-folk music, and country music.

More broadly, *Bob Dylan and the British Sixties* will examine Bob Dylan's influence within the historical context of major social, cultural, and political change in Britain during that decade. In doing so, it will follow a broadly traditional model and approach of historical periodisation, involving linearity and chronological order. In exploring that particular historical period, the book draws upon relevant secondary literature in the form of social- and cultural-historical studies of Britain during the 1960s.

Most of the many existing published works on Bob Dylan are mainly biographical, literary, or musicological in their nature and approach. In some cases, too, they have been religious or political in their emphasis. I quote from, and reference, many of these varied, and frequently interesting and insightful, works in the following pages. What I hope is distinctive or even innovative about this particular study is that it is cultural-historical in its approach and specifically British in its focus.

In charting the various stages of Bob Dylan's musical development as it affected British popular music and musicians during the 1960s, through his prolific songwriting, his studio albums, and his live concert performances, I have in places interspersed my historical study with a relevant biographical narrative of that period. While some of that may well be familiar to some readers through the principal biographies of Dylan, which I refer to at various points, I believe that it provides the necessary historical context within which Dylan's influence on British popular music during the 1960s should be viewed. To some younger readers that biographical and broader historical material may well, in any case, be largely unfamiliar.

While researching this book, I have found among many other studies three recently published works particularly helpful and informative with regard to the specific British focus of the book. Two of those, while essentially excellent reference books, also contain perceptive commentary. They are Andy Gill's *Bob Dylan: The Stories behind the Songs 1962–1969* (2011) and Nigel Williamson's *The Dead Straight Guide to Bob Dylan*. The third, John Hughes' *Invisible Now: Bob Dylan in the 1960s* (2013), is an illuminating and more detailed commentary which, like Gill's, covers the same historical period as this study.

Bob Dylan himself might well be irritated by this book's historical focus upon the 1960s. His musical work and career have, after all, spanned with distinction six decades. While I was researching and writing the book, that artistic lifetime achievement was itself recognised by his being awarded the Nobel Prize for Literature in October 2016. Dylan received it from the Swedish Academy for creating 'new poetic expression within the great American song tradition'. Sara Danius, the Academy's permanent secretary, also at the time compared Dylan in that respect to Homer and Sappho, who 2,500 years earlier in ancient Greece, she stated, 'wrote poetic texts that were meant to be listened to, they were meant to be performed, often with instruments, and it's the same way with Bob Dylan'.[1]

Nine years before that prestigious award, in late September 2007, when the poetic lyrics of Dylan's songs had become a subject of online study on English secondary schools' curriculum, the poet Andrew Motion, the British Poet Laureate from 1999 to 2009, also recognised the high quality of Dylan's lyrics when he wrote:

> You don't have to be approximately of his age to see that his lyrics are simply better than those by most other songwriters – better because they are more concentrated, more allusive, more memorable (even without the melodies), more surprising, more risk-taking, more willing to engage with the whole range of human experience.[2]

Three years earlier, referring to the powerful personal impact of Dylan's songs, Motion had also written, in words that ring true for this particular author:

> For my money, songs accumulate an even larger baggage of associations than poems. The time I first heard them, the people who introduced them to me, or who I know also like them; all these things become attached to the lyrics as well as the melody, at once broadening the experience and making it more intimate. Turning over the pages of *Bob Dylan's Lyrics 1962–85* is like opening a Pandora's box crammed with life's delights, winces, blushes, broodings, geographies.[3]

Turning again to this book's focus on the 1960s, it should be noted that Dylan appeared in a 1997 interview to be more nostalgic about the 1950s, stating:

What's dear to me are the 'Fifties,' cause that's when I grew up…there was an innocence about it all, and I don't recall anything bad ever happening. That was the 'Fifties,' the last period of time I remember as being idyllic.[4]

In sharp contrast, the overdue emphasis upon the 1960s of many studies of Dylan's work was noted by Lee Marshall in his largely sociological study *Bob Dylan: The Never Ending Star* (2007), when he pointed out that: 'Dylan's career beyond the sixties has received woefully inadequate coverage (for example, Howard Sounes' biography has 300 pages on the sixties, 107 pages on the seventies, and 98 pages on the eighties and nineties).'[5] Marshall referred, too, to Dylan's 'idealised star image', imposed on him by his massive presence and influence during the 1960s, whereby in the eyes of his countless admirers he 'came to represent rock culture, the sixties, and the promises that both offered but ultimately never quite realised'. As a consequence of that, 'Dylan spent the next thirty years of his career being compared to this earlier self', which led, in Marshall's view, to a subsequent 'kind of "commercial conversation" of Dylan's work that sought to freeze him as a nostalgia act'.[6]

In a 1985 interview Dylan himself complained, too, that; 'I'm not really a nostalgia freak. Every time you see my name, it's "The sixties this, sixties that". It's just another way of categorising me.'[7] In an earlier 1978 interview, however, when asked how, looking back, he recalled the period of his transition from folk to rock in the mid-1960s, the period when he recorded *Highway 61 Revisited* and, later, *Blonde on Blonde*, years covered in this book in Chapters 5 and 6, Dylan recalled that:

> Those were exciting times. We were doing it before anybody knew we would – or could. We didn't know what it was going out to be. Nobody thought of it as folk-rock at the time. There were some people involved in it like the Byrds, and I remember Sonny and Cher and the Turtles and the early Rascals. It began coming out on the radio…The top ten was filled with that kind of sound – the Beatles, too – and it was exciting, those days were exciting. It was the sound of the streets. It still is. I symbolically hear that sound wherever I am.[8]

It is nonetheless certainly not the deliberate aim of this particular study to confine Dylan and categorise him strictly within the framework of the 1960s in the manner of which he had complained in 1985, and no doubt many times since then. I am also mindful of Paul Williams' recognition of the shortcomings of purely chronological accounts of Dylan's work, treating each musical performance 'as though it is part of a process of development, part of some heroic saga of artistic growth (or decline)'. Such an approach, in Williams' view, 'can distract us from the fact that each work, each performance, also exists outside of time, and in fact derives its primary power from its content rather than its context'.[9] In an illuminating study with a similar emphasis to Williams', that is, on Dylan as a performing musician, Keith Negus has also observed that:

For many critics who grew up listening to Dylan from the early 1960s, his songs may be irredeemably linked to particular albums. But, they are not frozen in time. As recorded artefacts they continue to circulate and connect with new fans in different circumstances, while the songs in concert are drawn from a repertoire that dissolves the arbitrary distinction between one album and another, making it permeable and irrelevant.[10]

In spite of the perceptive nature of such observations, I would stress the fact that this book does not purport to be a broader study, biographical, literary, or musico-logical, of Dylan's life and work as a whole. Rather, it comprises instead an histor-ical study focused on a specific well-defined, yet transient, period in which Dylan developed a remarkable body of work in the form of songs, studio albums, and concert performances, all of which had a deep-running impact on British popular music and culture during that time of significant change in British society.

In support of my focus on Bob Dylan's musical impact during the 1960s, I would cite John Hughes' statement in his commendable study *Invisible Now: Bob Dylan in the 1960s* that: 'I have chosen to concentrate on this decade because it offers such an obvious narrative arc and displays Dylan's gifts so forcibly'.[11] In similar vein, Mike Marqusee maintained in 2003, from a more overtly political perspective, that: 'However you measure Dylan's subsequent achievements (and they are substantial), they do not enjoy the same umbilical relation to the turmoil of the times as the work of the sixties. This is a body of song tied to the unfolding drama of its era in a way that the later work is not.'[12]

With a less directly political emphasis, since the times in the British Sixties were, on the whole, less overtly turbulent than in the United States, this study takes a broadly similar view to that of Hughes and Marqusee concerning the special rela-tionship between that decade of change and the distinctive quality and force of the music produced by Dylan within its brief span.

I would broadly agree, too, with Sean Wilentz's view in his historical study *Bob Dylan in America* (2010) that the 1960s were clearly among 'Dylan's most concentrated periods of powerful creativity, including the most powerful of all, between 1964 and 1966'.[13] To that view Wilentz added his consideration that, ' interesting as his later endeavours have been, I think that Dylan completed by far his strongest work, mixing tradition and utter originality, in the mid-1960s and mid-1970s, a judgement he himself seems to share'.[14]

That reference to Dylan's fusion of tradition and originality, combined, I would add, with his strong sense of individuality, points to a wider historical truth, namely, that decades as historical periods are not, of course, hermetically sealed units, for they spring from, and spill over into, the decades that precede and succeed them. In Dylan's case, both parts of that process of historical continuity became apparent in terms of, first, his early musical and literary influences and, later, his own profound influence on the nature of modern popular music, particularly its songwriting. That kind of his-torical reality was recognised more generally by Arthur Marwick in his major study of the 1960s in the West, in which he referred to the 'long sixties', 'beginning', in his view, 'in 1958 and ending broadly speaking – many of the new trends of the sixties continued throughout the seventies, and right on to today – in 1973–74'.[15]

The main emphasis of this book nevertheless lies on the relatively short British Sixties, a period relating to Bob Dylan that begins with his first visit to London in the winter of 1962–63 and concludes with his last concert performance in Britain during that decade, at the Isle of Wight in late August 1969. That periodisation thus has a certain inherent coherence and symmetry. Indeed, Dylan was not to tour and perform in Britain again until 1978, most notably at an open-air rock concert which he headlined (and which I attended, along with about 200,000 other people) at Blackbushe Airport in Hampshire, southern England, in mid-July of that year.

Finally, in support of my concentration here on Dylan's impact upon a vibrant period in British popular music during the 1960s, I tend also to agree with a judgement made by Ian MacDonald in 2003, though I concede that in my case some degree of nostalgia may well play its part. In his collection of writings *The People's Music*, MacDonald wrote that during that decade:

> rock was at its peak both as a new, half-invented art form and as a recep-
> tacle for rebellious social impulses. The energy level (and the work rate of
> the artists involved) was then…uniquely high, the speed of development in
> every facet of the scene being astonishingly rapid and intense…the essentials
> of modern popular music were laid down during a period of less than ten
> years…the foundation decade for all that's followed.[16]

That phase of outstanding musical creativity was particularly evident in Britain, especially in the second half of the 1960s. Those years also witnessed, under Bob Dylan's dominant influence, a sea-change in the qualitative nature of songwriting in British popular music, a significant development that will be examined later in these pages.

As Alan Franks wrote in 2009:

> There had been plenty of great songwriters before Dylan, none more so than
> Cole Porter. From him and his peers came sublime marriages of wit and
> passion…but there had never been popular music with stanzas of such literate
> complexity or wild flights of expressionism. That is where the great change
> came, that is what set the critics going and keeps them at it.[17]

All those considerations justify, therefore, I believe, my focus on Dylan's musical output in the 1960s and his extensive influence on British popular music throughout that decade. As for the British Sixties, so much has been written about those years, with contrasting assessments and judgements. In this book I shall try to avoid mythologising or idealising that era, though I admit that that is not a straightforward task when writing in retrospect about the period that shaped the early part of my youth. At the same time, I shall generally steer clear of the opposite approach of de-mythologising or debunking the British Sixties, an equally one-sided approach pursued in recent years by some younger historians who, significantly, as I note later, did not personally live through those years.[18] In a recently published history of Britain in the 1960s, its editors, while not explicitly adhering to that latter school of thought, wrote, with some justification but arguably in rather overstated terms:

> Many people who lived through the Sixties...as they remember them, are actually giving personal value to, and attempting to experience in the present, something which they did not experience in the past. In short, for many people today, the relationship with the Sixties is dominated by *nostalgia*: the desire to re-create the past, or an idealized version of it, from extant materials in the present.[19]

In more measured terms, Gerard DeGroot in his history of the 1960s, published in 2008, stated at the outset that: 'My thesis is very simple: I feel that too much has been left out of the Sixties portrait, and the omissions have given rise to a misleading, reductive image.'[20] Later in that work, while drawing sombre conclusions about some highly damaging aspects of the 1960s' legacy, DeGroot also made a perceptive observation about Bob Dylan's running commentary on parts of that era, pointing out that:

> The really unsettling thing about Dylan was that he turned out to be right about so much – war, racism, hypocrisy, greed. He seemed to anticipate so eloquently all the problems of a troubled decade. No wonder, then, that people were quick to label him the voice of a generation.[21]

Referring in a similar manner to what, for DeGroot, amounted to selective or reductionist accounts of the 1960s, Mark Donnelly in his 2005 study *Sixties Britain: Culture, Society and Politics* maintained that the very phrase that provided the main title of his book was itself 'a heavily edited and reworked concept that is saturated in symbolism, meanings and myths'.[22] Indeed, the 1960s were, in his view, 'the most richly mythic decade of the twentieth century'. In his generally sympathetic cultural history of the 1960s, Jonathon Green largely concurred with that judgement, in relation at least to the recent past, when he wrote in 1999:

> We live in the shadow of the Sixties. Of all the artificial constructs by which we delineate our immediate past, the 'Sixties' have the greatest purchase on the mass imagination. They stand, rightly or not, as the dominant myth of the modern era.[23]

Marwick in his 1998 historical study of the 'long sixties' had underlined, too, the conflicting interpretations of that 'mythic decade' when he observed that:

> For some it is a golden age, for others a time when the old secure framework of morality, authority and discipline disintegrated...What happened between

the late fifties and the early seventies has been subject to political polemic, nostalgic mythologizing, and downright misrepresentation.[24]

In similar vein, DeGroot noted of the 'short sixties' that: 'The decade has been transformed into a morality play, an explanation of how the world went astray, or, conversely, how hope was squandered. Problems of the present are blamed on myths of the past.'[25]

For a final, concise observation on such ambiguities inherent in the 1960s, in Britain and elsewhere, one can cite Jon Savage's study of popular music in 1966, the particular year, in his view, when the decade 'exploded'. Of the 1960s he thus wrote that:

> Everyone thinks they know about the Sixties. It was a golden age; it was the moment everything started going downhill. It was the start of the alternative society; it was only a couple of hundred people in London, while 'real life' – whatever that is – went on elsewhere.[26]

In this book I shall attempt, then, to provide, in Hughes' phrase, a 'narrative arc' covering Bob Dylan's wide-ranging and deep-rooted influence on much of British popular music and culture during the 1960s. That was something of which I started to become aware, vaguely at first and later much more strongly, in the years immediately after I was intrigued by the raw directness of Dylan's first, eponymous album, hearing it for the first time in a small yet inviting multi-genre music record shop (of the kind that in Britain, sadly, no longer widely exists) in Harrow, north-west London, in 1962. I was even more impressed a year later when I first heard, and bought, I think in the same place, Dylan's second album, *The Freewheelin' Bob Dylan*. Those early experiences engendered and shaped a subsequent, longstanding admiration and respect for Bob Dylan and his music, and hence an enduring interest in the subject matter of this book. Its historical narrative, namely, that of his musical development and impact during the British Sixties, is one that I shall seek to develop and elaborate in the pages that follow.

Notes

1 Cited in Edna Gundersen's interview with Bob Dylan, 'The Nobel…Whoever Dreams About Something Like That?', *Daily Telegraph*, October 29, 2016. Asked by Gundersen about his view of Sara Danius' statement, Dylan responded: 'I suppose so, in some way. Some (of my) songs – 'Blind Willie', 'The Ballad of Hollis Brown, Joey', 'A Hard Rain', 'Hurricane', and some others – definitely are Homeric in Value.'

2 Andrew Motion, 'The Lessons They Are A-Changin', *The Times*, September 22, 2007.

3 'Andrew Motion's Top 12 Dylan Lyrics', *The Times*, December 4, 2004.

4 Bob Dylan, interview with Alan Jackson, 'Bob Dylan Revisited', in *The Times on Saturday*, November 15, 1997; cited in David Dalton, *Who Is That Man? In Search of the Real Bob Dylan* (London: Omnibus, 2012), p. 9.

5 Lee Marshall, *Bob Dylan: The Never Ending Star* (Cambridge: Polity, 2007), p. 13.

6 Ibid., p. 173.

7 Bob Dylan, interview with David Fricke, 1985; cited in Marshall, op. cit., p. 173.

8 Bob Dylan, interview with Ron Rosenbaun, *Playboy*, March 1978; reprinted in Jonathan Cott (ed.), *Dylan on Dylan: The Essential Interviews* (London: Hodder and Stoughton, 2006), p. 209.

9 Paul Williams, *Bob Dylan Performing Artist 1960–1973: The Early Years* (London: Omnibus, 2004 [first published 1990]), pp. 110–111.

10 Keith Negus, *Bob Dylan* (London: Equinox, 2008), pp. 70–71.

11 John Hughes, *Invisible Now: Bob Dylan in the 1960s* (Farnham: Ashgate, 2013), p. xv.

12 Mike Marqusee, *Chimes of Freedom: The Politics of Bob Dylan's Art* (New York/London: The New Press, 2003), p. 3.

13 Sean Wilentz, *Bob Dylan in America* (London: Vintage, 2011), p. 7.

14 Ibid. pp. 8–9. Wilentz was referring, for instance, to Dylan's comments in a 2004 interview with Ed Bradley. See, too, below Ch. 4, n. 18.

15 Arthur Marwick, *The Sixties: Cultural Revolution in Britain, France, Italy and the United States, c. 1958–c. 1974* (Oxford: Oxford University Press, 1998), p. 3.

16 Ian MacDonald, *The People's Music* (London: Pimlico, 2003), pp. viii–ix.

17 Alan Franks, 'How we Learnt to Trust in Bob', *The Times*, April 18, 2009.

18 See, for instance, James Obelkewich's review of Arthur Marwick's *The Sixties* in *Twentieth Century British History*, 11 (3), 2000, pp. 333–6; and in some respects Dominic Sandbrook's *White Heat: A History of Britain in the Swinging Sixties* (London: Little, Brown, 2006).

19 Introduction to Trevor Harris and Monia O'Brien Castro (eds.), *Preserving the Sixties: Britain and the Decade of Protest* (Basingstoke: Palgrave Macmillan, 2014), p. 2.

20 Gerard DeGroot, *The 60s Unplugged: A Kaleidosopic History of a Disorderly Decade* (London; Macmillan, 2008), p. 3.

21 Ibid., p. 231.

22 Mark Donnelly, *Sixties Britain: Culture, Society and Politics* (Harlow: Pearson Longman, 2005), p. 1.

23 Jonathan Green, *All Dressed Up: The Sixties and the Counterculture* (London; Pimlico, 1999), p. ix.

24 Marwick, op. cit., p. 3.

25 DeGroot, op. cit., p. 3.

26 Jon Savage, *1966: The Year the Decade Exploded* (London: Faber & Faber, 2015), p. x.

1

FIRST TIME IN LONDON

Winter 1962–63

Bob Dylan arrived in London, and in Britain, for the first time a week before Christmas on December 18, 1962, during the bitterly cold British winter of 1962–63. He had been invited by Philip Saville, a young BBC television director, to act in a play by the contemporary Jamaican playwright Evan Jones, entitled *Madhouse on Castle Street*. Saville had seen Dylan perform in 1960 at Pastor's Place, a club in Greenwich Village, New York City, which he had visited on the recommendation of the poet W.H. Auden, a New York resident at that time.[1] Saville had been working on a television production in New York with the American folklorist Alan Lomax, whom he had asked to produce a soundtrack of folk songs for a play entitled *Dark of the Moon*.[2]

Impressed at the time by Dylan, Saville later recalled that: 'I suddenly had the idea that it would be exciting to cast this young American poet in the role of an anarchistic young man.'[3] He therefore struck a deal with Albert Grossman, Dylan's manager since August 1962, for the young singer to appear in *Madhouse on Castle Street*. The deal was at a cost of 2,000 US dollars plus expenses and airfare, a generous offer at the time since no one at the BBC in 1962 had any idea who Bob Dylan was. As far as the Corporation was concerned, Saville later added, 'Bob Dylan was just an unknown'.[4]

In Britain in December 1962, outside a small number of folk-music enthusiasts in London and elsewhere, Bob Dylan was indeed largely unknown. His musical career had been launched just over a year before his arrival in London by two related fortuitous developments. Robert Shelton, folk-music critic of the *New York Times* had written a highly favourable review of Dylan's performance on September 26, 1961, at Gerde's Folk City in Greenwich Village, where he was supporting The Greenbriar Boys, a popular bluegrass group. Shelton's review appeared under the headline 'Bob Dylan: A Distinctive Folk-Song Stylist' in the *New York Times* on September 29, 1961. Dylan's then girlfriend Suze Rotolo recalled in her memoir of

Greenwich Village in the 1960s how she and Dylan eagerly bought several copies of the early edition of the *New York Times* from the newspaper kiosk on Sheridan Square and went across the street to an all-night deli to read Shelton's glowing review.[5] Suze Rotolo was to be an influential figure in Dylan's early cultural and political education. A young woman with wide artistic interests, she was also a left-wing political activist, working at the time for the civil rights pressure group CORE, the Congress of Racial Equality. She was in many ways Dylan's muse during three formative years in New York City, remaining in a close relationship with him from the summer of 1961 until their painful split in March 1964.[6]

A second fortunate development in September 1961 was the major opportunity provided for Dylan by the Texan folk singer Carolyn Hester. He had already met her and her then husband Richard Farina both in New York City and in Cambridge, Massachusetts. Hester subsequently invited Dylan to play harmonica on three tracks on her third album, her first for a major label, Columbia. (Dylan had previously played harmonica professionally at a recording session for Harry Belafonte.) During rehearsals and at the recording session itself on September 29 Dylan met Hester's producer John Hammond Sr.

A legendary figure in the record music industry, Hammond had discovered, launched, or promoted major jazz and blues stars such as Billie Holliday, Count Basie, Benny Goodman, Lionel Hampton and many others. Interested in finding new figures in the folk-music revival, Hammond was drawn to Dylan's potential raw talent. As Carolyn Hester later recalled: 'I could tell Hammond was hooked from the very start. The longer we worked, the more I could see Hammond's interest in Bob developing, until the two of them were thick as thieves.'[7] Dylan was also able to show Hammond Shelton's review in the *New York Times*, published by a stroke of good fortune the very day of Hester's recording session. Invited by Hammond to a demo session later that day, Dylan, in spite of his somewhat undisciplined studio technique, impressed the veteran producer to the point where he was offered a contract with Columbia Records that afternoon. Dylan was understandably elated. 'I couldn't believe it', he later recalled. 'I left there and I remember walking out of the studio. I was like on a cloud…It was one of the most thrilling moments in my life'.[8] Hammond later told Columbia's new Director of A&R, David Kapralik: 'Dylan's an extraordinary young man. I don't know if he's going to sell, but he has something profound to say.'[9] Kapralik trusted Hammond's judgement in view of his massive reputation, and Dylan was signed as a Columbia recording artist at the age of 20 at the end of October 1961.

His first album, the eponymous *Bob Dylan*, was recorded, with Hammond as producer, in a couple of afternoons in late November 1961 at a cost of only $402. It consisted mainly of traditional folk and country blues classics with only two original songs, notably 'Song for Woody', a tribute to Dylan's original musical mentor Woody Guthrie, the celebrated Oklahoma-born folk singer, songwriter, and drifter. *Bob Dylan* was eventually released by Columbia, under pressure from Hammond, in March 1962 with minimal promotion and sold only 5,000 copies in its first year, reinforcing the view of many in the Columbia building on Sixth Avenue that Dylan was 'Hammond's Folly'. Subsequent developments were to vindicate emphatically Hammond's initial artistic judgement.

When Bob Dylan arrived in London over a year later, in December 1962, he was initially booked into the May Fair Hotel on Stratton Street, but after an uneasy stay there he moved for a while to Philip Saville's house in Hampstead, north-west London. There, early one morning, Saville witnessed Dylan playing a song he had never heard before, 'Blowin' in the Wind', to the rapt attention of Saville's two Spanish au pairs.[10] Dylan had earlier composed the draft of what was to become one of his most famous, anthemic songs in April 1962, in a coffee house on MacDougal Street in Greenwich Village, New York City. But as Saville later recalled, although Dylan had written the song there, 'planned it in his mind...he still seemed to be working it out in my house'.[11] Saville thereupon asked Dylan to perform the song in Evan Jones' play *Madhouse on Castle Street*.

Uncomfortable with dialogue in the play in his assigned role of a young anarchist student living in a boarding house, Dylan was asked by Saville instead to sing some songs for the play, including 'Blowin' in the Wind', which was sung over the opening and closing credits, and 'Ballad of the Gliding Swan' written by Evan Jones. David Warner, a young Royal Shakespeare Company actor, played the part of the anarchist student. Dylan appeared in the play as Warner's roommate, in Saville's words, as 'a rather uncommunicative American who's very articulate in song'.[12] *Madhouse on Castle Street* was eventually broadcast by the BBC on January 13, 1963, but the recording tape of the play was later wiped, to Saville's regret, by the Corporation in 1968.[13]

Soon after Dylan had first arrived in London it was obvious to Philip Saville that the young singer 'loved London' and was 'very excited about the "new" England' of the early 1960s, a period when young people's 'ideas were spilling out in design, graphics, architecture, clothes'.[14] While in London Dylan was also eager to visit its various folk clubs. In particular, he had earlier been told by Pete Seeger to look up Anthea Joseph, who organised London's oldest folk club, the Troubadour, on Old Brompton Road in Earl's Court, south-west London.[15] Pete Seeger had performed just over a year before, in November 1961, at the Royal Albert Hall to a capacity audience of 5,000. It was the first folk-music concert proper, and by a major American folk singer, staged there, apart, that is, from the annual festival of the English Folk Dance and Song Society. Seeger's concert had been co-sponsored and assisted by key London folk-club organisers, as well as by Topic Records, founded in 1939 and associated with the Workers' Musical Association, and by Collet's Bookshop on New Oxford Street. Politically, both Topic Records, at that time the only significant record label in Britain dealing in traditional folk music, and Collet's Bookshop were widely regarded as 'stalwarts of the hard left'.[16]

Bob Dylan consequently visited the Troubadour soon after arriving in London, and Anthea Joseph was taking money on the door that evening. As she later recalled:

The day before I'd been in Collet's and read the article by Bob Shelton about Bob Dylan. I listened to that first album [*Bob Dylan*] in the shop… The following day I saw these feet coming down the stairs, cowboy boots and jeans, which was quite unusual, and I thought, Oh God, it's one of the Southend hillbillies, I can't bear it. Then he came down a little further and I saw the face, and thought, I know that face. He pushed some money at me and said 'Can I come in?' 'Hang on, you are Bob Dylan?' 'Yes, I am.' 'Right, if you play, you can come in for nothing.' Half the audience loved it, the other half hated it.[17]

At other times in late December 1962 Dylan visited other London folk clubs, notably, at the King and Queen pub in Foley Street, Fitzrovia, and the Singers' Club at the Pindar of Wakefield pub on Gray's Inn Road.[18] His visits to the Singers' Club were to hold particular significance for his later musical development, as in a different way were his visits to the King and Queen. The Singers' Club had been founded in January 1961 by Ewan MacColl, the highly prominent British folk singer and songwriter, and was run by himself and his third wife Peggy Seeger, half-sister of Pete Seeger, along with A.L. (Bert) Lloyd, the leading English folklorist since the late 1950s. The Singers' Club had superseded MacColl's earlier Ballads and Blues Club, established at the Princess Louise pub on High Holborn in 1957. The latter, as Colin Harper has observed, 'had the sheen, even then, of a forum for folksong as a particularly intellectual activity', yet it laid 'the foundation of the whole British folk club explosion' in the 1960s.[19]

MacColl's later Singers' Club from 1961 onwards became his 'command centre for the fight against mediocrity and commercialism'.[20] In October 1962 the club moved from its previous venues to the Pindar of Wakefield on Gray's Inn Road, and it was there on December 22, 1962 that Bob Dylan was photographed in performance by Brian Shuel, the only professional photographer who documented to a significant extent the London folk-club scene during the 1960s.[21] What proved musically controversial about the Singers' Club was its imposed 'policy rule' whereby its singers could only sing songs from their own country of origin in a language that they spoke and understood. In justification of that rule, MacColl later explained:

Our problem was English, Scots, Irish and American performers singing songs whose idiom, whose language, they did not understand, hence mishandling the songs…We were also intent on proving that we had an indigenous folk music that was as muscular, as varied and as beautiful as any music anywhere in the world.[22]

According to MacColl, therefore, his folk club ought to be fostering a national musical identity and, as he later put it, 'not just becoming an arm of American cultural imperialism'.[23] That belief reflected his own political convictions. Like his colleague Bert Lloyd, MacColl had, since his youth, been a supporter of the Communist Party of Great Britain. In 1957 the CPGB had published a pamphlet entitled 'The American Threat to British Culture', which claimed that 'American Big Business' was the force underlying American mass popular culture and its media of expression: pulp fiction, comics, films, and popular music. MacColl's form of cultural and musical nationalism was thus very much in tune with the CPGB's ideological approach.[24]

Underlying such beliefs, and the Singers' Club's 'policy rule' which they inspired, was the notion of the authenticity and purity of traditional folk music as opposed to the commerciality and tainted nature of popular music and culture. Furthermore, the authenticity of folk music, according to MacColl, Lloyd and other British folk-music purists and activists, stemmed from their historical interpretation of folk music as an expression of the collective experience of the industrial and agricultural working classes.

In defence of the leading British folk-music revivalists, and notably MacColl and A.L. Lloyd, it may be said that it was clearly to their credit that, as Paul Du Noyer has noted, 'they preserved so much that might otherwise have disappeared into the oubliette of cultural history'.[25] In criticism, however, of their inflexible approach to a particular musical genre, some cultural and social historians have made at least two pertinent observations. First, while the British folk revivalists portrayed folk songs as an authentic distillation of the lives of working-class people, the consequence of that portrayal, it has been argued, was really a break-down of the relationship between art and life. As Greil Marcus has observed, instead of folk music being viewed as a form of popular art: 'Rather, life – a certain kind of life – equaled art, which ultimately meant that life replaced it. The kind of life that equaled art was life defined by suffering, deprivation, poverty and social exclusion…the poor are art because they sing their lives without mediation and without reflection, without the false consciousness of capitalism and the false desires of advertising.'[26]

A second criticism of the British folk revivalists' approach was that they were engaged in an ideologically driven and highly selective reconstruction of the past experience of the British working class. As Michael Brocken has maintained, by the early 1960s the revivalists 'were beginning to represent a rather degraded collective gazing upon a present "ghastly" world and then back towards a putative time in the past, merely reconstructing an idealised past history that was once itself a grim present'.[27]

In similar vein, Michael Jones has observed of not only Ewan MacColl but also Pete Seeger that:

> They both worked tirelessly in the present by urging that an imaginary future could be created from materials which were, simultaneously, recoverable from the (imagined) past but also retrievable from a (substantially imagined) present – just so long as the tides of commercial music could be driven back and quietened long enough for the people's music to be heard, for traditional music to be embraced and for the transformative power of collective music-making to be experienced.[28]

Jones, however, went on to argue that:

> The true contrast between the US and UK folk revivals is…that Seeger could claim a closer connection to a *living* tradition. If we take Woody Guthrie as a touchstone for this contrast, Guthrie was not someone who collected songs in the way that MacColl and A.L. Lloyd did.[29]

It is not difficult to see how Bob Dylan, as an individualistic troubadour, would relate more to the American notion of a *living* folk-music tradition, epitomised by his mentor Woody Guthrie and indeed by the Delta blues singers. Dylan had been introduced by his first producer John Hammond Sr. to a collection of recordings by Robert Johnson in the mid-1930s that had been discovered by Hammond and released in 1961 as the compilation *King of the Delta Singers*. Dylan's understanding of the folk-music tradition was shaped by both of these powerful influences. As Mike Marqusee has pointed out:

> He [Dylan] was never the kind of folk singer who sought to disappear from the song and present it as an artifact. His approach, from the beginning, was with the blues singers for whom adding yourself to the tradition was what the tradition was all about.[30]

Moreover, Robert Johnson in particular, Marqusee notes, became for Dylan and friends such as Dave Van Ronk and Eric Von Schmidt 'an icon of the kind of authenticity that they were seeking, an authenticity in which the individual and the music became a seamless whole'.[31] All of that had been evident in Dylan's raw and direct interpretations of traditional country blues on his first, at the time underrated, eponymous album. A later favourable review of that album, just over a year after its release, had underlined its virtues as Dylan's 'electrifying and mercurial inventiveness (both as a songwriter and an interpreter) and a natural gift for genuine directness and simplicity in the finest folk-derived sense'.[32]

Feeling, then, ever since that first album, part of a living folk-music tradition, Dylan much later explained his own ambivalent relationship with it. It was a tradition that he was immersed in, and yet he rejected that strand of the folk revival which presented folk songs as artefacts. He recalled that:

> some people seemed to think that listening to songs should be like listening to dull sermons. I didn't want my songs to be like that. But at the same time I felt very much a part of the folk music tradition. All the lyrics I wrote came out of that idiom.[33]

Dylan later, too, expressed in his 2004 memoir his distaste for what he called 'the folk police', 'the classic traditional folk snobs'[34] on his own side of the Atlantic, who tended to selectively choose which of those artefacts, those 'dull sermons', should be performed, heard and evaluated. As he had earlier recalled:

It was just a clique, you know. Folk music was a strict and rigid establishment. If you sang southern mountain blues, you didn't sing southern mountain ballads and you didn't sing city blues. If you sang Texas cowboy songs you didn't play English ballads. It was really pathetic.[35]

But at the same time, in 1985, Dylan had also explained a major reason for his having turned to folk music at the start of the 1960s, after his devotion to the rock'n'roll of Elvis Presley, Buddy Holly, Little Richard and others in his late adolescence in Minnesota:

The thing about rock'n'roll is that for me anyway it wasn't enough…I knew that when I got into folk music it was a more serious type of thing. The songs are filled with more despair, more sadness, more triumph, more faith in the supernatural, much deeper feelings…There is more real life in one line than there was in all the rock'n'roll themes. I needed that. Life is full of complexities and rock'n'roll didn't reflect that.[36]

It was nonetheless a *living* folk tradition, personified by Woody Guthrie, to which Dylan was drawn. As Suze Rotolo later recalled: 'Bob's songs were in the folk idiom yet they were definitely and undeniably written in the present. The writing was timeless and timely – explosively so – and the audience gasped in recognition.'[37]

In London in the winter of 1962–63 Ewan MacColl's the Singers' Club in many ways exemplified the kind of dogmatic inflexibility with regard to folk music, regulated by 'the folk police', with which Dylan and others in the 1960s felt little sympathy. Unsurprisingly, then, his visits there in late December 1962 were not well received by its organisers Ewan MacColl and Peggy Seeger.[38] Peggy Seeger later expressed some degree of regret about this: 'Ewan and I were rather stand-offish at that time and perhaps we were not welcoming enough.'[39] They were not alone, however, in their indifferent response to Dylan's performance. At the time, for example, to Karl Dallas, who had been since 1957 the writer on folk music for *Melody Maker*, the leading and most substantial periodical on popular music in Britain during the 1960s, Dylan seemed merely 'a very poor Woody Guthrie imitator'.[40]

But elsewhere in London Dylan met with a more favourable response, particularly from the popular English folk singers Martin Carthy, a highly influential figure on the English folk-music scene during the early 1960s, and Bob Davenport. Dylan met Martin Carthy at the King and Queen pub on Foley Street just before Christmas 1962. Carthy had recognised Dylan from his photograph on the cover of the latest copy of *Sing Out!* magazine, which had printed the lyrics of 'Blowin' in the Wind', and which Carthy had recently seen in Collet's Bookshop.[41] A regular performer with The Thameside Four at the the King and Queen, Carthy invited Dylan to perform there that evening. The first-time visitor, Carthy recalled, 'was electrifying. He was brilliant…he took the place apart.'[42]

Carthy also suggested to Dylan that he should visit the Troubadour since he, Carthy, regularly performed there on Saturdays. It was either there or at the King and Queen that Carthy recalled Dylan singing 'A Hard Rain's A-Gonna Fall', which the young American had first performed at the Gaslight in Greenwich Village in September 1962, just a month before the Cuban Missile Crisis. Dylan's song was, in terms of melody line and verse pattern, largely a reworking of the traditional Anglo-Scottish border ballad 'Lord Randall', Child Ballad no. 12.[43] Carthy remembered that when Dylan started singing the song in London in late December 1962, he thought after the first two lines that he was indeed going to sing the traditional ballad 'Lord Randall', but that he then 'just took off on this great song, "Hard Rain…" And in 1962 that song was revolutionary.'[44]

From Martin Carthy, Dylan learned in London the melodies of the traditional English folk songs 'Scarborough Fair' and 'Lady Franklin's Lament', which he later used for his own songs 'Girl from the North Country' and 'Bob Dylan's Dream', both of which appeared on his second album, *The Freewheelin' Bob Dylan*, released in May 1963.[45] Both Carthy and Anthea Joseph also recalled Dylan singing 'Masters of War' at the Troubadour and the Singers' Club respectively.[46] This powerful song, 'the bluntest condemnation in Dylan's songbook',[47] which castigated what the outgoing US President Dwight Eisenhower had first called the military-industrial complex in January 1961, was based on the melody of 'Nottamun Town', which Carthy has called 'one of the great songs of lies'.[48] This was itself an Appalachian adaptation of an old English mummers' play. Dylan had probably learned the tune from the American singer Jackie Washington, a close friend of Eric Von Schmidt. Washington's version of the song had appeared on his first, eponymous album, released in December 1962.[49] Jean Ritchie, however claimed that Dylan had appropriated her version of the song, which she regarded as family property, and even became litigious on the matter.[50] Dylan later performed 'Masters of War', adopting the melodic delivery of Jackie Washington's version of 'Nottamun Town', in New York City, at Gerde's Folk City, in mid-January 1963.[51]

Both Martin Carthy and Anthea Joseph also recalled Dylan singing 'The Ballad of Hollis Brown', based on the melody of the traditional English song 'Pretty Polly', at the Troubadour and the Singers' Club just before Christmas 1962.[52] Dylan's song appeared on his third, and most politically engaged, album, *The Times They Are A-Changin'*, recorded from August to October 1963 and released in January 1964. So, too, did his 'The Lonesome Death of Hattie Carroll', which was based on the melody of the 16th century Scottish ballad 'Mary Hamilton'. In addition, the Scottish folk singer Nigel Denver might possibly have provided Dylan with the melody of Dominic Behan's Irish republican song, composed in the late 1950s, 'The Patriot Game', which Dylan used as the melodic basis for his song 'With God on Our Side', and which also appeared on *The Times They Are A-Changin'*. Denver recalled singing 'The Patriot Game' regularly between 1960 and 1962 at the Troubadour in London, whilst always acknowledging on stage Behan's authorship of the song. Behan himself later, according to Denver, accused Dylan of plagiarising and parodying his song, and even threatened legal action.[53] Since, however, Behan's melody of 'The Patriot Game' was itself based on the traditional song 'The Merry Month of May', previously recorded by, for instance, Burl Ives as 'The Nightingale', Behan was vulnerable to the historic defence of the practice of the use and adaptation of melody within the folk-music tradition.

It seems more likely that Dylan might well have heard 'The Patriot Game' performed earlier, not in London but in New York City by his friends The Clancy Brothers. That raises the broader point that Dylan had been exposed to traditional British and Irish songs well before his visit to London in the winter of 1962–63 – first in Minneapolis, when he was briefly a student at the University of Minnesota between 1959 and 1960, and then later, from January 1961, in New York City when he visited and often sang at the clubs and bars around Greenwich Village. As he later commented in his memoir, he had learned, for instance, from Harry Weber, a graduate student in Latin literature and traditional ballad scholar in Minneapolis,[54] 'mostly roving ballads…stern ballads, ones that meant cruel business…I loved these ballads right away.'[55]

Dylan's later exposure in London to British and Irish ballads was thus, as Hughes has noted, 'merely a consolidation and extension of a dependence on British idioms and song modes'[56] during that formative period of his artistic development. At any rate, he was clearly absorbing and displaying these traditional musical influences in London folk clubs during his brief stay in the city in the winter of 1962–63. He was, as Martin Carthy has recalled, 'a piece of blotting paper. He'd walk into a club and just sit there and listen all evening. It was all going in. He was wide-open to influences *all* the time…Then go home and write…And change things around. He was very imaginative.'[57]

The extent to which Dylan was absorbing such influences and utilising and adapting the melodies and verse patterns of traditional British and Irish songs did also raise, as the examples of 'Masters of War' and 'With God on Our Side' demonstrated, the question of alleged plagiarism on Dylan's part. But as Heylin has noted, in London at that time 'Carthy and Davenport were prepared to accept Dylan as a troubadour who utilised – but was not mired in – the folk tradition'.[58] Robert Shelton observed, nonetheless, that by the end of 1963 there was a debate within the folk-music scene over 'whether Dylan was a song cribber or a composer working in the accepted tradition of building new songs on the skeletal remains of old folk songs'.[59]

The balance of historical evidence surrounding that debate appears to be clearly in Dylan's favour. In his biography Robert Shelton quoted the American ethnomusicologist Charles Seeger, father of Pete, Peggy and Mike, as stating that artistic creation was characterised by 'conscious and unconscious appropriation, borrowing, adapting, plagiarizing and plain stealing', and that 'the folk song is, by definition, and, as far as we can tell, entirely a product of plagiarism'.[60] Consistent with that approach, Dylan was working, as the historian Sean Wilentz has maintained, 'in the same tradition as the minstrels (a tradition that includes vaudeville as well as the southern songster performers, among them Blind Willie McTell) – copying other people's mannerisms and melodies and lyrics and transforming them and making them his own, a form of larceny that is as American as apple pie'.[61] Dylan was thus 'simply, as Pete Seeger had described himself, a "link in a chain" of folk singers', adding himself to that musical tradition.[62] Even a hidebound traditionalist such as Ewan MacColl made the same historical point as Charles Seeger and Wilentz when considering the British folk-music tradition. 'In a sense', MacColl conceded, 'all folk-songs are forgeries. There is, as far as we know, no Ur 'Barbara Allan' or Ur 'Lord Randall'. All that we possess is a body of texts and tunes in a state of constant change, of evolution and devolution.'[63]

Dylan's absorption and adaptation of British and Irish folk-music influences during his first visit to London were not just in tune with the adaptive and transformative tradition of troubadours, minstrels, and country blues singers. His exposure to such influences also enabled him to suffuse his new songs with a timeless quality. Daniel Mark Epstein vividly recalled that aspect of, for instance, 'Boots of Spanish Leather', broadly based on the traditional English song 'Scarborough Fair', when he heard Dylan perform it in December 1963: 'There was not a line in the lyric that marked it as contemporary; there were many lines that sounded timeless, like stones worn smooth in a riverbed from centuries of water coursing over them.'[64]

In addition, this sense of timelessness conveyed by Dylan's new songs helped to loosen them, as Hughes has noted, away 'from the political and personal contexts and imagery associated with Guthrie',[65] his first great musical influence, whose early impression on the young acolyte had been profound.[66] As Dylan later recalled in his memoir, the moment that he first heard Woody Guthrie's solo records in Minneapolis had been for him 'an epiphany, like some heavy anchor had just plunged into the waters of the harbor…I felt like I had discovered some essence of self-command…feeling more like myself than ever before.'[67]

As the 1960s progressed, Guthrie's influence became less overt or pervasive. Yet Dylan's respect for his first great mentor remained deep-rooted and lasting. Later, after Dylan's motorcycle accident in July 1966, the only musical event that lured him out of his prolonged withdrawal from touring to perform on stage again was a memorial concert for Guthrie, who had died in 1967, at New York's Carnegie Hall in January 1968.

At the start of 1963 Bob Dylan flew from London to Rome on January 5 to meet his manager Albert Grossman, who was on tour with Odetta, one of the other recording artists on his roster. Dylan then flew back to London to spend time with his friends Eric Von Schmidt and Richard Farina, who were staying at a hotel in South Kensington. He joined them on January 14 and 15 for a fairly inebriated recording session for the small Folklore record label in the basement of Dobell's record shop on Charing Cross Road, playing harmonica under the pseudonym 'Blind Boy Grant'. He later performed again at 'The Troubadour'.[68] On January 6 he flew home to New York.

Dylan and Martin Carthy, who had been such a significant English musical influence, formed what was to be a lasting friendship during that short first visit to London. Dylan stayed several times at the home of Carthy and his first wife Dorothy in Belsize Park, north-west London. During the bitter winter of that time Dylan and Martin Carthy even cut up a non-functioning piano with a samurai sword to make a fire to keep themselves warm.[69] On what was to be Dylan's next visit to London, in May 1964, to play a sold-out Royal Festival Hall, he phoned Martin Carthy soon after he got off the plane. 'Are you there, Martin? Have you still got the piano?' Dylan asked. 'No, no, the piano all got burned up', Carthy recalled was his reply.[70]

The significance of Dylan's four-week visit to London in December 1962 and January 1963 for his artistic development in the immediate future was far-reaching. As Martin Carthy recalled in 1991:

> I've read a lot of books about him and not one of them talks in any detail about his time in England. As far as I can hear, by listening to his records, his time in England was absolutely crucial to his development.[71]

In particular, Carthy maintained, a comparison between Dylan's second album, *The Freewheelin' Bob Dylan*, recorded between July 1962 and April 1963 and released in May 1963, and his third album, *The Times They Are A-Changin'*, recorded between August and October 1963 and released in January 1964, revealed 'an enormous difference in the way he's singing, in the sort of tunes he's singing, the way he's putting words together'.[72]

From a different perspective, but in a similar vein, Heylin has described Dylan's visit to London in the winter of 1962–63 as the completion of 'the final part of his not-so-formal degree in folk music, making his first trip to England the font of the Anglo-American folk tradition'.[73] Martin Carthy, Bob Davenport and others in the London folk-club scene had thus introduced Dylan to the traditional British and Irish versions of songs he had probably known before in America mainly from their Appalachian derivatives.

Several of Dylan's new songs, with their melodies and verse patterns derived from those traditional models, were soon to be widely described as the 'protest songs' of his formative musical period of 1962–63. That was most obviously the case with the anthemic title song of his third album, *The Times They Are A-Changin'*. But the lyrical development that gave rise to the 'protest song' label could really be traced back to what was to become his most widely covered song, 'Blowin' in the Wind', which he had composed in April 1962 in New York City. Later, shortly before his second album, *The Freewheelin' Bob Dylan*, was released in May 1963, he had told a friend: 'I'm going through changes. Need some more finger-pointin' songs in it, 'cause that's where my head's at right now.'[74]

But more broadly Dylan's new songs of that period, strongly influenced by his first visit to England, were also themselves expressions of a creative adaptation of the traditional music of historic English-speaking popular cultures. That develop-ment was to be repeated throughout the 1960s in historically more recent forms of popular music, and in different ways, by Dylan as well as by other British and

American musicians in, as Marqusee and others have noted, a complex transatlantic process of mutual influence.[75] In what was to be a profoundly significant indicator of that process, The Beatles made their musical breakthrough just a month after Dylan's first visit to London when their second single, 'Please Please Me', entered most of the British pop-music charts at number 1 in February 1963. When Dylan next visited Britain, to play at the sold-out Royal Festival Hall in London in May 1964, that musical cross-fertilisation was beginning, in a changing British social and cultural climate, to acquire vibrant new forms of expression.

Notes

1 John Hughes, *Invisible Now: Bob Dylan in the 1960s* (Farnham: Ashgate, 2013), p. 73.

2 Philip Saville, 'Bob Dylan in the Madhouse' (from an interview with Elizabeth Thomson and David Gutman, May 10, 1989), in Elizabeth Thomson and David Gutman (eds.), *The Dylan Companion* (London: Macmillan, 1990), pp. 66–67.

3 Ibid., p. 67.

4 Ibid.

5 Suze Rotolo, *A Freewheelin' Time: A Memoir of Greenwich Village in the Sixties* (London: Aurum Press, 2009), p. 149.

6 For Bob Dylan's relationship with Suze Rotolo, see Rotolo, op. cit.; among many other sources, for a brief account, see Nigel Williamson, *The Dead Straight Guide to Bob Dylan* (London: Red Planet, 2015), pp. 31–32.

7 Cited in Andy Gill, *Bob Dylan: The Stories behind the Songs 1962–1969* (London: Carlton, 2011), p. 10.

8 Bob Dylan quoted in Cameron Crowe, liner notes for *Biograph* (Special Rider Music/Columbia Records, 1985), p. 8.

9 Cited in Gill, op. cit., pp. 10–11.

10 See J.P. Bean, *Singing from the Floor: A History of British Folk Clubs* (London: Faber & Faber, 2014), pp. 81–83.

11 Philip Saville quoted in 'Dylan in the Madhouse', in Thomson and Gutman (eds.), op. cit., p. 69.

12 Ibid., p. 68.

13 On the television play *Madhouse on Castle Street*, see Michael Gray, *The Bob Dylan Encyclopedia* (London: Continuum, 2006), pp. 447–449.

14 Philip Saville quoted in 'Dylan in the Madhouse', in Thomson and Gutman (eds.), op. cit., pp. 69, 67, 66.

15 See Derek Barker, 'One Time in London', in Derek Barker (ed.), *Isis: A Bob Dylan Anthology*, rev. edn. (London: Helter Skelter, 2004), p. 69.

16 See Colin Harper, *Dazzling Stranger: Bert Jansch and the British Folk and Blues Revival* (London: Bloomsbury, 2000), pp. 27, 72.

17 Anthea Joseph quoted in Harry Shapiro, *Alexis Korner: The Biography* (London: Bloomsbury, 1996), pp. 157–158.

18 On Dylan's time in London and its folk-music scene during December 1962/January 1963, see in particular: Derek Barker, 'One Time in London', in Barker (ed.), op. cit., pp. 65–72; 'A Chat with Martin Carthy' (interview by Matthew Zuckerman, January 1999) in Barker (ed.), op. cit., pp. 73–82; Bean, op. cit., Ch. 4, pp. 80–97; David Hajdu, *Positively Fourth Street: The Lives and Times of Bob Dylan, Joan Baez, Mimi Baez Farina and Richard Farina* (London: Bloomsbury, 2001), pp. 125–142; Clinton Heylin, *Behind the*

Shades: The 20th Anniversary Edition (London: Faber & Faber, 2011), pp. 105–111; Howard Sounes, *Down the Highway: The Life of Bob Dylan*, rev. edn. (London: Doubleday, 2011), pp. 130–132.

19 Harper, op. cit., pp. 35, 39.

20 Ibid, p. 39.

21 Ibid., p. 111.

22 Ewan MacColl, *Journeyman: An Autobiography*, re-edited with an introduction by Peggy Seeger (Manchester: Manchester University Press, 2009), p. 279.

23 Ewan MacColl quoted in Robin Denselow, *When the Music's Over: The Story of Political Pop* (London: Faber & Faber, 1989), p. 26. On MacColl and the British folk-music revival of the late 1950s/early 1960s, see Denselow, op. cit., pp. 22–23, 25–29.

24 On this point, see C.P. Lee, *Like the Night: Bob Dylan and the Road to the Manchester Free Trade Hall* (London: Helter Skelter, 1998), pp. 29–35.

25 Paul Du Noyer, *In the City: A Celebration of London Music* (London: Virgin Books, 2009), p. 156.

26 Greil Marcus, *Invisible Republic: Bob Dylan's Basement Tapes* (London: Picador, 1997), pp. 27–28. On this point, see, too, Georgina Boyes, *The Imagined Village: Culture, Ideology and the English Folk Revival* (Manchester: Manchester University Press, 1993), pp. 237–240.

27 Michael Brocken, *The British Folk Revival 1944–2002* (Aldershot: Ashgate, 2003), p. 41.

28 Michael Jones, 'Judas and the Many "Betrayals" of Bob Dylan', in David Boucher and Gary Browning (eds.), *The Political Art of Bob Dylan*, 2nd edn. (Exeter: Imprint Academic, 2009), pp. 82–83.

29 Ibid., p. 84.

30 Mike Marqusee, *Chimes of Freedom: The Politics of Bob Dylan's Art* (New York/London: The New Press, 2003), p. 39.

31 Ibid., p. 40.

32 Paul Nelson and Jon Pankake, *The Little Sandy Review* (Minnesota), reprinted in Carl Benson (ed.), *The Bob Dylan Companion: Four Decades of Commentary* (New York: Schirmer Books, 1998), pp. 20–23.

33 Bob Dylan, interview with John Preston, *Sunday Telegraph*, September 26, 2004.

34 Bob Dylan, *Chronicles Volume One* (London: Simon & Schuster, 2004), pp. 248, 253.

35 Bob Dylan quoted in Crowe, op. cit., p. 8.

36 Ibid., p. 26.

37 Rotolo, op. cit., pp. 231–232.

38 See Robert Shelton, *No Direction Home: The Life and Music of Bob Dylan*, rev. and updated edn., ed. Elizabeth Thomson and Patrick Humphries (London: Omnibus, 2011), p. 107; Sounes, op. cit., p. 131; Bean, op. cit., p. 89; Hughes, op. cit., p. 74.

39 Peggy Seeger quoted in Sounes, op. cit., pp. 131–132.

40 Bean, op. cit., p. 89.

41 *Sing Out!* is a US journal of folk music and folk songs that has been published since May 1950. Irwin Silber was its co-founder and editor from 1951 to 1967.

42 Martin Carthy quoted in Bean, op. cit., pp. 84–85.

43 The Child Ballads were a collection of traditional ballads from England and Scotland, together with their American variants, anthologised by the American scholar Francis Child during the second half of the 19th century. They were later published in five volumes, edited by Child and entitled *The English and Scottish Ballads*, which appeared between 1882 and 1898.

44 Martin Carthy quoted in Bean, op. cit., p. 85.

45 On the original story behind 'Lady Franklin's Lament', see Heylin, op. cit., p. 107.

46 See Hughes, op. cit., p. 74.

47 Gill, op. cit., p. 32.

48 'A Chat with Martin Carthy', in Barker (ed.), op. cit., p. 78. For Dylan's own confirmation of the fact that the military-industrial complex was his target in 'Masters of War', see his 2004 interview by Robert Hilburn, cited in Lee Marshall, *Bob Dylan: The Never Ending Star* (Cambridge: Polity, 2007), p. 121.

49 See Hughes, op. cit. p. 205, n. 25.

50 See Sounes, pp. 136–137.

51 Hughes, op. cit., p. 73. Dylan himself claimed that he wrote the first version of 'Masters of War' in London. See Clinton Heylin, *Revolution in the Air: The Songs of Bob Dylan, Vol. 1 (1957–73)* (London: Constable, 2009), p. 117.

52 Bean, op. cit., p. 85; Hughes, op. cit., p. 74.

53 See Bean, op. cit., p. 91.

54 See Shelton, op. cit., p. 56.

55 Dylan, op. cit., pp. 239–240.

56 Hughes, op. cit., p. 75.

57 'A Chat with Martin Carthy', in Barker (ed.), op. cit., p. 78.

58 Heylin, *Behind the Shades*, p. 108.

59 Shelton, op. cit., p. 125.

60 Ibid.

61 Sean Wilentz, *Bob Dylan in America* (London: Vintage Books, 2011), p. 266.

62 Ibid., p. 310. For further discussion of this contentious matter, and for a defence of Dylan, including in his later work, see ibid., pp. 308–313.

63 MacColl, op. cit., p. 281.

64 Daniel Mark Epstein, *The Ballad of Bob Dylan: A Portrait* (London: Souvenir Press, 2011), p. 19.

65 Hughes, op. cit., p. 75.

66 On Woody Guthrie's influence on Bob Dylan, among many sources, see for concise accounts Gill, op. cit., pp. 15–19; Williamson, op. cit., pp. 23–26. For Dylan's own recollection of Guthrie's influence, see Dylan, op. cit., pp. 243–248.

67 Dylan, op. cit., p. 244.

68 See Heylin, *Behind the Shades*, p. 111.

69 'A Chat with Martin Carthy', in Barker (ed.), op. cit., p. 78; Bean, op. cit., p. 94.

70 Bean, ibid.

71 Martin Carthy quoted in Barker, 'One Time in London', in Barker (ed.), op. cit., p. 67. (The author hopes that this chapter will help to rectify that omission.)

72 Ibid.

73 Heylin, *Behind the Shades*, p. 105.

74 See Anthony Scaduto, *Bob Dylan* (London: W.H. Allen, 1972), p. 141.

75 See Marqusee, op. cit., p. 69.

2

TRANSATLANTIC INFLUENCES
Folk, beat music, and R&B

The Beatles' British breakthrough with their second single, 'Please Please Me', in February 1963 was intensely sustained throughout that year. Their first studio album, named after that single, released in March 1963 and recorded in a one-day session in London, reached number 1 in the UK album charts, as did all but one of their subsequent 11 studio albums. Their second, *With the Beatles*, recorded between July and October and released in November 1963, not only reached number 1, too, but also became only the second album in UK popular-music history to sell a million copies. Earlier that year, in August, the group's fourth single, 'She Loves You', became the fastest-selling record in the UK, eventually recording sales of 1.3 million. By Christmas 1963 The Beatles held the top two spots in the UK pop singles chart with 'She Loves You' and their fifth single 'I Want to Hold Your Hand', which sold 1.25 million copies.

The Beatles' dramatic and commercially massive success throughout 1963 formed the most conspicuous part of the so-called British beat boom that lasted until at least late 1966.[1] During that period the terms 'beat groups', 'British beat music', and, in the case of The Beatles' native city of Liverpool, 'Merseybeat' were widely used to refer to a genre of popular music that was essentially a fusion of early rock'n'roll, rhythm and blues, and soul music. The typical musical format for that hybrid was built around a group consisting of lead, rhythm, and bass guitars, drums, and a lead singer or sometimes solo singers. The most popular, influential, and enduring of such groups was unquestionably The Beatles. But prominent among many others were The Searchers, Gerry and The Pacemakers, Billy J. Kramer and The Dakotas, and The Swinging Blue Jeans, all from Liverpool, The Hollies from Manchester, and The Dave Clark Five, Brian Poole and The Tremeloes, and Cliff Bennett and The Rebel Rousers, all from, or based in, London.

What the British press was increasingly calling 'Beatlemania' in 1963, to describe the intense popular and media interest in The Beatles, had also spread to the United

States by the end of that year, particularly with the release there in late December of their fifth single 'I Want to Hold Your Hand'. (The release of their previous singles in the USA had been held up by legal issues over royalties and publishing rights.) By late January 1964 'I Want to Hold Your Hand' had reached number 1 in the US pop charts, selling one million copies.

In early February 1964 The Beatles arrived in New York City for a short tour on their first visit to the United States. Two days later they performed live on US television for the first time on the networked *Ed Sullivan Show*, watched by approximately 73 million people, at that time just over a third of the total US population, and reckoned to be the largest audience ever recorded for a US television programme.[2] By April 1964, with their previous songs by then released, The Beatles held a total of 12 positions, including the top five, on the US Billboard top 100 singles chart.

On first hearing 'I Want to Hold Your Hand' and other Beatles songs, Bob Dylan later stated:

> When we were driving through Colorado we had the radio on and eight of the ten top songs were Beatles songs. In Colorado! 'I Wanna Hold Your Hand,' all those early ones. They were doing things nobody was doing. Their chords were outrageous, just outrageous, and their harmonies made it all valid.[3]

Dylan added, too, in a partial explanation of his own change of musical direction from 1965 onwards, and with an awareness of The Beatles' significance:

> I knew they were pointing the direction of where music had to go...it seemed to me a definite line was being drawn...You see there was a lot of hypocrisy all around, people saying it either had to be folk or rock. But I knew it didn't have to be like that. I dug what The Beatles were doing, and I always kept it in mind from back then.[4]

With regard to 'I Want to Hold Your Hand', as Ian MacDonald later observed, Dylan was thus 'able to see past the song's naivety to the epoch-making spirit animating it'.[5] The immense popularity and commercial success generated by that spirit sparked what the US media soon referred to as the 'British invasion', beginning later in 1964 and running into subsequent years in a second wave, in which other British beat groups enjoyed considerable success in the United States. Among these were The Searchers, The Dave Clark Five, Herman's Hermits, and Wayne Fontana and The Mindbenders, and later, in the second wave, more blues-based groups such as The Rolling Stones, The Animals, The Yardbirds, Manfred Mann, and The Spencer Davis Group. In the earlier wave throughout 1964 British artists had captured 30 per cent of the US record market. In broader cultural terms, the 'British invasion' of the United States in many cases involved, as Robert Cantwell has noted, 'the return of America's socially and politically repressed rock-and-roll music, carried by young English aficionados'.[6]

The British beat group boom of the early 1960s was thus accompanied by a second movement of British popular music – rhythm and blues – that was in significant respects distinct from, and grittier than, British beat music. Most prominent of the British rhythm and blues, or R&B, groups at that time, and in subsequent years, were The Rolling Stones, based in London, who made their eventual breakthrough in Britain in 1964. But conspicuous and popular, too, were other blues-based groups such as The Animals from Newcastle, Them from Belfast, The Spencer Davis Group from Birmingham, and The Pretty Things, The Yardbirds, and Manfred Mann, all from, or based in, London. In addition, The Kinks and The Who, both also from London, played a hard-edged form of beat music that drew heavily on rhythm and blues.

British rhythm and blues had a number of musical strands, but the dominant one in the early to mid-1960s was rooted in black American Chicago-style electric urban blues, as performed since the late 1940s by musicians such as Muddy Waters, John Lee Hooker, Howlin' Wolf, Memphis Slim, T-Bone Walker, Bo Diddley, Jimmy Reid, Chuck Berry, and others.[7] British rhythm and blues developed in response to the recordings of such musicians, often on the Chess label in Chicago, which were difficult for young British blues enthusiasts to obtain at that time in Britain, even in London.[8] In many cases such records were brought across the Atlantic to major British ports by merchant sailors or American servicemen based in Britain.

The major forerunners and pathfinders of British rhythm and blues were Alexis Korner and his group, formed in early 1962, Blues Incorporated, the first real full-time British electric blues band. Yet Blues Incorporated had its deeper roots in the British jazz and skiffle scenes of the 1950s, with which Korner was associated, specifically in London. The leading British jazz bandleaders at that time, Humphrey Lyttleton, Ken Colyer and, in particular, Chris Barber had during the 1950s attempted to promote blues to their Dixieland jazz audiences. Alexis Korner, who had become enamoured of blues ever since his English schooldays during the Second World War, and had a zealous commitment to its active promotion, had played occasionally for Chris Barber's Jazz Band in London on banjo, when its regular banjoist, Lonnie Donegan, was unavailable.[9]

Korner later, in 1954, joined Ken Colyer's Skiffle Group on guitar and mandolin. Skiffle music, which Colyer and Chris Barber had used as an interval vehicle for presenting blues to their jazz audiences, was essentially a 1950s British hybrid genre of country blues, Anglo-American folk music, and elements of traditional jazz. It was performed with a combination of guitars, banjos, and double bass, and often washboards, tea chests, and drums, in a rudimentary musical style resembling that of American jug bands. Its influences included black American folk and blues musicians such as Josh White, Big Bill Broonzy, Lonnie Johnson, and Leadbelly. Lonnie Donegan, Chris Barber's regular banjoist, who became the leading and most popular British skiffle artist, had recorded and released in 1956, as The Lonnie Donegan Skiffle Group, a frenetic hit version of Leadbelly's song 'Rock Island Line'. It spent 22 weeks in the UK pop charts and even entered, highly unusually at that time, the US top 20.[10] The record's success was a major factor in fuelling the British skiffle boom of the second half of the 1950s, involving the formation of thousands of skiffle groups throughout Britain. Among their number, significantly, was the early incarnation, in Liverpool in 1957, of The Beatles, appearing as The Quarrymen, originally formed and led by John Lennon.

Earlier, in London in late 1955, Cyril Davies, a burly metalworker from the north-west London suburb of South Harrow, who was an accomplished twelve-string acoustic guitarist, had formed the London Skiffle Centre, based at the Roundhouse pub on the corner of Wardour and Brewer Streets in Soho, London, where Alexis Korner regularly played. But by 1957, tiring of skiffle, Davies decided, with Korner, to convert his Skiffle Centre into an acoustic blues club at the Roundhouse, which they called the Blues and Barrelhouse Club, and which was to run on into 1961. Among the club's distinguished visitors and visiting performers were black American blues musicians such as Big Bill Broonzy, Sonny Terry, and Brownie McGhee, and later Muddy Waters and Otis Spann.[11]

After the closure of the blues club at the Roundhouse pub, Alexis Korner in March 1962 opened Britain's first dedicated rhythm and blues venue, the Ealing Club, situated in a room below the ABC teashop and opposite Ealing Broadway underground station in the west London suburb of Ealing. Korner had decided to distance himself from the prejudice against electric blues harboured by purist jazz enthusiasts in central London, particularly at the National Jazz League's own Marquee Club, located since 1958 on Oxford Street.[12]

Korner's band Blues Incorporated, resident at the Ealing Club, was a loosely knit ensemble jointly fronted by himself on electric guitar and Cyril Davies on amplified harmonica, with regular sideman Dick Heckstall-Smith on saxophone. It also often featured Jack Bruce, later bass guitarist for the rock supergroup Cream, on double bass, and sometimes Charlie Watts, later of The Rolling Stones, on drums, when he was not studying at Harrow Art College in north-west London. Alexis Korner was also a considerate mentor for young British rhythm and blues musicians such as Mick Jagger, Keith Richards, and Brian Jones, all later of The Rolling Stones, Keith Relf, later of The Yardbirds, and Paul Jones, later vocalist of Manfred Mann. In fact Mick Jagger gave his first public performance at the Ealing Club soon after its opening in 1962, singing Chuck Berry's 'Around and Around'. He subsequently became Blues Incorporated's second-string vocalist when their main singer, Long John Baldry, was unavailable.[13]

In the light of the increasing popularity of the Ealing Club, and the exodus to it from central London of many paying customers, Harry Pendleton, manager of the Marquee Club, suppressing his prejudice against electric blues, offered Alexis Korner's Blues Incorporated a vacant Thursday-night spot at the Marquee, starting in May 1962. It was there, in July 1962, that the newly formed Rolling Stones played their first gig, with Mick Jagger as lead vocalist.

In November 1962 Cyril Davies left Blues Incorporated, which by then had in his view become more jazz-oriented, and formed his own rhythm and blues All Stars, often playing at the Railway Hotel in Wealdstone, Harrow, north-west London, with Long John Baldry as lead vocalist. Davies and his All Stars recorded two highly regarded singles, 'Preachin' the Blues' and 'Country Line Special'. The latter clearly demonstrated why Davies was at that time widely regarded as Britain's most virtuoso performer on amplified blues harmonica. He died prematurely of leukaemia, aged only 32, in January 1964. Yet as Colin Harper has observed, 'it is as much for the platforms he provided for others as for his own musical work that he remains an icon of British blues and folk'.[14]

Alexis Korner, too, who died in January 1984, as Davies' fellow musician at the Blues and Barrelhouse Club, and in Blues Incorporated, was unquestionably one of the founding fathers of British blues, in both its acoustic and electric forms, which had been grounded in the London jazz and skiffle scenes of the 1950s, in which Korner was closely involved. Indeed, while the lifespan of British skiffle during that decade was short, as Michael Brocken has maintained: 'It was, without doubt, the foundation upon which the next two decades of British popular music were built.'[15]

———————

The British beat group and rhythm and blues movements of the early 1960s, as has been noted, overlapped and yet were in certain ways distinct. Van Morrison, at that time lead singer of Them, the R&B group from Belfast, later even maintained that the British rhythm and blues movement had originally been 'an anti-establishment stance against The Beatles...It was in no shape or form meant to be a commercial entity at all. Well, this was later picked up by the record companies and regurgitated into something that was called rock. But when it started it had nothing to do with rock. It was actually *against* the rock/pop movement.'[16]

Common ground in at least two respects nonetheless existed between the beat/ pop-rock[17] and rhythm and blues movements – first, in terms of performed and recorded material, and, second, in terms of a shared desire for some degree of artistic authenticity. With regard to shared musical material, most of the British beat groups at that time within their repertoire regularly performed and recorded rhythm and blues numbers, using that term in its broad sense as meaning urban black American popular music, which since the 1950s had encompassed genres such as electric blues, rock'n'roll, gospel, and soul. Throughout 1963 UK top 20 hits were achieved by The Searchers with 'Sweets for My Sweet', originally recorded by The Drifters; by The Hollies with both 'Searchin', originally recorded by The Coasters, and 'Stay', originally recorded by Maurice Williams and The Zodiacs; by Brian Poole and The Tremeloes with both 'Twist and Shout', previously recorded in a hit version by The Isley Brothers, and 'Do You Love Me', originally recorded by The Contours; and by Bern Elliot and The Fenmen with 'Money (That's What I Want)', originally recorded by Barrett Strong.

Moreover, The Beatles, the preeminent British beat group of their era, recorded no fewer than ten R&B songs, viewed in the above broad sense, on their first two studio albums *Please Please Me* and *With the Beatles*, released in March and November 1963 respectively. These included, on *Please Please Me*, 'Anna', originally recorded by Arthur Alexander, 'Baby It's You' and 'Boys', originally recorded by the black American girl group The Shirelles, 'Chains', originally recorded by another black American girl group, The Cookies, and The Isley Brothers' 'Twist and Shout'. *With the Beatles* contained powerful and authoritative vocal interpretations by John Lennon of three early Motown songs, 'Please Mr. Postman', originally recorded by The Marvelletes, 'You Really Got a Hold on Me', originally recorded by Smokey Robinson and The Miracles, and Barret Strong's 'Money (That's What I Want)'. The second Beatles album also included covers of The Donays' 'Devil in Her Heart' and of Chuck Berry's 'Roll over Beethoven'.

With regard to the desire for greater artistic authenticity, we have already seen how for Bob Dylan and his American friends in the early 1960s country blues singers such as Robert Johnson and folk singers such as Woody Guthrie personified the kind of authenticity to which they aspired, representing in their eyes a *living* blues and folk-music tradition. In similar spirit, many young British popular musicians during that period – particularly in the newly formed rhythm and blues groups, but also in many beat groups – were keenly aware of a *living*, albeit more recently developed, American popular-music tradition, one rooted in early rock'n'roll and in rhythm and blues, both broadly and narrowly conceived, and to which they sought to add themselves. The Beatles, in particular, were clearly, as Bob Stanley has noted, 'pop fans, happy to raise the profile of other artists, thrilled to be part of pop's big picture. They believed in some continuity in pop—through rock'n'roll and the Brill Building and girl-group scenes to the nascent Motown'.[18] In their relation to that musical tradition, The Beatles were, in Harper's description, 'a foursome of ex-skifflers and rock'n'rollers from Liverpool whose transformation of R&B muscle, rock'n'roll swagger and doo-wop harmonies into something singularly identifiable as British "beat" was comparable to the transatlantic journey of jazz, folk and blues into skiffle a few years earlier'.[19] It was more broadly comparable, too, in terms of such transatlantic cross-fertilisation, to Bob Dylan's adaptation of British and Irish folk-music melodies and influences to his own newly composed songs throughout 1963.

At any rate, early American influences on The Beatles, evident both in their live performances and in their studio albums, enabled them to project an aura of musical authenticity, one that was perceived to be inherent in early American rock'n'roll and in the sounds of early Motown and black American girl groups. The latter, after all, comprised musical sub-genres that, as Andrea Cossu has noted, 'came from a racial periphery, and had little to share with the bubblegum music that characterized the tailor-made products for teenagers in the early 1960s'.[20]

The leading British rhythm and blues groups from 1962 onwards were as aware as The Beatles of a living American musical tradition. But in the case of The Rolling Stones and others the most vital part of that tradition was blues, both country blues and, more overtly, rhythm and blues, conceived in its more specific form of black American electric, Chicago-style urban blues.[21] The raw authenticity of both country and urban blues appeared to those young British musicians to overshadow even the appeal and energy of early white American rock'n'roll. Indeed, for the young Mick Jagger during his schooldays in north Kent, once he had discovered black American blues, his love of it 'was as passionate and sincere as he'd ever been about anything in his life'.[22] He was, then, according to Philip Norman, able to see:

> just what an impostor rock was in so many ways; how puny were its wealthy young white stars in comparison with the bluesmen who'd written the book and, mostly, died in poverty; how those long-dead voices, wailing to the beat of a lone guitar, had a ferocity and humour and eloquence and elegance to which nothing on the rock'n'roll jukebox even came close.[23]

To Jagger and other young British R&B musicians the perceived authenticity of blues did indeed stem from those qualities, together with its directness, including its sexual explicitness; its alternative, socially marginalised appeal; and its highly individualistic tone and character, evident, for instance, in its persistent theme of the alienated outsider or misfit. For the bluesmen, in Harry Shapiro's words, 'were often wanderers of the waste in their own land; jumping trains, drinking, womanizing, and spending time in jail for crimes of violence.' Much of their music was thus 'simply their own sense of "otherness" as much as social commentary'.[24]

Furthermore, it was domestically significant that in Britain the rhythm and blues boom of the early 1960s was itself closely associated with British art schools or colleges – particularly in the London suburbs. At that time those institutions offered learning opportunities, often in an informal setting, in what was then referred to as commercial art, which covered fields such as graphic design and illustration. Many leading members of the most prominent British R&B groups had been students at such art schools or colleges – notably, for example, Keith Richards and Charlie Watts of The Rolling Stones from those at Sidcup and Harrow respectively, Phil May of The Pretty Things also at Sidcup, Keith Relf and Eric Clapton of The Yardbirds at Kingston, Pete Townshend of The Who at Ealing, and Ray Davies of The Kinks at Hornsey.[25]

All of those musicians had their musical roots in the London art college jazz and blues scene. As Dominic Sandbrook has observed, too, of that cultural connection: 'Rhythm and blues fitted nicely with the dissenting spirit of the art schools. As the music of the black American city, it allowed suburban British bohemians to portray themselves as cosmopolitan rebels.'[26] In more directly musical terms, rhythm and blues exerted a strong appeal to those young, artistic individualists. They were strongly drawn to the distinctive and alternative qualities of a compelling and vibrant, yet in Britain at that time largely unfamiliar, genre of popular music.

In addition to shared musical material and a common search for authenticity, there was another distinct factor that united the British rhythm and blues groups and the beat groups of the early 1960s, a factor that became evident from 1963 onwards and was to become even more apparent as the 1960s progressed, when British groups, especially The Beatles, began to write and perform their own song material. That factor was the development which Ian MacDonald later described as the 'democratisation of popular music', whereby the balance of power in deciding the direction and content of pop music began to shift from a corps of professionals—managers, songwriters, publishers, record executives, radio station proprietors and record shop owners—to a body of young amateurs whose connection with the industry's audience was as close *as could be*: those young amateurs were that audience cast in proto-professional form.

That decisive shift also involved a simultaneous transfer of economic power to consumers 'in the business of identifying what is popular…Those who had previously made the decisions and led the market began to follow the market and have the decisions made for them'.[27]

The most significant change accelerating that shift of power, or at least influence, to recording artists and their youthful audience and market was the growing tendency of British popular musicians to write their own songs, following the outstanding examples of The Beatles and Bob Dylan. In the period before 'the 1963 watershed', MacDonald noted, pop stars had been 'groomed and processed by managers and producers, their songs provided for them by professional writers',[28] and, it should be added, with those pop stars supplied with fabricated names designed to project an aura of glamorous, youthful stardom – for example, Adam Faith, Billy Fury, or Lance Fortune – that distanced them from the young, mainly working-class consumers of their pop singles.

In contrast, the growing autonomy of young British popular musicians in the 1960s was most clearly exemplified by The Beatles. From their very first studio album, *Please Please Me*, released in 1963, they composed their own songs. Indeed, their third album, *A Hard Day's Night*, released in August 1964, consisted entirely of original song material. Their own compositions were to comprise the bulk of the tracks on their subsequent eight albums. The Beatles also determined the choice of musical genre in their studio recordings and, more broadly, the course of their own future musical development. They thereby set new standards for their contemporaries in British popular music. They did so as well, later in the 1960s, in their innovative use of recording studio techniques.

The socio-cultural effect of the shift of power and influence to musical performers and recording artists, evident in such developments, from 1963 onwards was, as MacDonald observed, to narrow the gap between professional popular musicians and their paying audience, a gap that had been much wider from about the late 1950s to 1962, following the dissipation of the initial impact of early rock'n'roll in the mid-to-late 1950s.[29] The Beatles, for example, became national, and from 1964 international, pop stars partly because they had already been in 1960–61 *local* stars in their native city of Liverpool. Brian Epstein, their manager from January 1962 until his death in 1967, had been a local record shop owner in Liverpool who in late October 1961 was asked by three customers on the same day whether he stocked a record, 'My Bonnie', by a local group, The Beatles, of whom he had never heard. Prompted by those enquiries, Epstein had visited the Cavern Club, one of their most frequent performing venues, in nearby Matthew Street two weeks later to watch them play for the first time. After being appointed as The Beatles' manager, two months later, he subsequently signed them to EMI's Parlophone record label in April 1962.[30]

The growing democratisation of popular music in Britain during the 1960s is, however, a thesis which, while reflecting such realities, should not be overstated. Record company executives and producers, and performers' managers and agents, still exercised considerable commercial power. But the transfer of at least significant economic influence to young performers and consumers did coincide with important socio-economic and demographic trends in Britain during the 1960s. By the beginning of the decade there were more than five million teenagers in Britain, and, as Dominic Sandbrook has observed: 'In an era of free education and healthcare, teenagers were bigger, healthier and more culturally assertive' than in previous decades. As an age cohort they accounted for 10 per cent of national personal income and more than £800 million of consumer spending, mostly on clothing and entertainment, in Britain per annum.[31] A report by the high-circulation national newspaper the *Daily Mirror* in October 1963 stated that the, by that time, five-and-a-half million teenagers in Britain were buying more than 50 million pop singles a year and spending an annual total income of £1 billion.[32]

In national economic terms, the consequence of such developments was much greater market attention to an age group – broadly, those aged 25 or younger – that had previously been socially marginalised but was now far more economically independent, with greatly increased disposable income and hence consumer purchasing power, than in previous decades. In broader social terms, the growth of that age group, both economically more significant and numerically much larger and more socially visible than before, also gave rise in many cases to a growing and unprecedentedly wide generational gap – in attitudes, outlook, and lifestyle – between the sons and daughters of the 'baby-boomer' generation – those born in Britain in the mid-to-late 1940s and who came of age in the 1960s – and their parents. That gap was to widen as the 1960s progressed, with significant cultural consequences.

All of these factors, therefore, fuelled the increased national and media attention to what was generally termed 'pop music' in Britain during the early to mid-1960s. Of that development there were, in addition to the scale of pop-record sales, at least two other specific indicators. First, on early Friday evenings from August 1963, and running until December 1966, a new pop-music television programme, *Ready Steady Go!*, was launched by Independent TV's London broadcaster Rediffusion. Each programme began with the striking tagline 'The weekend starts here'. Featuring live music acts and a youthful studio audience, it was the first British television programme to reflect accurately the musical and fashion tastes, styles, and preoccupations of a developing youth culture which large sections of its audience were embracing. The programme provided a crucially important vehicle for British beat groups and R&B groups such as The Beatles, The Rolling Stones, The Animals, Manfred Mann and many others, as well as for British solo performers such as Dusty Springfield, and later for American recording artists. In response to the great success of *Ready Steady Go!*, the BBC launched its rival programme, *Top of the Pops*, on New Year's Day, 1964.

A second indicator of the increasing centrality of pop music in British society and culture was the establishment by the spring of 1964 of pirate radio stations, beginning in March of that year with Radio Caroline, which broadcast pop music from ships anchored just off British territorial waters. In spite of their popularity, they were eventually closed down in 1967 by the British government under the Marine Broadcasting (Offences) Act. Attempting to atone for its previous neglect of pop music and its growing significance, the BBC then belatedly opened its own new pop radio station, Radio One, serviced in many cases by former pirate radio station presenters.

This flourishing of youth culture in Britain during 1963–64, in which popular music played a central part, was demonstrably related to the economic and demographic factors that have been noted. But historically it was also in large part a cultural reaction against the Britain of the 1950s. What were to become some of the dominant features of Britain in the 1960s – the emphasis on social and cultural change; an optimistic, even idealistic, belief in progress; an awareness of increased affluence; a greater focus on personal freedom rather than on social conformity – appeared in stark contrast to the key social and cultural features of the British 1950s. Even if to the parents of the 'baby boomers' that decade had appeared to offer stability and security after the horrors and deprivations of the Second World War, to many of their sons and daughters the 1950s had left only a deeply unappealing legacy. In Arthur Marwick's view, that consisted of such social realities as:

> rigid social hierarchy; repressed attitudes to sex; racism; unquestioning respect for authority in the family, education, government, the law and religion;…a strict formalism in language, etiquette and dress codes; a dull and cliché-ridden popular culture, most obviously in popular music, with its boring big bands and banal ballads.[33]

Of the British 1950s, Ian MacDonald, too, observed that:

> Any domestic film of the period will convey the genteel, class-segregated staidness of British society at the time. The braying upper-class voices on newsreels, the odour of unearned privilege in parliament and the courts, the tired nostalgia for the war, all conspired to breed unrest among the young. [John] Lennon, in particular, loathed the Fifties' stiff and pompous soullessness, revelling in the surreal satirical attacks on it by Spike Milligan, Peter Sellers, et al., in BBC radio's *The Goon Show*.[34]

With regard to the emergence of John Lennon and The Beatles, together with that of The Rolling Stones, during 1963–64, MacDonald also perceptively wrote:

> If it's difficult to understand the initial impact of The Beatles without understanding the nature of their times and society, it's quite impossible to understand The Rolling Stones for the same reasons. Without the greyly

restrained and deferential culture of the fifties (which endured until 1963), the Stones would have had no context for their outrageous story to be played out against, nothing to oppose or complain about (and, in turn, be opposed and complained about)…They needed stuffiness, pomposity, snobbery and social inertia as the theatre in which they acted out their drama.[35]

In contrast to what appeared to many young people in Britain during the early 1960s to be the residual features of a drab, traditional, and class-bound society, there was, as the 1960s progressed, in Dominic Sandbrook's words, 'a palpable sense of confidence that life was getting better, transformed by full employment, mass education, new technology and rising living standards'.[36] The spirit of that era, suffused, in MacDonald's view, with both 'a sense of rejuvenating freedom comparable to the joy of being let out of school early on a sunny afternoon' and a widespread 'soaring optimism', was thus shaped by far-reaching social, cultural, and economic forces. But that animating spirit was expressed most clearly by the freshness, variety, and energy of much of British popular music at that time, and, for MacDonald, 'nowhere more perfectly than in the music of The Beatles'.[37]

The Beatles, The Rolling Stones, and other British groups during that period were effecting, as Gordon Thompson has also noted, 'dramatic changes' in British popular music, changes that 'transformed an often pale imitation of Americana into a robust culture of their own making'.[38] Yet many of those groups on their tours of the United States from 1964 onwards were also amazed to discover the lack of familiarity among young white Americans with either early rock'n'roll or black American rhythm and blues. The Animals, for instance, on their first tour of the United States in September 1964, were, as Sean Egan has noted, dismayed by the 'astonishing ignorance of the Americans about their own musical heritage'.[39] Hilton Valentine, the group's lead guitarist, thus recalled that: 'When we went to America, people said, "What's the source of your material?" And we said, "What do you mean, it's American music." And they hadn't heard it.'[40]

In the period between Bob Dylan's first visit to London in the winter of 1962–63 and his next trip in May 1964, such was the changing musical, social, and cultural climate of the Britain of those times. Dylan himself had become an important early musical influence on some of the most popular and influential British groups of that fruitful period.[41] Pete Townshend of The Who, for example, has recalled how he and Richard Barnes, his friend and fellow-student at Ealing Art School in west London, 'discovered Bob Dylan, and listened intently to his first two albums. There was something extraordinary there but I wasn't sure what it was.'[42]

After his exposure to *Bob Dylan* and *The Freewheelin' Bob Dylan*, Townshend, who 'had already written a couple of decent songs', was now 'using an old tape recorder to write new ones in the style of Bob Dylan'.[43] Indeed, the first song that Townshend wrote for The Who, 'Can't Explain', was described at the time by Richard Barnes as 'Bob Dylan with a hint of Mose Allison'.[44] Later it was the release of Dylan's fourth album, *Another Side of Bob Dylan*, in August 1964, which, Barnes also recalled, Townshend 'played endlessly, especially the track "All I Really Want to Do"', that 'spurred him on with his own songwriting'.[45]

Two of the tracks on Dylan's first album were also admired and even covered in recordings by The Animals, the R&B group from Newcastle, in one case in a dramatic manner and with long-running consequences. The first of those tracks was 'Baby Let Me Follow You Down', the traditional song that Dylan had first heard from Eric Von Schmidt. The Animals' drummer John Steel later pointed out: 'We knew the song from the Dylan version on the first album [*Bob Dylan*] so that was okay by us 'cos we loved that album.'[46] The Animals recorded their version of the song under the title 'Baby Let Me Take You Home' in London in February 1964, with Mickie Most as producer. Released in March 1964, the record reached number 21 in the UK charts.

The second track from Dylan's first album covered by The Animals was 'House of the Rising Sun'. Dylan's version, concerning a brothel in New Orleans, was based on the traditional 'Rising Sun Blues', a song that the folklorist Alan Lomax had collected in Kentucky in 1937 and had contributed to Leadbelly's repertoire.[47] It was probably a derivative of a 16th century English ballad. Ten years later it had appeared as a track on an album by Josh White, the celebrated blues and folk singer from South Carolina. But for The Animals it was Dylan's version, in John Steel's view the 'outstanding track' on *Bob Dylan*, on which they based their own electric adaptation, 'no matter what you hear about Josh White'.[48] In support of Steel's recollection, Richard Green, in an interview with The Animals in the pop-music paper *New Musical Express*, had observed in 1964: 'Certainly every time I have visited The Animals in the past few months, out has come a Bob Dylan LP and "House of the Rising Sun" has been played.'[49] Steel later recalled, however, that:

> Even though Bob Dylan was really fresh and new then, as far as we were concerned it wasn't cool to say that we'd pinched the song from his album. We'd much prefer it to be thought that we were delving into some really obscure stuff.[50]

The resulting Animals' version of 'House of the Rising Sun', with the lyrical setting of the song transformed from a brothel into a gambling den, was recorded in London on May 18, 1964, with Mickie Most again as producer, in, according to John Steel, just one take and with the whole recording process lasting only ten minutes.[51] At four minutes and 27 seconds it was at that time, in an era when two-and-a-half minute singles were the norm, one of the longest popular-music singles ever recorded. But to his credit its length was approved and promoted commercially by producer Mickie Most.[52]

Although The Animals had taken the chord sequence of 'House of the Rising Sun' from Dylan's version, his initial acoustic guitar strumming was replaced in their version by Hilton Valentine's arpeggiated chord sequence. In Sean Egan's vivid and evocative description, the record thus began with Valentine's 'stately, circular arpeggios' and proceeded with Alan Price's organ:

> Alternatively pulsing away like a heartbeat under [Eric] Burdon's brooding, bitter reading, then heightening the drama with spectacular crescendos as Burdon's emotions boil over. Price also provides a conceptually perfect ending, his final shimmering wash sounding like the first rays of dawn creeping over a horizon.[53]

The artistic result, a record which Egan has described, with considerable justification, as 'one of the greatest ever made',[54] certainly in the history of modern popular music, reached number 1 in the UK charts in June 1964. Two months later it reached number 1 in the US charts, albeit in a butchered, clumsily edited version which cut in half Alan Price's outstanding organ break. The commercial success of the record nonetheless led to The Animals' participation in the 'British invasion' through their tour of the USA in September 1964.[55]

During that tour The Animals first met, through an arrangement, Bob Dylan, 'another of their heroes', in his manager Al Grossman's New York City apartment. It turned out that their admiration of Dylan was reciprocated since he had been impressed by their electric version of the traditional song he had sung on his first album, to the extent that its impact influenced the future switch in his own musical direction.[56] As The Animals' drummer John Steel has recalled:

> This is from the horse's mouth. That is what he [Dylan] told us. He said he was driving along in his car and ['House of the Rising Sun'] came on the radio and he pulled the car over and he banged on the bonnet. That gave him the connection—how he *could* go electric. He might have been heading that way already but he said that was really a significant thing for him.[57]

Such a path was to lead, for that and other reasons, to Dylan's controversial and divisive decision to 'go electric', first at the Newport in July 1965 and later in his confrontational 1966 world tour. The Animals' electric adaptation of 'House of the Rising Sun', the genesis of which lay in their admiration for Dylan's acoustic version, thus contributed to what was to be a pivotal change in the entire future direction of rock music.

It should be added that Bob Dylan's acoustic version of 'House of the Rising Sun' drew heavily on his friend Dave Van Ronk's arrangement of the traditional song.[58] In his own memoir *The Mayor of MacDougal Street* Van Ronk much later recalled that, following the transatlantic success of The Animals' electric adaptation in 1964, Dylan himself eventually 'dropped the tune from his repertoire because he was sick of being asked to do "that Animals song—the one about New Orleans"'.[59]

Like The Animals and Pete Townshend, The Beatles, too, were highly impressed with Bob Dylan's early albums. George Harrison traced Dylan's influence to the day they first heard *The Freewheelin' Bob Dylan*, which they played over and over again in their rooms in the George V Hotel in Paris in early 1964,[60] during a three-week engagement at the Olympia Theatre, beginning in mid-January. 'Right from that moment', Harrison later recalled, 'we recognised some vital energy, a voice crying out somewhere, toiling in the darkness.' When they finally met Dylan in person, in New York City in August 1964, that 'had a certain effect on us', but he considered that 'the seed was already sown by the album'.[61] 'The content of the song lyrics and the attitude' which it contained seemed to them 'just incredibly original and wonderful.'[62] Paul McCartney, too, later made clear that The Beatles were 'great admirers of Dylan' ever since his first album, a copy of which McCartney had in Liverpool, and John Lennon, notably, had 'been very influenced'.[63]

Dylan's influence on The Beatles, and on Lennon in particular, was to become evident from midsummer 1964 onwards in their songwriting on their fourth, fifth, and sixth studio albums, *Beatles for Sale*, *Help*, and *Rubber Soul* respectively. The process of transatlantic cross-fertilisation of popular music, of mutual musical influence, that Bob Dylan had helped to ignite following his first visit to London in the winter of 1962–63, at that time in the genre of traditional acoustic music, was to proceed in more complex, and later more contentious, ways after his next visit to Britain, to London's Royal Festival Hall in May 1964.

Notes

1 See Bob Stanley, *Yeah Yeah Yeah: The Story of Modern Pop* (London: Faber & Faber, 2014), pp. 131–143.

2 Jonathan Gould, *Can't Buy Me Love: The Beatles, Britain and America* (London: Portrait, 2007), pp. 3–4.

3 Bob Dylan to Anthony Scaduto, quoted in Anthony Scaduto, *Bob Dylan* (London: W.H. Allen, 1972), p. 175.

4 Ibid.

5 Ian MacDonald, *Revolution in the Head: The Beatles' Records and the Sixties* (London: Pimlico, 1995), p. 78.

6 Robert Cantwell, *When We Were Good: The Folk Revival* (Cambridge, MA: Harvard University Press, 1996), p. 308.

7 On black American electric urban blues, see, for example, Dick Weissman, *Blues: The Basics* (New York and London: Routledge, 2005), Ch. 4, pp. 82–99.

8 On the youthful Mick Jagger's efforts to obtain such records, see Philip Norman, *Mick Jagger* (London: Harper Collins, 2013), p. 42.

9 On Alexis Korner's personal background and subsequent musical development, see in particular Philip Norman, op. cit., pp. 54–63; Philip Norman. *The Stones*, updated edn. (London: Sidgwick & Jackson, 2001), pp. 44–52; Harry Shapiro, *Alexis Korner: The Biography* (London: Bloomsbury, 1996), passim.

10 On Lonnie Donegan, see Colin Harper, *Dazzling Stranger: Bert Jansch and the British Folk and Blues Revival* (London: Bloomsbury, 2000), pp. 21–23; Michael Brocken, *The British Folk Revival 1944–2002* (Aldershot: Ashgate, 2003), pp. 71–73, 76–77.

11 See Harper, op. cit. pp. 29–31; John Platt, *London's Rock Routes* (London: Fourth Estate, 1985), pp. 13–17; Chas McDevitt, *Skiffle: The Definitive Inside Story* (London: Robson Books, 1997), pp. 90–93.

12 On this point, see Norman, *Mick Jagger*, pp. 55, 63, 67; Norman, *The Stones*, p. 48.

13 Norman. *The Stones*, p. 51. On the early association of Jagger and other subsequent members of The Rolling Stones with Korner and the Ealing Club, see Norman, *The Stones*, pp. 47–51; Norman, *Mick Jagger*, pp. 54–63.

14 Harper, op. cit., p. 30.

15 Brocken, op. cit., p. 76. On later prominent British rock musicians as early skifflers, see ibid., p. 77. On British skiffle in general, see Brocken, op. cit., pp. 67–88; McDevitt, op. cit., passim; Ronald D. Cohen, *Folk Music: The Basics* (London: Routledge, 2006), pp. 98–100.

16 Van Morrison quoted in Bill Flanagan, *Written in My Soul: Candid Interviews with Rock's Great Songwriters* (London: Omnibus, 1990), p. 411.

17 For the view that The Beatles 'largely invented', as a new musical hybrid genre, 'pop-rock', see Ray Coleman, *McCartney: Yesterday and Today* (London: Boxtree, 1995), p. 7.

18 See Stanley, op. cit., p. 124. The Brill Building, situated on 49th Street in Manhattan, New York City, contained the offices and studios of popular-music industry professionals during the late 1950s and 1960s. It was there that many of the pop-music hits of that period were composed, usually by songwriter partnerships. Notable among those, for example, were Gerry Goffin and Carole King, Jerry Leiber and Mike Stoller, Burt Bacharach and Hal David, and Barry Mann and Cynthia Weil.

19 Harper, op. cit., p. 135. On The Beatles' adaptation of that American popular-music tradition, see, too, Charlie Gillett, *The Sound of the City*, rev. edn. (London: Souvenir, 1983), p. 263.

20 Andrea Cossu, *It Ain't Me, Babe: Bob Dylan and the Performance of Authenticity* (Boulder, CO: Paradigm Publishers, 2012), p. 42. The guiding thread of Cossu's study of Bob Dylan is the relationship between 'performance, reputation and authenticity' in his work (ibid., p. xviii).

21 On the early impact of black American country and electric blues upon The Rolling Stones, see Norman, *The Stones*, pp. 33–48; Norman, *Mick Jagger*, pp. 34–38, 41–42; Keith Richards with James Fox, *Life* (London: Weidenfeld & Nicolson, 2010), pp. 103–110.

22 Norman, *Mick Jagger*, p. 36.

23 Ibid. On the nature of the appeal of black American electric blues at that time to young British rhythm and blues musicians, see, too, Shapiro, op. cit., pp. 100–103.

24 Shapiro, op. cit., p. 103.

25 See Dominic Sandbrook, *White Heat: A History of Britain in the Swinging Sixties* (London: Little, Brown, 2006), pp. 128–131; Simon Frith and Howard Horne, *Art into Pop* (London: Methuen, 1987), p. 73.

26 Sandbrook, op. cit., p. 131.

27 Ian MacDonald, *The People's Music* (London: Pimlico), pp. 192, 193.

28 Ibid., p. 193.

29 Ibid., p. 196. I recall seeing Keith Moon, drummer of The Who, outside the Fender Club in the Churchill Hall, in Kenton, north-west London, where The Who had been playing, some time in 1964. He was engaged in conversation with about a dozen male, at that time, fellow Mods, in similar dress and with similar hairstyles. The scene seemed to indicate a cultural affinity between a performer and his audience, one that was rooted in popular recognition and appreciation of local, in that instance, north-west and west London stardom.

30 See Philip Norman, *Shout! The True Story of the Beatles*, rev. and updated edn. (London: Sidgwick & Jackson, 2003), pp. 125–127, 130–131. 'My Bonnie' was in fact a record by

Tony Sheridan, recorded in Hamburg in 1961 on the German Polydor label, with The Beatles named as 'The Beat Brothers' as his backing group.

31 Sandbrook, op. cit., p. 97.

32 Ibid.

33 Arthur Marwick, *The Sixties: Cultural Revolution in Britain, France, Italy and the United States, c. 1958–1974* (Oxford: Oxford University Press, 1998), p. 3.

34 MacDonald, *Revolution in the Head*, p. 9.

35 MacDonald, *The People's Music*, p. 51.

36 Dominic Sandbrook, 'Foreword', in Trevor Harris and Monia O'Brien Castro (eds.), *Preserving the Sixties: Britain and the 'Decade of Protest'* (Basingstoke: Palgrave Macmillan, 2014), p. xv.

37 MacDonald, *Revolution in the Head*, p. 1.

38 Gordon Thompson, *Please Please Me: Sixties British Pop, Inside Out* (Oxford: Oxford University Press, 2008), p. 13.

39 Sean Egan, *Animal Tracks: The Story of the Animals, Newcastle's Rising Suns* (London: Helter Skelter, 2001), p. 50.

40 Hilton Valentine quoted in ibid., p. 51. On the early lack of exposure of many white American rock musicians to black American music in the early 1960s, see, too, Richards, op. cit., p. 160.

41 As Ray Coleman has noted, the term 'groups' was commonly used at that time in popular music, not being replaced by the term 'bands' until the late 1960s. In the early 1960s 'bands' as a term was 'reserved for brassy dance orchestras or jazz line-ups' (Coleman, op. cit., p. 7).

42 Pete Townshend, *Who I Am* (London: HarperCollins, 2012), p. 65. See, too, Richard Barnes, *The Who: Maximum R&B* (London: Plexus, 1982), p. 8.

43 Townshend, op. cit., p. 68.

44 Ibid., p. 75.

45 Barnes, op. cit., p. 8.

46 John Steel quoted in Egan, op. cit., p. 40.

47 See Cantwell, op. cit., p. 308.

48 John Steel quoted in Egan, op. cit., p. 42.

49 Richard Green, 'The Animals Score Big Hit by Toning Down the Lyric', *New Musical Express*, June 26, 1964, p. 5; cited in Thompson, op. cit., p. 84, n. 15.

50 John Steel quoted in Egan, op. cit., p. 42.

51 See Egan, op. cit., p. 44. On the development of The Animals' 'House of the Rising Sun,' see ibid., pp. 42–47. For another account of its recording, see Thompson, op. cit., pp. 84–85.

52 See Egan, op. cit., pp. 44–45.

53 Ibid., pp. 46–47.

54 Ibid., p. 6.

55 See ibid., pp. 50–51.

56 See ibid., p. 51.

57 John Steel quoted in ibid., p. 51.

58 On this point, see Andy Gill, *Bob Dylan: The Stories behind the Songs 1962–69* (London: Carlton, 2011), p. 12; Howard Sounes, *Down the Highway: The Life of Bob Dylan* (London: Doubleday, 2001), p. 96.

59 Dave Van Ronk with Elijah Wald, *The Mayor of MacDougal Street* (Cambridge, MA: Da Capo, 2005), p. 177.

60 See Graeme Thomson, *George Harrison: Behind the Locked Door* (London: Omnibus, 2013), p. 85.

61 George Harrison quoted in Derek Taylor, *It Was Twenty Years Ago Today* (London: Bantam Press, 1987), p. 92.

62 George Harrison interviewed in *Mojo* magazine, December 1993; quoted in Mark Blake (ed.), *Dylan: Visions, Portraits and Back Pages* (London: DK/Mojo, 2005), p. 46.

63 Paul McCartney quoted in Barry Miles, *Paul McCartney: Many Years from Now* (London: Secker & Warburg, 1997), p. 187.

3

SECOND TIME IN LONDON

May 1964

Bob Dylan's third studio album, *The Times They Are A-Changin'*, lyrically his most politically and socially engaged, was released in January 1964. Apart from its anthemic title track, it also contained another song that was to acquire classic status and to be categorised at the time as another of Dylan's early 'protest songs', namely, 'With God on Our Side'.[1] In addition, the album contained four other songs of social or political commentary, 'The Ballad of Hollis Brown' and 'North Country Blues', concerned with respectively the human effects of rural poverty and industrial decline, 'Only a Pawn in Their Game', with its focus on institutionalised racism, and 'The Lonesome Death of Hattie Carroll', concerned with injustice following the death by manslaughter, according to the subsequent judicial verdict, of a black American Baltimore female bartender.

Several of the songs on the album, as had been the case with *The Freewheelin' Bob Dylan*, were based on traditional British folk-song melodies. 'The Ballad of Hollis Brown', for example, was based on the melody line of the traditional English song 'Pretty Polly', while 'The Lonesome Death of Hattie Carroll' was based on that of the 16th century Scottish ballad 'Mary Hamilton'.

The release of *The Times They Are A-Changin'* in January 1964, with its stark, often austere tone and subject matter, consolidated Dylan's growing reputation as the leading writer and performer of 'protest' and topical songs dealing with political and social issues of the day, even if he was shortly to renounce, or at least step away from, that elevated status which had been widely assigned to him during that period. But such a reputation had already been established by July 1963 at the Newport Folk Festival, where, making several appearances, he had been the outstanding performer, duetting on one occasion with Joan Baez on 'With God on Our Side'. At that time Dylan was beginning to form a somewhat uneasy relationship with Baez, giving rise to the widespread popular description of them as 'the King and Queen of Folk'. Dylan had accepted an offer from Baez, who then enjoyed a more substantial musical reputation and a larger audience than his own, to appear as a guest performer on her 1963 tour. By October of that year, the fact that Dylan's reputation had grown to rival that of Baez was marked by his acclaimed solo concert at Carnegie Hall in New York City.

It was already clear, however, by mid-to-late 1963 that Dylan was disturbed personally by his growing fame. At Newport in July he had told friends that: 'The attention is too much commotion for my body and head.'[2] In particular, he was troubled, too, by the label or image of 'spokesman of a generation' that was increasingly being imposed on him, together with the need urged on him by many activists in the American civil rights movement of that time to demonstrate his social responsibility as a leading, if not the preeminent, topical songwriter of the day.

With regard to the civil rights movement, Dylan had agreed to fly down to Greenwood, Mississippi, in July 1963 to perform, along with Pete Seeger, Josh White, and Theodore Bikel, at a voter-registration rally, designed to encourage greater black American voting in that state. At the rally, organised by the Student Non-violent Coordinating Committee (SNCC), of which his friend Jim Foreman was a leading member, Dylan sang his 'Only a Pawn in Their Game', a song prompted by the murder a month before of Medgar Evers, the chief organiser in Mississippi of the National Association for the Advancement of Colored People (NAACP). Dylan's appearance at the rally, together with that of his fellow performers, was not without courage in view of the Kennedy administration's reluctance at that time to provide federal protection for voter registration in the Deep South.

The following month, August 1963, Dylan appeared and performed, along with Joan Baez, before 200,000 people at the March on Washington, during which Martin Luther King Jr. delivered his historic 'I Have a Dream' speech. Dylan again sang 'Only a Pawn in Their Game', while the folk trio Peter, Paul and Mary sang his 'Blowin' in the Wind'. The previous month their cover version of the song had sold 300,000 copies in the first week of its release. By mid-August 1963 the record had reached number 2 in the US Billboard chart, with sales exceeding one million copies.

Yet in the aftermath of such events Dylan faced increasing pressures to demonstrate further political commitment and social responsibility, which were judged by many of his peers and admirers to be consonant with his qualities and status as an outstanding young topical songwriter. In spite of such pressures, Dylan recorded his third album *The Times They Are A-Changin'* between August and October 1963. It consisted wholly of original self-compositions, most of which were, in his own description, 'finger-pointing' songs reflecting the social and political turmoil of that period.

The title track exemplified the tenor of the album as a whole: its underlying emphasis of political and social concern and of the pressing need for radical change. In spite of Dylan's later movement away from his association with his early 'protest' or topical song material, 'The Times They Are A-Changin'' as a song, with its melody influenced by the traditional Irish and Scottish ballads 'Come All Ye Bold Highwaymen' and 'Come All Ye Tender-Hearted Maidens', undoubtedly assumed anthemic status for large sections of the generation that had come of age in the 1960s. As John Hughes has observed:

> For all Dylan's disavowals of the role of spokesman, this is a conscious, no-holds-barred anthem for a generation. It articulates the incalculable yet irresistible movement of the present into the future, condensing into five verses a political vision swept along with the current of the times.[3]

The declaration in the song that 'Your sons and your daughters are beyond your command' summed up, too, the widening generational gap that had appeared in the 1960s between many of the unprecedentedly more independent and affluent 'baby boomers' and their parents. Specifically, the song's exhilarating tone, one, in Hughes' words, of 'uncompromising assurance—declaiming vision as reality underway',[4] lucidly expressed the concerns of the interrelated civil rights and folk-music movements, with which Dylan was closely associated at that time.

There were, however, two aspects of the song content of the album as a whole that provided significant indicators of Dylan's future changes of artistic direction. In the first place, Dylan's topical songs on the album were, with the exception of the title track, essentially individualist in their tone and emphasis. 'The Ballad of Hollis Brown', 'The Lonesome Death of Hattie Carroll', and 'North Country Blues' were all commentaries on contemporary social and political issues. But they were composed from the perspective of particular individuals, and were evocations of subjective experience and individual feelings. In contrast, the predominant emphasis of much of the folk-music movement of that period, both in the United States and in Britain, most conspicuously, for instance, at the Singers' Club in London, was on the collectivity – the 'folk', the 'people', the industrial and rural working classes – rather than on the individual. As Lee Marshall has observed:

> A crucial element of folk authenticity is that performers are understood to be part of the group they represent, part of the folk…As such,…each singer was merely one representative of the people. In this understanding it is the song not the singer (let alone the writer) that matters.[5]

In so far, too, as traditional folk songs were treated in much of the folk-music movement as artefacts, to be revered as authentic expressions of collective, working-class experience, the people in those songs were often, Marshall added, made to 'serve as representative characters, intended to reflect a particular social type… rather than being treated as individual human beings'.[6]

As Elijah Wald has also noted in respect of the contrasting, individualist focus of Dylan's topical songs: 'He was not writing "We Shall Not Be Moved" or "We Shall Overcome". He was writing about individuals, and often difficult, complex individuals.'[7] 'Only a Pawn in Their Game', for example, was another Dylan song that 'expressed a sensibility at odds with any mass movement'.[8] The song was not, admittedly, composed mainly from the perspective of a particular individual, unlike the previous songs mentioned above. Although it began with a specific event, the murder of Medgar Evers, it was not merely concerned with condemning his killer. Rather, it focused more on the underlying social and political causes that lay behind the murder. In its lack of didacticism, its subtlety and breadth of vision, Dylan's song was thus very different in kind and quality from most of the other topical song material of the day. In the light of those differences of approach in Dylan's song-writing, including in particular the individualist emphasis of his early topical songs, it is not difficult, therefore, to see how they would sit uneasily with the collectivist ethos of much of the British and American folk-music movements of the early 1960s. Nor is it hard to understand why a mutual unease or tension would arise from those different perspectives and approaches, and become more acute during the following years, particularly in 1965 and 1966.

There was also a second aspect of the song content of *The Times They Are A-Changin'* that pointed towards further future developments in Dylan's songwriting. The album contained two highly personal and introspective songs, 'Boots of Spanish Leather' and 'One Too Many Mornings', that were quite unrelated to topical social or political issues. 'Boots of Spanish Leather', like 'Don't Think Twice, It's All Right' on *The Freewheelin' Bob Dylan* album and the unreleased 'Tomorrow Is a Long Time', was inspired by his girlfriend Suze Rotolo's seven-month absence in Italy, transposed in the song to Spain. Evoking feelings of loss and regret, the song had been written by Dylan in early January 1963 during his short visit to Italy with his manager Albert Grossman and the folk singer Odetta, before he returned briefly to London. He had failed to meet up with Suze Rotolo, who had left for New York a few weeks earlier. The song's melody, like that of 'Girl from the North Country' on the *Freewheelin'* album, drew broadly on the traditional English song 'Scarborough Fair', which Dylan had learned from Martin Carthy in London.[9]

The other highly personal song on *The Times They Are A-Changin'*, 'One Too Many Mornings', was reflective, introspective, and melancholic. In its tone and con-tent, again it was very different from the 'finger-pointing' songs that comprised the bulk of the album. As Michael Gray has observed, it was 'a song that should have served notice on Dylan's early cult followers that Dylan was not going to be a graphic protest singer. But no one seemed to notice'.[10]

Of the highly personal nature of the earlier song 'Don't Think Twice It's All Right' and 'Boots of Spanish Leather', Dylan's friend Dave Van Ronk later remarked: 'Bobby was rolling it out like a soap opera for everyone to hear. The songs were so damn self-pitying—self-pitying but brilliant.'[11] Van Ronk might well have formed at the time a similar judgement about 'One Too Many Mornings', also inspired by his relationship with Suze Rotolo. She herself much later, in her memoir of 2008, alluding to those songs, recalled:

> The old songs [of Dylan's], from the early time of his life in which I participated, are so recognizable, so naked, that I cannot listen to them easily. They bring back everything. There is nothing mysterious or shrouded with hidden meaning for me. They are raw, intense, and clear.[12]

Earlier, too, she had told Dylan biographer Howard Sounes: 'If you listen to all the songs, they couldn't be more clear. Anything about our relationship, about our life together, is very clearly in the songs.'[13] Later, however, in her memoir, mindful of the dynamic tension between artistic creation and personal experience in song-writing, Rotolo added: 'Hearing Bob sing songs that were close to home was always strange for me…I began to feel that people knew more about my life than I did. Gradually I learned to let go and accept the abstraction of his art.'[14]

More broadly, too, she observed that:

> The songs are translations of moods and sensations he experienced. They are fictions that allude to those experiences…He once told me that he couldn't have written certain songs if he hadn't known me. But that doesn't neces-sarily mean a particular song. It means I served as a muse during our time together, and that I don't mind claiming.[15]

The 'raw, intense, and clear' nature in Rotolo's recollection of songs such as 'Boots of Spanish Leather' and 'One Too Many Mornings', contrasting starkly with Dylan's 'finger-pointing songs' on *The Times They Are A-Changin'*, was complemented in a different manner by the album's final track, 'Restless Farewell', the last to be recorded for it, in late October 1963. The valedictory tone of the song, the melody of which was based on the Irish drinking song 'The Parting Glass', often sung by the Clancy Brothers in New York City, reflected the pressures of fame and the desire on Dylan's part both to protect his own privacy from the 'dirt of gossip' and the 'dust of rumors' and to resist the encroachments on his autonomy by those who sought to assimilate him for their own political or social purposes or causes.

Musically, 'Restless Farewell' also marked the formal end of Dylan's frequent use of British and Irish folk modes and melodies that had been evident from 1962 until the close of 1963.[16] The song could be interpreted, too, in Andy Gill's view, as pro-viding 'a fitting epilogue to Dylan's protest period, even though he would continue to be viewed predominantly in that light for another year or two'.[17]

It was not, however, until his next (fourth) album, *Another Side of Bob Dylan*, released in August 1964, that a more explicit recantation of that period appeared in the form of his song 'My Back Pages', with its striking paradoxical chorus line, 'Ah, but I was so much older then. I'm younger than that now.'

When Bob Dylan arrived in London in May 1964, for the first time in the city since his initial visit in the winter of 1962–63, he phoned Martin Carthy soon after his plane had landed and visited his friend at his home in north-west London, bereft by then, Dylan was told, of Carthy's non-functioning piano. Dylan then played Carthy his new song 'Mr. Tambourine Man', which was eventually to appear on his fifth studio album *Bringing It All Back Home*, released in March 1965. In his response to the song, Carthy later recalled: 'I was absolutely thunderstruck. I'd never heard a song like that.'[18] 'Where [the hell]', he thought, 'is this man going?'[19]

This remarkable, introspective, and meditative song Dylan had begun writing on a cross-country trip that he undertook with friends in February 1964, travelling down to New Orleans, then to Texas, and eventually on to California. He completed the song a month or so later, at the home of his journalist friend Al Aronowitz in New Jersey.[20] Dylan's subsequent sole London concert on Saturday, May 17 at the Royal Festival Hall, sold out to its capacity audience of 2,700, allowed him to give a debut concert performance of 'Mr. Tambourine Man'. The concert's set-list also included 'It Ain't Me Babe', in another concert debut, and 'All I Really Want to Do', both of which were to appear on Dylan's fourth album *Another Side of Bob Dylan*, as well as 'The Lonesome Death of Hattie Carroll' from *The Times They Are A-Changin'*, which, by the time of the London concert, had already broken into the UK top 20 album chart.

Of Dylan's performance on May 17, Martin Carthy later stated that Dylan 'was just fantastic'.[21] With regard to Dylan's performance of 'The Lonesome Death of Hattie Carroll' in particular, Carthy recalled: 'He just started to sing it and it was just like the place caught fire...But the roar when he came to the end of it I'll never forget it...I just knew I'd heard something quite extraordinary. And I didn't care that he'd taken the idea from Brecht. Hooray that he knows who Bertolt Brecht is.'[22]

Dylan's song, which drew on the melody of the 16th century English ballad 'Mary Hamilton', had indeed also used a verse pattern based on Brecht's song 'Pirate Jenny' from *The Threepenny Opera*, co-written by Brecht and Kurt Weill and produced in 1928.[23] Carthy added to his view of Dylan's composition that: 'It's an absolutely wonderful song, written, I'm quite sure, in a rage, but also with a great sense of form. Whatever he did, and whatever he does, there's always form there.'[24] As Sounes has also concisely noted, in the song Dylan 'related the story with the economy of a news reporter and the imagery of a poet'.[25]

During the intermission of the two-hour concert, John Lennon sent a telegram to Dylan, saying that The Beatles had wished to be at the concert but had a filming commitment for *A Hard Day's Night*.[26] At the end of the concert, leaving the Royal Festival Hall, Dylan had his first experience of young fan adulation, to which he reportedly reacted with mixed feelings.[27]

During Bob Dylan's short visit to London, lasting from May 9 to 18, he stayed at the May Fair Hotel, off Piccadilly. In the course of his stay, he was also taken around some London folk clubs by Bill Leader, a London folk-club organiser, and Bert Jansch, the rising Scottish folk and blues guitarist. The clubs included the Roundhouse on Wardour Street and the Broadside at the Black Horse pub in Rathbone Place, where Dylan was subsequently barred, apparently for drinking his own bottle of red wine.[28] After leaving London, Dylan flew to Greece, in the company of the singer Nico, for a working holiday during which he composed, in a village near Athens, many of the songs for his fourth, and, as it was to prove, transitional, album *Another Side of Bob Dylan*. It was recorded in New York in early June 1964 and released in August of that year.[29]

With regard to the other songs on that album, all 11 of which were self-compositions, Dylan told the journalist Nat Hentoff: 'There aren't any finger-pointing songs. Me, I don't want to write *for* people any more. You know—be a spokesman. From now on I want to write from inside me'.[30] Many of those new songs were indeed highly personal in tone and content.

The title of the album, all the tracks of which were recorded in one six-hour, beaujolais wine-fuelled session, appeared superficially to indicate an abandonment of his past social concerns and commitments. But as Dylan later pointed out, he was very uneasy about the album's title, which had been conceived by his producer Tom Wilson. Dylan recalled that: 'I begged and pleaded with him [Wilson] not to do it…I knew I was going to have to take a lot of heat for a title like that and it was my feeling that it wasn't a good idea coming after *The Times They Are A'Changin'*… It seemed like a negation of the past which in no way was true.'[31]

The main themes of *Another Side of Bob Dylan*, as Dylan's first biographer Anthony Scaduto noted, were 'love and personal freedom', laced with 'caustic comments on human relationships'.[32] Furthermore, the love songs on the album were themselves radical and groundbreaking at the time. 'All I Really Want to Do' and 'It Ain't Me Babe', for example, were, as Michael Gray has observed, 'historically important songs: they questioned the common assumptions of true love and the male–female relationship; they not only avoided possessiveness and macho strut but explained why as well'.[33]

Another song on the album, 'My Back Pages', was, however, historically important for a different reason. It indicated more clearly than any other of Dylan's songs to date why he had changed the course of his artistic direction, away from his early 'finger-pointing' songs. 'My Back Pages' made clear Dylan's renunciation of what he considered to be his youthful certitude, which was bound up with the tenure of one-dimensional, doctrinaire positions characteristic of the protest-song movement and its direct and simplistic mode of address. As has been noted, however, Dylan himself never fully succumbed to the latter simplicities in his own songwriting. The fact that the subtlety and individualist emphasis of most of his early topical songs arguably precluded the need for such an unqualified recantation was later aptly crystallised in British jazz singer George Melly's comment that those songs, even 'the most overt' of them, 'suggested a complicated universe where cause and effect, greed and exploitation, revolution and reaction are part of our fibre, not just nasty bogeymen who can be exorcised with a guitar and a lyric'.[34]

'My Back Pages' is nonetheless clearly a personal apologia, Dylan's explicit 'mea culpa' in its tone, content, and celebrated refrain, 'Ah, but I was so much older then. / I'm younger than that now'. But that chorus line also conveyed a firm sense of his personal and creative liberation from those previous entrapments. The song was thus, in Hughes' description, 'a signpost, pointing away from the past, and expressing a powerful ethical recoil from false temptations: to preach and pontificate;…to serve other people's agendas; and to mistake one's motives'.[35]

Another Side of Bob Dylan did, however, consequently provoke a hostile reaction from many of Dylan's admirers and supporters for his apparent renunciation of topical songs. Irwin Silber, the leftist editor of *Sing Out!*, in an open letter in the October/November edition of the magazine, which came out in September

1964, thus rebuked Dylan for his change of musical direction. His new songs, Silber maintained, were 'all inner-directed now, inner-probing, self-conscious—maybe even a little maudlin or a little cruel on occasion'.[36]

Much later, Joan Baez recalled that when in the past she had asked Dylan why he had written 'protest' songs in the first place, he had replied cynically: 'Hey, news can sell, right?...I was never into that stuff.' Baez stated that at the time:

> I didn't believe him. That was a pile of shit. Actually I'll give you a good old English word. It was codswallop and I told him. Nobody could have written those songs and not meant it. Whether he likes it or not, he goes down in the history books as a leader of dissent and social change.[37]

That view was confirmed by friends and colleagues such as John Hammond, Phil Ochs, and Dave Van Ronk.[38] Hammond stated that when he first got to know him in late 1961, Dylan was 'thinking and talking about injustice, and about social problems. Bobby really wanted to change things. He was uptight about the whole set-up in America, the alienation of kids from their parents, the false values.'[39]

Dave Van Ronk, too, told Dylan's first biographer, in a rather more nuanced manner, that Dylan 'was no opportunist. He really believed it all. I was there. He absorbed what was around him, believed it, but he didn't really understand it. He only absorbed the superficialities.'[40]

Van Ronk, much later, also observed shrewdly that:

> One of the great myths of that period is that Bobby was only using the political songs as a stepping stone, a way to attract attention before moving on to other things...The fact is, no one—and certainly not Bobby—would have been stupid enough to use political music as a stepping stone, because it was a stepping stone to oblivion...As for the charge that Bobby was 'selling out' when he stopped writing protest music, or when he went electric [in 1965–66], it makes no sense in the context of that moment, because there was no reason to think that there could be any buyers. It never occurred to me that he was scuttling his artistic vision in a cynical grab at fame and fortune, and if he had been, I would have been very dubious about it working.[41]

In any case, Van Ronk added, 'Bobby's model was Woody Guthrie, and Woody had written a lot of political songs but also songs about all sorts of other subjects, and Bobby was doing the same thing'.[42]

Anthony Scaduto in 1971 added his own view that 'Dylan may have been an opportunist on occasion, but he did not lend his voice to the civil rights movement as part of his design to increase his popularity'. Moreover, black American music had 'touched him deeply' during his adolescence in Hibbing, Minnesota, and 'the black experience had touched his very strong feelings for the oppressed. Maybe he was simply romanticizing it all, as he had romanticized the hobo, but he was totally sincere about it.'[43]

Quite apart, then, from the unjustified charge that Dylan had been using his early topical songs as a career stepping-stone, he was also facing intense popular and media pressures by the time of the release of *Another Side of Bob Dylan*, pressures that made him feel that his perceived image and identity as the foremost topical songwriter of the day were imposing on him, against his will, a personal and artistic straitjacket. Besides, *Another Side of Bob Dylan* contained love songs that were, as has been noted, radical and unconventional in their questioning nature. Moreover, the album's long-term musical impact was far-reaching in that it paved the way for a highly personal, even confessional, style and school of singer-songwriting in the late 1960s and early 1970s, evident in the work of James Taylor, Joni Mitchell, Carole King, Tim Hardin, Cat Stevens, and many others.

In the period between the recording and the release of *Another Side of Bob Dylan*, the British rhythm and blues movement continued to thrive, both in live performance and with recorded material, mainly covering black American R&B originals. The Animals' electric version of 'House of the Rising Sun', probably the first example of what was later referred to as 'folk-rock', had reached number 1 in the British charts in June 1964. The Rolling Stones, too, secured their first UK number 1 hit with their cover version of Bobby and Shirley Womack's 'It's All Over Now' in July of that year, as did Manfred Mann the same month with their cover version of The Exciters' 'Do Wah Diddy Diddy'.

Meanwhile, The Beatles' immense commercial success and growing popularity rapidly increased, and on an international scale. In the spring of 1964 they began filming for *A Hard Day's Night*, a mock-documentary feature film directed by Dick Lester. The film was accompanied by a soundtrack album, released by EMI in July 1964 and consisting of 13 original songs by John Lennon and Paul McCartney composed against a very tight schedule. The film was premiered in London in July 1964 and in New York the following month, and subsequently enjoyed both widespread critical approval and great commercial success on both sides of the Atlantic. The soundtrack album, which was melodically strong in its song content and ebullient in tone, met with a similar response.

After a worldwide tour in June and July 1964, The Beatles revisited the United States in August for a nationwide 20-concert tour. Earlier that year, in the spring, they had made public their admiration for Bob Dylan in an article in *Melody Maker* headed 'The Beatles Dig Dylan'. In August they had the opportunity to meet him for the first time. John Lennon had earlier asked Al Aronowitz, a New York-based journalist who had written sympathetic articles on the Beat poetry and folk-music scenes in San Francisco and New York City, and who had interviewed and befriended Dylan in 1962, to arrange a meeting with The Beatles while they were in New York during their American tour. Dylan, accompanied by his roadie Victor Maimudes and by Aronowitz, consequently met The Beatles at the Delmonico Hotel on Park Avenue, Manhattan, on August 28 after the first of their two concerts at the West Side Tennis Stadium, Forest Hills, Queens. Of that meeting's significance

Aronowitz later wrote: 'I was well aware at the time that I was brokering the most fruitful union in the history of pop music…I was engineering, participating in and chronicling a milestone moment in history.'[44]

Among other things at that meeting, Dylan introduced The Beatles for the first time to marijuana and was very surprised that they had never smoked pot before. 'But what about your song, the one about getting high?' Dylan had asked. 'And when I touch you, I get high, I get high.' Of the lyrics of 'I Want to Hold Your Hand', John Lennon explained to him: 'It goes, "I can't hide, I can't hide".'[45]

As Jonathan Gould has pointed out, Al Aronowitz had by 1964 'come to see Dylan and The Beatles as the charismatic leaders of two flourishing musical subcultures, folk and pop'. In his view, Dylan's core audience was composed of college- or university-educated young people, with, in Gould's words, 'artistic or intellectual leanings, a dawning political and social idealism, and a mildly bohemian style'. In contrast, The Beatles' core audience at that time consisted largely of 'teenyboppers' 'whose lives were totally wrapped up in the commercialized popular culture of television, radio, pop records, fan magazines and teen fashion. They were seen as idolaters not idealists.' Nevertheless, Dylan's core audience was at the same time 'entranced by the allure of a newly energized and autonomous pop culture'.[46]

British groups such as The Beatles and The Animals had clearly, to Dylan's own stated approval, served to revitalise that culture, and the place of rock'n'roll and rhythm and blues within it. The subsequent musical interaction between Dylan and The Beatles in particular meant that their core audiences, already in Britain in 1964 never so starkly distinct or as mutually exclusive as Aronowitz had broadly depicted them, were increasingly to overlap as the 1960s progressed, when, in his own words, 'The Beatles' words got grittier and Bob invented folk-rock'.[47] That development will be explored here later.

Soon after their hotel meeting in Manhattan, Dylan's influence on The Beatles started to become apparent. That could be seen in clear changes in their style of songwriting as well as in the sound of their fourth album, *Beatles for Sale*, recorded between August and October 1964 and released in December of that year. In their early work, certainly in the original songs on their first three albums, The Beatles had written their lyrics to convey a particular mood or tone designed to complement or embellish the melody, harmony, and overall musical sound of their songs. As John Lennon later put it, in that early period 'we were writing songs à la Everly Brothers, à la Buddy Holly, pop songs with no more thought to them than to create a sound. And the words were almost irrelevant.'[48] The Beatles did that, moreover, as Ian MacDonald later observed, by composing their songs not through the structured verse forms of traditional popular music lyric-writing but rather by a method that 'worked more as chains of phrases, some inspired, some hackneyed, some randomly surreal'.[49]

The effect of Dylan's growing influence on The Beatles from 1964 onwards was really twofold. First, it impressed on them the importance of lyrics in actually saying something significant, rather than just embellishing the melody of their songs. Second, it widened the range of the themes and subjects of their songs beyond the central concern of most previous pop-song lyrics with boy–girl romance. It was on John Lennon in particular that Dylan exerted the greatest influence during the mid-1960s, helping to make his lyrics more personal, reflective, and introspective. In their encounters, following the Beatles' first meeting with Dylan in August 1964, Lennon recalled: 'I remember the early meetings with Dylan, he was always saying "Listen to the words, man" and I said "I can't be bothered. I listen to the sound of it, the overall sound".'[50]

It was indeed the case that at first, when listening to Dylan, Lennon, as Steve Lowe has noted, 'preferred to revel in the songs' overall tone of solid self-possession'.[51] Lennon biographer Ray Coleman, who knew his subject well personally, and who interviewed him many times, pointed out that later 'Lennon did admit, though, that…Dylan helped him to think for himself and inject more honesty into his own lyrics'.[52]

Lennon maintained, for instance, that he wrote the title track, recorded in April 1965, of the Beatles' fifth studio album, *Help*, in the style of Bob Dylan, though, he added, 'later we Beatle-fied it'.[53] Another early Beatles song, 'I Should Have Known Better', recorded in February 1964 and sung by Lennon on the album *A Hard Day's Night*, might also, in sound rather than lyric, have been partly influenced by Dylan. It was, in MacDonald's description, 'a cheery potboiler based on an imitation of Bob Dylan's huffing harmonica style and developed into a melody composed largely of one note'.[54] Like most of the tracks on that third Beatles album, it was nonetheless a song that conveyed an overall sense of vital energy and youthful ebullience.

It was, however, on The Beatles' fourth album, *Beatles for Sale*, released in December 1964, and on one particular track, 'I'm a Loser', sung by Lennon and recorded in August of that year, that Dylan's influence became more clearly apparent, both in sound and mood and in Lennon's more realistic lyrics. In the last major interview he gave before he was murdered on December 8, 1980, Lennon recalled of his song: 'That's me in my Dylan period.' Asked by David Sheff whether the song was a personal statement, Lennon replied by saying: 'Part of me suspects I'm a loser. Part of me thinks I'm God Almighty.'[55]

Certainly the recurring chorus of the song, 'I'm a loser / and I'm not what I appear to be', revealed the former sensibility. In its verses, too, amid a series of commonplace reflections on lost love, Lennon suddenly asks, 'Is it for her or myself that I cry?', while elsewhere he sings: 'Although I laugh and I act like a clown, / Beneath this mask I am wearing a frown'. Such words reflected a mood of critical self-appraisal, uncommon in The Beatles' previous pop lyrics and very rare, too, for that matter, in most previous pop lyrics in general.

Confirming his more personal approach to songwriting that was gradually emerging in 1964, Lennon told David Sheff 16 years later: 'I'm not interested in writing third-party songs. I like to write about me; 'cause I *know* me.'[56] His biographer Ray Coleman later wrote of 'I'm a Loser', the first early, Dylan-influenced indication of that approach, that the song 'may not match Dylan's searing sense of loneliness and loss evoked by his contemporary "Boots of Spanish Leather" or "Ballad in Plain D", but it was an attempt to inject some honesty and genuine emotion into the fairy-tale world of The Beatles'.[57] In Coleman's view, too, the opening 'pretty bleak trilogy' of songs on *Beatles for Sale* – 'No Reply', 'I'm a Loser' and 'Baby's in Black' – 'displayed the bleaker side of the Lennon persona'.[58]

Shortly after the release of *Beatles for Sale* in December 1964, Lennon told the leading British popular-music paper *Melody Maker* that both 'I'm a Loser' and 'I Don't Want to Spoil the Party' on the album reflected Bob Dylan's increasing influence on The Beatles' songwriting in general, though the latter song also clearly displayed rockabilly and country-music influences. But as Gould has suggested, Lennon at that time 'was presumably referring more to the general tone of Dylan's music than to his words, since neither the content nor the style of the lyrics to either song, apart from their vaguely introspective cast, bear much resemblance to anything specific in Dylan's work'.[59] In similar vein, MacDonald observed that in 'I'm a Loser' Lennon 'merely adopts a tone. A touch of rough harmonica, some strummed acoustic guitar, slightly more thoughtful and hard-bitten lyrics—this was the extent of his "Dylan influence" when the song was recorded',[60] that is, in August 1964, just a fortnight before The Beatles' first meeting with Dylan in New York City.

But Dylan's growing influence on The Beatles was more than just a matter of tone and attitude, important as those factors were. His influence also extended, as has been noted, to the very nature and content of lyrics and the scope of their subject matter. That was tentatively apparent in most of the eight original Lennon/McCartney songs on *Beatles for Sale*. In his study of The Beatles, Gould also noted, for example, that Paul McCartney's simple but tuneful song on the album, 'I'll Follow the Sun', which had actually been conceived by him before The Beatles were formed,[61] might in its finished, recorded version, featuring some acoustic instrumentation, have reflected Dylan's influence at the time since: 'In keeping with his vagabond persona, one of Dylan's favorite song-forms on his early albums was a type of rueful fare-thee-well patterned on the many traditional blues and folk ballads that address the vicissitudes of "rambling" and the inevitability of moving on'.[62] 'Don't Think Twice, It's All Right' had been a clear early example of that song form.

Significantly, too, 'I'll Follow the Sun' and most of the other original compositions on *Beatles for Sale* demonstrated Dylan's songwriting influence in their moving away, at least to some extent, from the prevailing standards of boy–girl romance characteristic of most pop-music lyrics. They did so by expressing, for really the first time, a greater degree of realism, even pessimism, about interpersonal relationships, together with a greater awareness of romantic difficulties and frustrations. It was hardly surprising that one of The Beatles' favourite tracks on *Another Side of Bob Dylan* was, according to Gould, 'I Don't Believe You (She Acts Like We Never Have Met)',[63] very much a song of romantic disappointment, frustration, and bewilderment.

Partly because of the very tight schedule under which The Beatles had been working throughout 1964, involving touring, filming, and working on the soundtrack to *A Hard Day's Night*, *Beatles for Sale* contained six covers, five of which were of early American rock'n'roll, rockabilly, and R&B classics, namely, Carl Perkins' 'Everybody's Trying to be My Baby' and 'Honey Don't'; Buddy Holly's 'Words of Love'; 'Kansas City', composed by Leiber and Stoller and sung earlier by Little Richard; and Chuck Berry's 'Rock and Roll Music'. Just as The Animals on their first tour of the United States in September 1964 had encountered with astonishment the lack of familiarity among young white Americans with their own popular-musical heritage, so too, as Coleman observed in his biography of Lennon, were The Beatles, by championing those largely forgotten classics, able in effect 'to reacquaint American audiences with their own rock'n'roll history'.[64]

Bob Dylan's fifth studio album, *Bringing It All Back Home*, which was to be released in March 1965, itself bore a title that implicitly acknowledged the group's achievement in that significant respect, one that Dylan sought to reproduce in his own way with his new form of American electric music. The Beatles' early recognition, too, of Dylan's qualities as an outstanding songwriter would further shape their musical aspirations and achievements, and those of Lennon in particular, during that following year. In a continuing process of transatlantic cross-fertilisation, they in turn would influence Dylan's musical reorientation, which *Bringing It All Back Home* would herald in a distinctive and innovative artistic breakthrough.

Notes

1 On the origins of the melody of 'With God on Our Side', see Ch. 1 above, pp. 13–14. On the song itself, see Clinton Heylin, *Revolution in the Air: The Songs of Bob Dylan Vol. 1: 1957–73* (London: Constable, 2010), pp. 166–170; Andy Gill, *Bob Dylan: The Stories behind the Songs 1962–69* (London: Carlton Books, 2011), pp. 56–57.

2 Cited in Gill, op. cit., p. 49.

3 John Hughes, *Invisible Now: Bob Dylan and the 1960s* (Farnham: Ashgate, 2013), p. 79.

4 Ibid.

5 Lee Marshall, 'Bob Dylan: Newport Folk Festival, July 25, 1965', in Ian Inglis (ed.), *Performance and Popular Music: History, Place and Time* (Aldershot: Ashgate, 2006), pp. 23–24.

6 Lee Marshall, *Bob Dylan: The Never Ending Star* (Cambridge: Polity, 2007), p. 66.

7 Elijah Wald, *Dylan Goes Electric: Newport, Seeger, Dylan and the Night That Split the Sixties* (New York: Harper Collins, 2015), p. 107.

8 Ibid., p. 109.

9 On 'Boots of Spanish Leather', see Heylin, op. cit., pp. 147–150.

10 Michael Gray, *Song and Dance Man III: The Art of Bob Dylan* (London: Continuum, 2000), p. 4. On 'One Too Many Mornings', see Heylin, op. cit., pp. 205–207; Gill, op. cit., pp. 58–59.

11 Dave Van Ronk quoted in Bob Spitz, *Dylan: A Biography* (New York and London: W.W. Norton & Co., 1991), p. 200.

12 Suze Rotolo, *A Freewheelin' Time: A Memoir of Greenwich Village in the Sixties* (London: Aurum Press, 2009), p. 155.

13 Suze Rotolo quoted in Howard Sounes, *Down the Highway: The Life of Bob Dylan* (London: Doubleday, 2001), p. 159.

14 Rotolo, *A Freewheelin' Time*, p. 289.

15 Ibid., p. 290.

16 On the artistic benefit for Dylan of traditional British and Irish folk modes and melodies, see Hughes, op. cit., p. 75.

17 Gill, op. cit., p. 67. On 'Restless Farewell', see, too, Helyin, op. cit., pp. 207–211. Heylin notes that it had been one of Frank Sinatra's favourite Dylan songs, and that Sinatra had later personally asked him to perform it, which Dylan agreed to, at his 80th birthday bash in Los Angeles in 1995 (ibid., p. 210).

18 Martin Carthy quoted in J.P. Bean, *Singing from the Floor: A History of British Folk Clubs* (London: Faber & Faber, 2014), pp. 93–94.

19 Carthy cited in Heylin, op. cit., p. 223. On 'Mr. Tambourine Man', see ibid., pp. 219–226; Gill, op. cit., pp. 101–103.

20 On this point, see Heylin, op. cit., pp. 222–223; Gill, op. cit., p. 101.

21 Martin Carthy quoted in 'A Chat with Martin Carthy', interview by Matthew Zuckerman, January 1999, *ISIS*, 83, February 1999; reprinted in Derek Barker (ed.), *Isis: A Bob Dylan Anthology*, rev. edn. (London: Helter Skelter, 2004), p. 79.

22 Ibid.

23 See Heylin, op. cit., p. 184; Bob Dylan quoted in Cameron Crowe, liner notes for *Biograph* (Special Rider Music/Columbia Records, 1985).

24 Martin Carthy quoted in Barker (ed.), op. cit., p. 77. On 'The Lonesome Death of Hattie Carroll', see Heylin, op. cit., pp. 196–203; Gill, op. cit., pp. 64–65.

25 Sounes, op. cit., pp. 64–65.

26 Ibid., p. 160.

27 See Clinton Heylin, *Behind the Shades: The 20th Anniversary Edition* (London: Faber & Faber, 2011), pp. 155–156.

28 Colin Harper, *Dazzling Stranger: Bert Jansch and the British Folk and Blues Revival* (London: Bloomsbury, 2000), pp. 140–141.

29 On *Another Side of Bob Dylan*, see Nigel Williamson, *The Dead Straight Guide to Bob Dylan* (London: Red Planet, 2015), pp. 178–179; Gill, op. cit., pp. 69–85.

30 Bob Dylan quoted in Anthony Scaduto, *Bob Dylan* (London: Helter Skelter, 2001 [first published 1971]), p. 180.

31 Bob Dylan quoted in Crowe, op. cit., p. 10.

32 Scaduto, op. cit., p. 181.

33 Gray, op. cit., p. 4.

34 George Melly, *Revolt into Style: The Pop Arts* (Oxford: Oxford University Press, 1989), p. 114.

35 Hughes, op. cit., p. 95.

36 Cited in Gill, op. cit., p. 73.

37 Joan Baez quoted in Williamson, op. cit., p. 47.

38 See Scaduto, op. cit., p. 120.

39 John Hammond quoted in ibid., p. 120.

40 Dave Van Ronk quoted in ibid., pp. 120–121.

41 Dave Van Ronk with Elijah Wald, *The Mayor of MacDougal Street* (Cambridge, MA: Da Capo, 2005), pp. 204, 215.

42 Ibid., p. 204.

43 Scaduto, op. cit., p. 146.

44 Cited in Colin Irwin, *Bob Dylan: Highway 61 Revisited* (London: Flame Tree Publishing, 2008), p. 21.

45 Paul McCartney quoted, recalling that occasion, in Barry Miles, *Paul McCartney: Many Years from Now* (London: Secker & Warburg, 1997), p. 187.

46 Jonathon Gould, *Can't Buy Me Love: The Beatles, Britain and America* (London: Portrait, 2007), pp. 252–253; Gould's source: Al Aronowitz, Q, May 1994.

47 Al Aronowitz quoted in Irwin, op. cit., p. 22.

48 John Lennon quoted in David Sheff, *Last Interview: All We Are Saying* (London: Pan Books, 2001), p. 152. (This, the last major interview Lennon gave before he was murdered on December 8, 1980, was based on 20 hours of tapes, and conducted in New York City in September 1980.)

49 Ian MacDonald, *Revolution in the Head: The Beatles' Records and the Sixties* (London: Pimlico, 1995), p. xi.

50 John Lennon quoted in Ray Coleman, *Lennon: The Definitive Biography* (London: Pan Books, 2000), p. 399.

51 Steve Lowe, 'The Fab Five: Dylan and the Beatles', in Mark Blake (ed.), *Dylan: Visions, Portraits and Back Pages* (London: DK/Mojo, 2005), p. 46.

52 Coleman, op. cit., p. 399.

53 Cited in Wald, op. cit., p. 181.

54 MacDonald, op. cit., p. 85.

55 John Lennon quoted in Sheff, op. cit., p. 195.

56 Ibid., p. 197.

57 Coleman, op. cit., p. 400.

58 Ibid.

59 Gould, op. cit., p. 259. Lennon, cited in ibid., in *Melody Maker*, December 19, 1964.

60 MacDonald, op. cit., p. 98.

61 See John Lennon quoted in Sheff, op. cit., p. 174.

62 Gould, op. cit., p. 259.

63 Ibid., p. 267.

64 Coleman, op. cit., p. 401.

4

THE 1965 BRITISH TOUR

At the beginning of 1965 The Beatles' great admiration for Bob Dylan, and recognition of his growing influence on their own work, were again made crystal-clear in an article by Ray Coleman in *Melody Maker*, headed 'Beatles say – Dylan shows the way'.[1]

Towards the end of the previous year the fruitful process of mutual musical influence and interaction that was steadily developing between Bob Dylan and The Beatles was reproduced in a different kind of transatlantic cross-fertilisation that had been evident since 1963 – that is, between British rhythm and blues groups and American R&B, in both its broad and its more specific forms. In the case of the latter genre, electric Chicago-style blues, in November 1964 The Rolling Stones, contrary to most previous commercial norms in British popular music, released their cover version of a slow blues, Willie Dixon's 'Little Red Rooster', which had earlier, in 1961, been recorded by Howlin' Wolf. In a spirit that clearly exemplified a desire for greater musical authenticity, that wish to add themselves to a living blues tradition, Keith Richards, The Rolling Stones' lead guitarist, much later recalled:

> When we put out 'Little Red Rooster', a raw Willie Dixon blues with slide guitar and all, it was a daring move at the time, November 1964. We were getting no-no's from the record company, management, everyone else. But we were on the crest of a wave and we could push it. It was almost in defiance of pop. In our arrogance at the time, we wanted to make a statement…Mick [Jagger] and I stood up and said, come on, let's push it. This is what we're fucking about. And the floodgates burst open after that, suddenly Muddy and Howlin' Wolf and Buddy Guy were getting gigs and working. It was a breakthrough. And the record got to number one. And I'm absolutely sure what

we were doing made Berry Gordy at Motown capable of pushing his stuff elsewhere, and it certainly rejuvenated Chicago blues as well.[2]

'Little Red Rooster' did indeed reach number 1 in the UK singles charts on December 3, 1964. It was also the last Rolling Stones cover version to be released as a single during the 1960s. Their determination in the face of opposing commercial forces to push and record that slow blues bears out Elijah Wald's observation of The Rolling Stones that: 'They were long-haired pop stars, but also dedicated neo-ethnics, as immersed in authentic roots styles as the hardcore Village folk crowd, and far more purist than the Weavers or Peter, Paul and Mary.'[3]

In a manner that deviated less overtly from prevailing commercial standards, but which also acknowledged respect for the qualities of an ongoing black American popular-musical tradition, a month after the success of 'Little Red Rooster', in January 1965, the Birmingham group The Moody Blues reached number 1 in the UK singles charts with 'Go Now'. This was a compelling cover version of the black American singer Bessie Banks' original, released in November 1964.

In early 1965 this fertile musical development continued with The Animals' cover versions of Nina Simone's 'Don't Let Me Be Misunderstood' and Sam Cooke's 'Bring It on Home to Me', which reached number 3 and number 7 in the UK singles charts in January and March 1965 respectively, and, also in January of that year, with Them's version of Big Joe Williams' 'Baby, Please Don't Go', which reached number 10. In February 1965 The Rolling Stones released 'The Last Time', a Mick Jagger/Keith Richards composition which used a chorus by The Staple Singers. It became their first original single to reach the number 1 spot in the UK charts, achieving that status, for the third time, in March 1965.

It was against this background of a thriving British rhythm and blues scene, together with the continuing massive popularity and success of The Beatles, that Bob Dylan arrived at London Heathrow airport on April 26 for his first full-scale British tour, during which he would perform at eight concerts in seven British cities, including the capital. He arrived accompanied by Joan Baez, Albert Grossman, his manager, and others, as well as by a film crew for a documentary about Dylan's 1965 tour, to be directed by Donn Pennebaker.

Bob Dylan met the British press first at Heathrow airport and then two days later at the Savoy Hotel on the Strand in London, where he was staying. At Heathrow, in response to a question about the nature of his message, he replied: 'Keep a good head and always carry a light bulb.' In general, as Robert Shelton later recorded: 'The pop and national press had a carnival. Reporters were appalled, bemused, entranced. Dylan made good copy.' Meanwhile, Dylan himself, too, was 'bemused by it all'.[4] Just over a month before, in March 1965, Dylan's fourth studio album, *Bringing It All Back Home*, had been released. He had written the bulk of its songs between late November 1964 and early January 1965. The first side of the album was electric in sound and nature, the second side predominantly acoustic. Of the album Robert Shelton later wrote: 'If given a time limit to illustrate his gifts, I would play the 23 minutes of side two.'[5] The final versions of three of the songs on that second side, 'Mr.

Tambourine Man', 'It's Alright, Ma (I'm Only Bleeding)' and 'Gates Of Eden', were recorded in one long take, without even a playback between the tracks.

The album itself was groundbreaking in terms of both Dylan's musical career and the future direction of popular music, since, as Howard Sounes has observed, it 'integrated what he had learned from the success of British bands like the Beatles with his own, more poetic lyrics'.[6] Recorded in just three days, between January 13 and 15, 1965, the resulting music was 'a joyous fusion of freeform verse and good time rock'n'roll'. Moreover, the album's very title was 'a reference to the fact that this was American music British groups had borrowed'.[7]

As Andy Gill has also noted, with *Bringing It All Back Home* Dylan had devised

> a new mode of expression which took his primary poetic influences – the Symbolist poetry of Rimbaud and Villon, the folk vernacular of Woody Guthrie, the immediacy of beat writers like Ginsberg and Kerouac, the visionary awareness of William Blake, and the hipster slang of beat comics like Hugh ("Wavy Gravy") Romney and Lord Buckley – and lashed them to a driving beat.[8]

The first, electric side of the album was innovative at the time, since, as Michael Gray has commented, 'here was this folk singer committing the ultimate sacrilege of singing rock 'n' roll songs with electric guitars behind him'.[9] Yet it also contained four outstanding Dylan songs: 'Subterranean Homesick Blues' and 'Maggie's Farm', and two tender and subtle romantic songs: 'She Belongs to Me' and 'Love Minus Zero/No Limit'.

The album's opening track, 'Subterranean Homesick Blues', was influenced by Chuck Berry's 'Too Much Monkey Business'. But so, too, on that proto-rap track were, as Colin Irwin has observed, other influences such as the Woody Guthrie/ Pete Campbell collaboration 'Taking It Easy', recorded by Pete Seeger and The Weavers, as well as the 'machine gun' couplets of Kerouac and the Beat poets.[10]

Encouraged by the commercial success as a single of 'Subterranean Homesick Blues', which, as the first recorded example of his new electric musical style, reached number 9 in the UK singles charts in April 1965, Dylan, much later, in Martin Scorsese's 2005 documentary *No Direction Home*, stated that:

> British audiences were the first to accept what I was doing at face value. To that crowd it wasn't different at all; it was right in line with everything they've read in school from the Shakespearean tradition to Byron and Shelley.[11]

Although the track marked the start of a new stage of Dylan's musical development, it certainly did not imply an abandonment of social commentary or even protest on his part. Indeed, as Gill has maintained, the song was 'the most concise com-pendium of anti-establishment attitude Dylan ever composed…in which virtually every couplet can be abstracted as a slogan'. Furthermore, what was different from his earlier topical songs was the cynical, streetwise nihilism of the song, whose third and fourth verses condense a generation's disquiet with the American Dream lifestyle into a few succinct phrases, while offering only the most nugatory, absurd advice on how to deal with it. There was no specific victim in the song, and no message other than the recurrent "Look out, kid" to warn of society's manifold traps and dead-end diversions.[12]

The overall sense of a sardonic and aphoristic critique of contemporary American society conveyed in 'Subterranean Homesick Blues' was reproduced on the acoustic side of *Bringing It All Back Home* in a more profound manner in 'It's Alright, Ma (I'm Only Bleeding)', one of Dylan's greatest song-statements. It castigated the dark underside of a materialistic and dehumanising society in which manufacturers made 'everything from toy guns that spark / to flesh-colored Christs that glow in the dark'. But the song was delivered from the perspective of a defiant and alienated individual asserting his own autonomy and freedom. As Paul Williams has pointed out, 'while the song is in one sense a catalogue of horrors, it is not pessimistic or downbeat…rather it seems to speak of the individual's power to see through all this, endure it, survive it, and ultimately perhaps prevail against it'.[13]

That observation implicitly pointed to a second, existentialist aspect of the song that many critics and commentators have since tended to overlook. Among the few who have not done so, Keith Negus has perceptively described 'It's Alright, Ma (I'm Only Bleeding)' as 'a song that condenses social critique and existential anxiety into a stream of quotable, proverb-like lines'.[14] Clinton Heylin, too, has noted:

> On 'It's Alright, Ma' there is an air of futility absent from earlier songs, even the apocalyptic ones. It seems he [Dylan] had finally got around to reading Sartre and Kierkegaard, for here is the first evidence of an existential strain that suffuses much of what he would write in the coming year. This was Dylan's 'life and [his] life only' – the song's original subtitle, an existential statement if ever there was one.[15]

In similar vein, in his early biography Robert Shelton referred to, as one of the 'road maps' guiding Dylan in 1965, his espousal at that time of:

> a street existentialism that came less from ordered thinking than from emotional reaction. Dylan didn't discard earlier insights or orientations; he didn't spout Sartre or Heidegger. But if we take existentialism out of the seminar and onto the highway, we can find compass points throughout Dylan's 1965–66 work.[16]

That 'street existentialism' thus involved for Dylan 'an anguished search for honesty amid awareness of death and despair, to which one does not succumb. Out on the streets he was weighing his anguish and responsibility, pitting his loneliness against that of the lonely crowd.'[17]

Significantly, too, in a later, 2004 television interview with Ed Bradley, Dylan singled out 'It's Alright, Ma' as having represented a strange kind of artistic breakthrough, as one of those songs over whose composition he had appeared to have exercised little conscious control. 'Those early songs', he told Bradley, 'were almost magically written'. He then recited the remarkable opening verse of 'It's Alright, Ma': 'Darkness at the break of noon / Shadows even the silver spoon / The handmade blade, the child's balloon / Eclipses both the sun and moon.'

Dylan went on to suggest that such verses had not arisen from any self-conscious songwriting technique. 'Well, try to sit down and write something like that,' he said, 'there's a magic to that and it's not Siegfried and Roy kind of magic, you know? It's a different kind of a penetrating magic. And, you know, I did it. I did it at one time.' Asked by Bradley if it was something that he could do again, Dylan replied: 'I did it once, and I can do other things now. But I can't do that.'[18]

As for *Bringing It All Back Home* as a whole, the album, and its groundbreaking nature, at the time and indeed in the years since, exerted a widespread appeal, not least to John Lennon. For him, Dylan's significance during the mid-1960s, British rock journalist Ray Coleman later recalled, lay in:

> his spectacular command of words and ability to combine intelligent imagery with electric folk music. Lennon was quickly hypnotized by Dylan's album *Bringing It All Back Home*, a brave adventure by a former folk singer-guitarist into the world of rock. John played the album a lot at home but would not be drawn much on it. It was if he felt the presence of a genuine literary rival.[19]

With regard in particular to its opening track, 'Subterranean Homesick Blues', Coleman also recalled: 'John described it as "very Chuck Berry-ish." He and I spent a lot of time at his Weybridge home trying to work out the words.'[20]

Bob Dylan's 1965 British acoustic tour began on April 30 and concluded on May 10. It comprised eight concerts in seven British cities: Sheffield, Liverpool, Leicester, Birmingham, Newcastle, Manchester, and London, with two concluding appearances at the Royal Albert Hall on May 9 and 10. In those concerts, documented in a fragmentary manner in Donn Pennebaker's documentary *Don't Look Back*, Dylan played to about 50,000 people.

By the time the tour began Dylan's records were selling well in the UK for CBS, the British affiliate of Columbia Records. Three of his albums, *The Freewheelin' Bob Dylan*, *The Times They Are A-Changin'*, and *Another Side of Bob Dylan*, were in the UK album charts, while two of his singles were in the UK singles charts: 'The Times They Are A-Changin'' at number 9 in March 1965 and 'Subterranean Homesick Blues' also at number 9 in April. By late May 1965 his fifth album, *Bringing It All Back Home*, had reached number 1 in the UK album charts.

During the concerts themselves, playing to audiences composed of both folk-music enthusiasts and pop-music fans, Dylan, Coleman at the time observed, 'commanded utter silence...Even the noisy pop fans were stunned into silence by his words, the honesty of his performances', in which he 'consistently showed an endearing modesty. He wandered on stage with no sign of the "big star" atmosphere we had come to expect from pop immortals'.[21] His sole props consisted of a stool, an acoustic guitar, harmonicas, and a glass or two of water.

As a critic from the *Daily Telegraph* commented on one of Dylan's performances: 'There are better singers, better guitarists, better harmonica players, and better poets. But there is no other 23-year old who does all these things with even a semblance of the power, the originality or the fire.'[22] Furthermore, with regard to Dylan's songwriting, the same critic observed that 'this haystack-headed young American has achieved in an age of more and more pictures, and less and less text, of emotional noises rather than meanings, an astounding popular victory, for the word'.[23]

At Dylan's Leicester concert, in particular, Coleman vividly described the scene:

> When this slight, serious-faced and incredibly casual man walked on stage – with a guitar, seven harmonicas and two glasses of water his only company – there was silence. At the end of every song, the audience applauded – thunderously. No screams, no whistles, no talking. The applause almost switched off mechanically, like it was canned.[24]

For the second of the final two concerts of the tour at London's Royal Albert Hall, on May 10, the maximum capacity of 7,000 tickets had been sold out in March within two hours.[25] For the first concert on May 9, about 150 tickets were held back for members of the British rock and pop elite, notably The Beatles, The Rolling Stones, The Animals, and others. All three of those groups had called into Dylan's Savoy Hotel suite to pay their respects.[26] Manfred Mann had also dropped off a copy of their cover version of Dylan's 'With God on Our Side', which was in the UK singles charts,[27] and which the group had performed live on *Ready Steady Go!*, at that time the most popular and influential pop-music programme on British television. That was in itself a highly significant indicator of the extent of Dylan's lyrical impact.

Joan Baez, who had accompanied Dylan on his flight to London in late April, had previously introduced him to her American audiences and more recently, in 1964, had performed with him in the United States. She had hoped for a reciprocal arrangement from Dylan in Britain, where she was yet to be established, but he never invited her to join him on stage during his spring 1965 tour. As she later admitted: 'I was very, very hurt. I was miserable.'[28] Finding Dylan during the tour often petulant, self-obsessed, and surrounded by sycophants, and feeling estranged, too, from his entourage, she flew out of London to Paris, where her parents were then living. It was only after a long interval of nearly ten years, and having composed a cathartic song about their past relationship, 'Diamonds and Rust', that she renewed contact with Dylan, eventually performing with him in the Rolling Thunder Review of 1974.

Baez later described her interaction with Dylan on his spring 1965 British tour as 'the most demoralising experience of my life', adding that she had 'never understood how he could suddenly change, as if everything he had done before had never really happened'.[29] In her 1988 memoir, too, she sadly recalled:

> Sometimes I think you pulled away from all reality on that English tour of spring 1965. You were mantled with praise, sought after by hysterical fans, appealed to by liberals, intellectuals, politicians, the press, and genuinely adored by fools like me, and I don't think you ever really recuperated. You invited me to come, and I assumed you'd invite me up to sing with you.[30]

But in spite of Baez's deep sense of disappointment and exclusion at the time, Dylan's performances during that spring 1965 tour were, as Daniel Mark Epstein has observed, 'dark, hypnotic and intensely personal, a one-man tour de force. They left no space for Joan Baez's folk romanticism and earnest politics.'[31] As Dylan himself maintained with regard to his own musical development: 'Hey, I can fit into her music, but she doesn't fit into my music, my show. It would have been dumb, and it would have been misleading to the audience.'[32]

Joan Baez did later return to London, after the end of Dylan's British tour, for her own successful solo concert at a sold-out Royal Albert Hall on May 23, though, as she later recalled, in the circumstances she felt 'too sick to enjoy it'.[33] Dylan had promised to attend but was unable to do so since he was hospitalised in London at the time with a viral ailment. The prelude to her earlier departure from London, when she suddenly left Dylan's entourage gathered in his Savoy Hotel suite, was candidly captured on camera in Donn Pennebaker's *cinéma-vérité*-style documentary *Don't Look Back*. D.A. Pennebaker, an Illinois-born filmmaker, had originally, through the intervention of Sara Lowndes, a friend of Dylan's manager's wife Sally Grossman, been contacted by Albert Grossman to shoot a film of Dylan's 1965 British tour, *cinéma-vérité* style. Sara Lowndes, whom Dylan was later to marry in November 1965, was then working for Drew Associates, a film production company. Pennebaker later stated: 'I saw Dylan as a Byronesque pop figure, a guy who was inventing a whole new kind of mood in popular music.'[34]

When they began filming the 1965 tour, Pennebaker and his sound engineer Robert Van Dyke, in accordance with the principles of *cinéma-vérité*, strove to capture events as they took place in as unobtrusive a manner as possible, with the use of omnidirectional microphones placed outside the view of the subjects being filmed, and with hand-held cameras focused on Dylan himself over the course of 20 hours throughout the tour. The film thus sought to be an actual presentation of *cinéma-vérité* rather a simulation of that style, as had been the case with The Beatles' nonetheless highly popular and enjoyable mock-documentary *A Hard Day's Night*, released in July 1964. As Tim Riley later noted of that comparison, Donn Pennebaker 'manages in documentary form what The Beatles' *A Hard Day's Night* does as narrative comedy; it shows Dylan as the center of an uncorked youth scene sent reeling over the celebrity surrounding Dylan's talent, with Dylan as the bemused center of the storm'.[35]

Pennebaker's film starts memorably with what was in many ways the first, and iconic, pop-music video, with Dylan, against the soundtrack of 'Subterranean Homesick Blues', dropping a succession of large cue cards to the ground in an alley beside the Savoy Hotel. The young Scottish pop-folk singer Donovan Leitch, who had previously been introduced to Dylan by Joan Baez, had earlier, at the suggestion of Dylan's friend the poet Allen Ginsberg, helped to write out words and phrases from the lyrics of 'Subterranean Homesick Blues' on those pieces of card for Dylan to display to Pennebaker's camera. The sequence was thus, in David Hajdu's description, 'a wittily literal portrayal of Dylan the street poet'.[36]

The film then focused on scenes in hotel rooms, on Dylan's often humorous and sometimes caustic encounters with journalists, his meetings with fans and admirers, rail and road journeys across England, green-room activity, and snippets of footage from Dylan's concert performances. Among the film's many vivid and revealing scenes were those that documented, not always in camera shot, a succession of British rock stars of the moment – foremost among them The Beatles, The Rolling Stones, and The Animals – who came, in what seemed to be a never-ending party, to pay their respects to Dylan at the Savoy Hotel. As the singer Marianne Faithfull, who also joined that pilgrimage, later recalled:

> There was no doubt now who was the crown prince of rock; it was Bob. The Animals and the Stones had all come to visit, serious bad boys come to pay their respects and sit meekly on the couch as the mad dauphin came in and out talking of Apocalypse and Pensacola. And now, the confirming touch: the Beatles had come to pay him homage.[37]

The Beatles themselves, who astutely stayed out of camera shot, at the time were nervous and 'waiting for the oracle to speak'. But in their company, as well as that of The Rolling Stones, Dylan, in Faithfull's recollection, 'simply carried on as if none of them was present'.[38]

That hotel suite footage also included cameo performances by, among others, Alan Price, who had just left The Animals to start a solo career, and Donovan, who played his slightly Dylanesque song 'To Sing for You' to the modest approval of the gathering, including Dylan's. In his response, Dylan played the first two verses of his new song 'It's All Over Now, Baby Blue', which had appeared on *Bringing It All Back Home* and was itself a poignant farewell to past attachments, as he moved on personally and artistically.

Donovan himself appeared to have taken this encounter in a generous and level-headed manner. The American folk singer Derroll Adams had originally introduced him to Joan Baez at a folk concert in Newcastle in May 1965, Donovan later recalled, and Baez, with her 'amazing eyes, concerned and pleading, I felt, for sanity and compassion in a mad, greedy, violent world', had later set up, with Dylan's approval, a meeting in London at, for Baez, the ill-fated Savoy Hotel gathering.[39]

Dylan had already made public his approval of the young Scottish singer,[40] having often listened to his first album and liking in particular his song 'Catch the Wind'.

On first hearing Donovan in 1965, Dylan had said of him, in Donovan's own recollection, that 'he sounds like Jack Elliot', who had been Woody Guthrie's first disciple before Dylan, and Dylan had been correct in that view since 'I had really studied Jack's style of Guthrie interpretation'.[41] Donovan had added, not entirely convincingly, that while he loved Dylan's music, Dylan himself, 'the Hebrew shaman with the Celtic name', was 'one of hundreds of influences on me and most of those influences were in Dylan's music too'.[42] Donovan claimed, too, that he 'sounded like him [Dylan] for five minutes while trying out different styles'.[43] Dylan, for his part, increasingly aware, as he toured England, of Donovan's apparently ubiquitous cultural presence as an obvious imitator, the 'British Dylan', responded in his Leicester concert by altering a line of his 'Talking World War III Blues' to 'I turned on the radio – it was Donovan…whoever Donovan is'.[44] Dylan, Donovan later recorded, had told reporters backstage that he 'didn't mean to put the guy down', only intending the reference in a jocular manner,[45] and that 'Dylan accepted me with magnanimity at the height of all that craziness of comparison'.[46]

Of *Don't Look Back*, it may be said that it was the first rock documentary, and one of the leading examples of that film genre in the years that have followed. The final cut was not completed until April 1966. When first shown it, Dylan felt that quite a few alterations were needed. But on a second viewing he changed his mind and agreed to no cuts at all.[47]

It was eventually premiered in San Francisco in May 1967 and released in DVD format in 2000. As Michael Gray commented, of its time-frame of 1965, it was:

> an extraordinary document, capturing in an aptly fresh, cinéma-vérité style an artist coming to the peak of his powers, intensely active, intelligent and charismatic – and allowing unprecedented backstage rights to the cameras. It was a core part of the anti-showbiz stance Dylan was pioneering that you were allowed to see the very immediate moments before and after the artist was on stage.[48]

Probably the main shortcoming of the film, however, was its lack of extended concert performance footage. But that was later rectified by the 2005 bootleg release of a two-DVD set of outtakes, which provided many enthralling song performances. Moreover, Gray has also noted that with the passage of time *Don't Look Back* appears to have become 'an ever more valuable document', one which, like its much less accomplished and less effective successor of 1966 *Eat the Document*, also provided historically 'a now incongruous glimpse back at the Dickensian Britain that Dylan, the original spider from Mars, had descended upon'.[49]

As for the 1965 British concert tour that the film documented, commercially and artistically it had been a success. According to Tito Burns, the 1965 tour promoter, three facts underlay its success: Dylan's initial powerful appeal to a British folk–music audience; his actual performances; and CBS, Columbia Records' British affiliate, promoting Dylan's records, both albums and singles,[50] which from March 1965 throughout the rest of the year sold more than those of any other artist in the entire CBS catalogue. Following the British tour, Columbia Records in New York embarked on a major promotional campaign on Dylan's behalf in June 1965.

As for Dylan's 1965 concert performances, two of his biographers have described in particular the one at the Royal Albert Hall on May 9 as 'his most electrifying performance of the tour' and 'an intense, almost mesmeric performance, holding a vast audience inthralled',[51] while, at first hand, a disconsolate and estranged Joan Baez had nonetheless recognised, on another earlier occasion, that while she had 'cried through his entire concert', it 'was, by the way, a magnificent performance'.[52] Another Dylan biographer, Clinton Heylin, however, has maintained that while the concert performances were 'not exactly lacklustre, they sound almost formulaic, something of which Dylan himself was acutely aware'.[53] Against that view, Gray has pointed out that the 2005 bootleg release of outtakes from *Don't Look Back* yielded a 'treasure of many complete performances', in Britain in both 1965 and 1966, that 'blows away any lingering possibility of claiming that the Dylan captured in those concerts is "bored" with his concert material'.[54]

But there was nevertheless a deeper unease underlying Dylan's own experience of his 1965 British tour, during which his audiences still associated him with, and revered him for, his first four studio albums, for Dylan himself was becoming less and less comfortable with being confined to a purely acoustic mode of musical expression. In an interview later that year, in August 1965, with Nora Ephron and Susan Edmiston he explained, with regard to his recent acoustic concerts, that:

> I knew what the audience was gonna do, how they would react. It was very automatic. Your mind just drifts unless you can find some way to get in there and remain totally there. It's so much a fight remaining totally there all by yourself. It takes too much, I'm not ready to cut that much out of my life.[55]

Moreover, to a friend he had earlier expressed his dissatisfaction with what he increasingly considered to be the routinised nature of his recent acoustic performances:

> I play these concerts and I ask myself, 'would you come to see me tonight?' – and I'd have to truthfully say, 'no, I wouldn't come, I'd rather be doing something else, really I would.' That something else is rock. That's where it's at for me. My words are my pictures, and the rock's gonna help me flesh out the colors of the pictures.[56]

Such sentiments had indeed earlier inspired the recording of the electric side of *Bringing It All Back Home* in mid-January 1965. Four months later, at the end of his 1965 British tour, on May 12, Dylan had gone in similar spirit to Levy's recording studios on New Bond Street, London, for what turned out to be a brief, rather disorganised, and eventually inebriated recording session with John Mayall and his

Bluesbreakers. They, probably the most authentic and purist British rhythm and blues group of the day, included, apart from Mayall on vocals, John McVitie on bass guitar, Hughie Flint on drums, and their young lead guitarist, Eric Clapton. Indicating that something which could eventually be released might result from the session, Tom Wilson, Dylan's then current producer, had flown over from New York. The session, however, turned out to be unproductive. As drummer Hughie Flint later recalled:

> All through the session it was just messing around. I don't think we played a complete number. It was a real mess. There was a lot of booze there, crates and crates of wine – I'd never seen so much wine, and everybody got very pissed, very quickly, none more so than Dylan.[57]

At that session Dylan had in fact only three songs potentially ready for recording, two of which were outtakes from his *Bringing It All Back Home* album: 'I'll Keep It with Mine' and 'If You Gotta Go, Go Now'. But completed versions of them never materialised from the proceedings. An acoustic version of 'If You Gotta Go, Go Now', however, which Dylan later performed at a studio session for BBC TV in early June, was made into an acetate by his music publisher and offered to the British group Manfred Mann. They cut a folk-rock version of the song which reached number 2 in the UK singles charts in September 1965.[58] Apart from the future royalties derived from Manfred Mann's hit, the other benefit to Dylan that indirectly sprang from the abortive May 12 session was his realisation that individual blues musicians, rather than an entire blues band, might greatly enhance his own recorded work. That was to be achieved to dramatic effect on his next studio album, *Highway 61 Revisited*, which was to be recorded in New York between June and August 1965.

After a brief holiday in Portugal with Sara Downdes, Bob Dylan returned to London for the recording of two half-hour studio performances for BBC TV on June 8, which were eventually finished on tape on June 24.[59] In many ways they seemed to constitute, in Paul Williams' words, 'the last stand of Bob Dylan, folk star'.[60] Indeed, it seemed to be that the artistically and commercially successful 1965 British tour had produced a situation in which, as Ray Coleman, an eyewitness to the tour, later wrote to Robert Shelton, Dylan had 'emerged from the relative obscurity of the folk world to the wider, more dangerous world of pop idol. For Dylan it was fraught with trouble.'[61] That in turn posed an acute dilemma for him. He was becoming increasingly dissatisfied with his solo acoustic performances. As he later made clear: 'I was getting bored with that. I couldn't go out and play like that. I was thinking of quitting.'[62] Was he, then, to abandon his musical career, to walk away from all that? Or should he strike out in a new musical direction, which *Bringing It All Back Home* had in part heralded? The second half of 1965, and the following year, too, would create circumstances in which that dilemma would be resolved in a controversial and creatively groundbreaking manner.

Notes

1 Ray Coleman, 'Beatles Say – Dylan Shows the Way', *Melody Maker*, January 9, 1965.

2 Keith Richards with James Fox, *Life* (London: Weidenfeld & Nicolson, 2010), pp. 160–161.

3 Elijah Wald, *Dylan Goes Electric: Newport, Seeger, Dylan and the Night That Split the Sixties* (New York: Harper Collins, 2015), p. 177.

4 Ray Coleman quoted in Robert Shelton, *No Direction Home: The Life and Music of Bob Dylan*, rev. and updated edn., ed. Elizabeth Thomson and Patrick Humphries (London: Omnibus, 2011), p. 203.

5 Shelton, op. cit., p. 193.

6 Howard Sounes, *Down the Highway: The Life of Bob Dylan* (London: Doubleday, 2001), p. 170.

7 Ibid., pp. 171, 171–172.

8 Andy Gill, *Bob Dylan: The Stories behind the Songs 1962–1969* (London: Carlton Books, 2011), p. 90. On *Bringing It All Back Home* in general, see ibid., pp. 87–107.

9 Michael Gray, *Song and Dance Man III: The Art of Bob Dylan* (London: Continuum, 2000), p. 4.

10 Colin Irwin, *Bob Dylan: Highway 61 Revisited* (London: Flame Tree Publishing, 2008), p. 46.

11 Bob Dylan quoted in *No Direction Home* (directed by Martin Scorsese, 2005); cited in Irwin, op. cit., p. 47.

12 Gill, op. cit., p. 93.

13 Paul Williams, *Bob Dylan Performing Artist 1960–1973: The Early Years* (London: Omnibus, 2004), p. 132.

14 Keith Negus, *Bob Dylan* (London: Equinox, 2008), p. 37.

15 Clinton Heylin, *Revolution in the Air: The Songs of Bob Dylan Vol. 1: 1957–73* (London: Constable, 2010), p. 257.

16 Shelton, op. cit., pp. 189, 190.

17 Ibid., pp. 190.

18 Bob Dylan interviewed by Ed Bradley, *60 Minutes*, CBS TV, December 7, 2004; cited in Antony Decurtis, 'Bob Dylan as Songwriter', in Kevin J.H. Dettmar (ed.), *The Cambridge Companion to Bob Dylan* (Cambridge: Cambridge University Press, 2009), pp. 43–44.

19 Ray Coleman, *Lennon: The Definitive Biography* (London: Pan Books, 2000), p. 358.

20 Ibid., p. 359.

21 Ray Coleman quoted in Shelton, op. cit., p. 203.

22 Maurice Rosenbaum in the *Daily Telegraph*, quoted in Shelton, op. cit., p. 205.

23 Ibid.

24 Ray Coleman, 'A Beatle-Size Fever without the Screams', *Melody Maker*, May 8, 1965; cited in Andrea Cossu, *It Ain't Me, Babe: Bob Dylan and the Performance of Authenticity* (Boulder, CO: Paradigm Publishers, 2012), p. 54.

25 Shelton, op. cit., p. 203.

26 For a vivid first-hand account of their visits to the Savoy Hotel, see Marianne Faithfull with David Dalton, *Faithfull* (London: Michael Joseph, 1994), pp. 54–56.

27 Bob Spitz, *Dylan: A Biography* (New York and London: W.W. Norton & Co., 1991), p. 288.

28 Joan Baez quoted in Shelton, op. cit., p. 207.

29 Joan Baez quoted in David Hajdu, *Positively Fourth Street: The Lives and Times of Bob Dylan, Joan Baez, Mimi Baez Farina and Richard Farina* (London: Bloomsbury, 2001), p. 254. On Joan Baez' overall reaction to Dylan's 1965 British tour, see ibid., pp. 251–254.

30 Joan Baez, *And a Voice to Sing With: A Memoir* (London: Century, 1988), pp. 95–96.

31 Daniel Mark Epstein, *The Ballad of Bob Dylan: A Portrait* (London: Souvenir Press, 2011), p. 152.

32 Bob Dylan quoted in Shelton, op. cit., p. 296.

33 Baez, op. cit., p. 97.

34 D.A. Pennebaker quoted in Hajdu, op. cit., p. 249.

35 Tim Riley, *Hard Rain: A Dylan Commentary* (New York: Da Capo Press, 1999), p. 111. On D.A. Pennebaker's *Don't Look Back*, see Nigel Williamson, *The Dead Straight Guide to Bob Dylan* (London: Red Planet, 2015), pp. 289–291. For Pennebaker's recollections of the filming of *Don't Look Back*, see Epstein, op. cit., pp. 141–156.

36 Hajdu, op. cit., p. 249.

37 Faithfull, op. cit., p. 55.

38 Ibid., pp. 55, 56.

39 Donovan Leitch, *The Hurdy Gurdy Man* (London: Random House, 2005), p. 93.

40 See 'Dylan Digs Donovan', *Melody Maker*, May 8, 1965.

41 Leitch, op. cit., p. 89.

42 Ibid., op. cit., pp. 88–89, 77.

43 Donovan quoted in Anthony Farrell, Vivienne Guinness, and Julian Lloyd (eds.), *Rock 'n' Roll Remembered: An Imperfect History* (Dublin: The Lilliput Press, 1996), p. 58.

44 Cited in Gill, op. cit., p. 110.

45 Leitch, op. cit., p. 99.

46 Donovan quoted in Farrell et al. (eds.), op. cit., p. 59.

47 Williamson, op. cit., p. 291.

48 Michael Gray, *The Bob Dylan Encyclopedia* (London: Continuum, 2006), p. 188.

49 Ibid., pp. 188, 204.

50 Shelton, op. cit, p. 204.

51 Spitz, op. cit., p. 295; Sounes, op. cit., p. 179.

52 Joan Baez letter to her sister Mimi, May 5, 1965; cited in Hajdu, op. cit., p. 252.

53 Clinton Heylin, *Behind the Shades: The 20th Anniversary Edition* (London: Faber & Faber, 2011), p. 193.

54 Gray, *Bob Dylan Encyclopedia*, p. 195.

55 Interview by Nora Ephron and Susan Edmiston, August 1965; published in Jonathan Cott (ed.), *Dylan on Dylan: The Essential Interviews* (London: Hodder & Stoughton, 2006), p. 52.

56 Cited in Gill, op. cit., p. 89.

57 Hughie Flint quoted in Heylin, *Behind the Shades*, p. 201. On the May 12 London recording session, see Heylin, ibid., and Heylin, *Revolution in the Air*, pp. 260–261, 282–283.

58 The British electric-folk band Fairport Convention later recorded a French language version of Dylan's song, 'Si Tu Dois Partir', which reached number 21 in the UK singles charts in 1969. See Heylin, *Revolution in the Air*, pp. 260–261.

59 Shelton, op. cit., p. 207.

60 Williams, op. cit., p. 144.

61 Ray Coleman letter to Robert Shelton, cited in Shelton, op. cit., p. 203.

62 Dylan interview by Ephron and Edmiston in Cott (ed.), op. cit., p. 52.

5

GOING ELECTRIC

Folk-rock and The Beatles

Two weeks after he returned to the United States in early June 1965, Bob Dylan went into Columbia Records Studio A in New York City to begin recording his sixth studio album, *Highway 61 Revisited*, his first with wholly electric instrumentation, which was eventually released in early September 1965. The album's opening track, 'Like a Rolling Stone', was recorded on June 15 and 16 and produced by Tom Wilson. At just over six minutes long, the song was a breakthrough in the history of rock music. It was written upon Dylan's return from England while he was staying at Woodstock, upstate New York. It was a time when he was tired and recuperating from his illness at the end of his British tour, having been briefly hospitalised at St. Mary's Hospital, London. It was also a period during which he was seriously considering, as has been noted, quitting the music scene altogether. As he later, in March 1966, told the journalist Nat Hentoff:

> Last spring [1965], I guess I was going to quit singing. I was very drained…I was playing a lot of songs I didn't want to play. I was singing a lot of words I didn't really want to sing…It's very tiring having other people tell you how much they dig you, if you yourself don't dig you.[1]

In February 1966 Dylan stated in another interview, with regard to 'Like a Rolling Stone', that:

> I wrote that after I had *quit*. I'd literally quit, singing and playing – I found myself writing this song, this story, this long piece of vomit, twenty pages long, and out of it I took 'Like a Rolling Stone' and made it as a single. And I'd never written anything like it before and it suddenly came to me that this is what I should do.[2]

As for the lyrical content of 'Like a Rolling Stone', Dylan later told journalist Jules Siegel: 'In the end it wasn't hatred, it was telling someone something they didn't know, telling them they were lucky. Revenge, that's a better word.'[3] Moreover, the song reflected, too, a world-view on Dylan's part that had been evident, in a different manner and as only a few commentators have recognised, in 'It's Alright, Ma' on *Bringing It All Back home*. It, as Andy Gill has observed, amounted to 'a position which could loosely be described as existentialist', since 'Like a Rolling Stone' suggested strongly that 'truly to know yourself and find fulfilment, you must face the world alone, mould your future and your philosophy from your own experiences.'[4] From that standpoint, and in Dylan's own words, 'with no direction home', the subject of the song, 'invisible now…with no secrets to conceal', might eventually achieve a cathartic self-awareness.

The final recorded version of 'Like a Rolling Stone', which featured Mike Bloomfield on guitar, Paul Griffin on piano, Al Kooper on organ, and Bobby Gregg on drums, was completed after, uncharacteristically for Dylan, several takes and false starts on June 16.[5] Soon after it was released in July 1965, it reached number 2 in the US singles charts and number 4 in the UK.

Musically groundbreaking, Dylan's vocal performance was, in Gill's vivid description, 'utterly gripping, a semi-spoken blues rap delivered in a sour, offhand monotone which curled occasionally at the end of lines, like a sneer twisting the corner of his mouth as he gloated over a hipster's downfall'.[6]

Largely unprecedented in modern popular music were not only that tone of recrimination but also the song's sheer length and its surrealistic imagery. One of Dylan's most famous songs, 'Like a Rolling Stone' proved historically to be in many ways a musical milestone and turning-point. As Paul McCartney later recalled: 'It seemed to go on and on forever. It was just beautiful. He showed us all that it was possible to go a little further.'[7]

Nearly 23 years after 'Like a Rolling Stone' had been recorded and released, Bruce Springsteen, inducting Bob Dylan into the Rock and Roll Hall of Fame in January 1988, also recognised its historic significance, remembering when he had first heard the record, aged 15, travelling with his mother in the car and listening to the radio, 'and on came that snare shot', he recalled, 'that sounded like somebody kicked open the door to your mind: "Like a Rolling Stone"…Bob freed your mind the way Elvis freed your body. He showed us that just because the music was innately physical did not mean that it was anti-intellectual.'[8]

Dylan's first, highly controversial, and symbolically important live performance of 'Like a Rolling Stone' was at the Newport Folk Festival on July 25, 1965, only five days after the song had been released as a single. He had decided to perform at a predominantly acoustic folk-music festival live with electric instrumentation, backed by members of the Paul Butterfield Blues Band, whose brilliant guitarist Mike Bloomfield had played at the recording sessions of 'Like a Rolling Stone' just over a week before. The resulting, barely 15-minute appearance at Newport premiered live performances of 'Like a Rolling Stone' and 'Maggie's Farm', together with 'It Takes a Lot to Laugh, It Takes a Train to Cry', originally entitled 'Phantom Engineer'. Dylan's brief electric explosion at an acoustic folk event has subsequently assumed legendary status in historical terms. Greil Marcus has observed that: 'As music it was a non-event, after Elvis Presley's third, above-the-waist performance on the *Ed Sullivan Show* in 1957, and the Beatles' debut there in 1964; as a performance it has grown into perhaps the most storied event in the history of modern popular music.'[9]

Dylan received a stormy reception at Newport for 'going electric', though accounts differ about the extent of that hostile reaction and the reasons for it.[10] Among the various interpretations of the audience response to Dylan's brief performance, his friend Eric Von Schmidt recalled that the negative reaction and booing were really caused by the sheer volume of The Paul Butterfield Blues Band accompanying Dylan, together with the poor overall sound quality. 'The people', Von Schmidt maintained, 'who first started shouting were not putting Bobby down for playing electric; it was just that we couldn't hear him.'[11]

At any rate, having left the stage at Newport after only about 15 minutes, Dylan was eventually persuaded to return to perform by himself on acoustic guitar and played and sang 'It's All Over Now, Baby Blue', from the acoustic side of *Bringing It All Back Home*, and then 'Mr. Tambourine Man' from the same album. Much of the audience cheered him, failing, however, according to Dylan's first biographer Anthony Scaduto, to recognise that the first song 'was Dylan again bidding the old allegiance goodbye', while the second 'was calling for the razing of all barriers that keep a man from getting to the truth within him…The folk crowd knew only that he was using the *proper* guitar.'[12]

Dylan nonetheless appeared backstage, in the view of many eyewitnesses at the time, including his close friend the blues singer Maria Maldour, to be visibly shaken by the whole experience.[13] He was, Scaduto recalled, 'upset at the reaction, and upset that he had apparently misjudged his audience, had lost control'.[14] Dylan's friend and biographer Robert Shelton met him twice in New York a week after the festival and observed that: 'He still seemed stunned and distressed that he had sparked such animosity.'[15]

Dylan himself confirmed that observation eight months after the Newport Folk Festival, albeit adding a note of wry humour, when he stated that:

> I was kind of stunned…There were a lot of old people there, too…lots of whole families had driven down from Vermont…they just came to hear some relaxing hoedowns, you know, maybe an Indian polka or two. And then when everything's going all right, here I come on, and the whole place turns into a beer factory. There were a lot of people there who were very pleased that I got booed. I saw them afterward. I do resent, though, that everybody that booed said they did it because they were old fans.[16]

As for using electric instrumentation at Newport, Dylan told Nat Hentoff in that same interview that he had not recently started playing with a band 'for any kind of propaganda-type or commercial-type reasons. It's just that my songs are pictures and the band makes the sound of the pictures.'[17]

There appears, however, to be little historical doubt that his brief performance at Newport 1965 had exposed a deep division between, on the one hand, traditional folk-music enthusiasts who believed that Dylan had sold out to the forces of commercial music and, on the other, those who were strongly drawn to the new lyrically rich and inventive electric music that Dylan had unveiled four months before on the non-acoustic side of *Bringing It All Back Home*. That division of his audience was later to be reproduced dramatically on Dylan's next tour of Britain in May 1966.

In broader cultural terms, that polarisation of Dylan's audience represented a major development in modern popular music, one that seemed to support the view of Elijah Wald, and others, that Dylan's decision to perform live at Newport with a band and electric instrumentation, at a folk-music festival, was 'the moment of intersection, when rock emerged, separate from rock 'n' roll, and replaced folk as the serious intelligent voice of a generation'.[18]

That view of the widening gulf between the old and the new popular-music scenes seems to have been clearly recognised and comprehended at the time by Joe Boyd, the sound and stage manager at Newport in 1965, who recalled many years later that:

> There are a lot of occasions when you can look back and say, 'Well after that night, things were never the same.' But it's very rare that you're in a moment where you know it is at the time; you knew, as it was happening, that paths were parting.[19]

At Newport, in the light of Dylan's brief watershed appearance, Boyd's recollection, nearly 40 years after the event, was that: 'The old guard hung their heads in defeat while the young, far from being triumphant, were chastened…The festival would never be the same, nor would popular music and nor would "youth culture".'[20]

In agreement with that assessment of the significance of the occasion, Paul Rothschild, who was on the mixing desk at Newport, also recalled:

> To me that night at Newport was as clear as crystal. It's the end of an era and the beginning of another. There's no historical precedent. This is a folk festival, *the* folk festival, and you couldn't even say it's blues and the blues has moved to an electric format. This is a young Jewish songwriter with an electric band that sounds like rock 'n' roll. There were two very big passions happening here. It was an election. You had to choose which team you were going to support.[21]

Dylan's growing distance from the old guard of folk-music traditionalists had, then, been publicly underlined by his divisive performance at Newport. His own motives for 'going electric' there do not, however, appear to be supported by any clear evidence that his appearance with The Paul Butterfield Blues Band was either premeditated or carefully planned; hence his own reaction in its aftermath. As Paul Williams has commented: 'I don't think Dylan was deliberately confrontational (for once). He was just following his muse, his ear, moving out of a format that no longer worked for him and into a world rich with new possibilities.'[22] Dylan's brief appearance at Newport was thus in itself an assertion of his artistic independence, of his determination not to be co-opted for other people's causes or commitments.

Such a development in his musical approach stemmed in part, as we have seen, from his growing dissatisfaction with solo acoustic performance. But it sprang, too, from his increasing attraction to working with a band, which would, as he put it, make the sounds of the pictures that his songs portrayed. That feeling was clearly influenced by his favourable response to British groups such as The Beatles and The Animals. It also had deeper personal roots in his love of classic rock'n'roll in his early youth in Minnesota.

As for the charges of betrayal, apostasy, and capitulation to commercial market forces that were levelled at him by many folk traditionalists as a result of his changing musical direction, both at the time of Newport 1965 and even more vociferously during the following months, his friend Robert Shelton later maintained in Dylan's defence that:

> Dylan had not been surreptitiously manipulated. He alone decided to leap back into rock, taking with him folk song's storytelling and comment. The controversy over him adding a beat and subtracting topical sloganeering detracted from a significant development: Dylan was creating a new kind of expression, more sophisticated than that of his previous three years.[23]

Furthermore, Dylan's embrace of electric music in 1965, of what would soon be called 'folk-rock', was yet another stage in his musical development for which he would be disparaged and attacked by his critics. As Shelton noted:

> If Dylan worked in blues, he was a white man stealing black music. If he developed Woody's talking blues, he was an imitator. If he adapted Anglo-Irish folk songs, he was a thief. If he wrote topical-protest songs, traditionalists thought he was a traitor, yet if he turned subjective, he was a self-involved existentialist.[24]

Dylan's movement away from what was generally perceived to be acoustic folk music did not in any case imply his abandonment of the folk-music tradition. That was evident not just in 1965 and the following year but also in his songwriting and musical performance well after the 1960s had passed away. Indeed, he had an historically informed, youthful awareness in the mid-1960s of the essential, mythic reality of much of that folk-music tradition. As he told Anthony Scaduto:

> I know what folk music is, that's why I don't call myself a folk singer. Most of the people down on me because of folk music just don't know what

they're talking about. They always say that folk music should be simple so people can understand…But the truth is, there are weird folk songs that have come down the ages, based on nothing, or based on legend, Bible, plague, religion, just based on mysticism. Those songs weren't simple at all. What's happened is the labour movement people, they're talking about keeping it simple.[25]

In very similar, if more surreal, terms Dylan told Nat Hentoff in March 1966:

Traditional music is based on hexagrams. It comes about from legends, Bibles, plagues, and it revolves around vegetables and death. There's nobody going to kill traditional music. All these songs are about roses growing out of people's brains and lovers who are really geese and swans that turn into angels – they're not going to die…Songs like 'Which Side Are You On,' and 'I Love You, Porgy' – they're not folk-music songs; they're political songs. They're already dead.[26]

As for 'protest songs' and the messages inherent in them, Dylan considered 'protest' to be 'an amusement-park word', while the word 'message' struck him 'as having a hernia-like sound. It's just like the word "delicious." Also the word "marvellous."' In practical songwriting terms, too, his view was that 'anybody that's got a message is going to learn from experience that they can't put it into a song. I mean it's not going to come out the same message.' He added ironically: 'Myself, what I'm going to do is rent Town Hall and put about 30 Western Union boys on the bill, I mean, then there'll really be some messages.'[27]

Asked, too, on another occasion during the mid-1960s whether he himself was seeking to convey a message in his songs, he responded:

I'm just transferring my thoughts into music…All I can hope to do is sing what I'm thinking. Don't put me down as a man with a message. My songs are just me talking to myself. Maybe that's an egotistical thing to say but it's what it is. I have no responsibility to anybody except myself.[28]

Recoiling from being categorised still as a 'protest singer', Dylan responded thus to an interviewer in San Francisco in early December 1965 with barbed humour:

Interviewer: 'How many people who labour in the same musical vineyard in which you toil, how many are protest singers?…That is, people who use their music, use the songs, to protest the social state in which we live today…'
Dylan: '…How many?'
Interviewer: 'Yes, there are many?'
Dylan: 'Yeah, I think it's about 136.'
Interviewer: 'You mean exactly 136?'
Dylan: 'Uhhh, either 136 or 142.'[29]

The genre of contemporary popular music which was then developing, instead of so-called 'protest songs', in 1965 – on the electric side of *Bringing It All Back Home*, with 'Like a Rolling Stone', and at Newport – soon became labelled 'folk-rock'. According to Dylan biographers Scaduto and Heylin, the term, which Dylan strongly disliked, was probably coined by Eliot Tiegel of *Billboard* magazine a few months after The Animals had topped both the US and UK singles charts in May 1964 with their electric version of 'House of the Rising Sun'.[30] Just over a year later, from June 1965 onwards, the term started to be more widely used, in both the media and the popular-music business, after the success of The Byrds' electric version of Dylan's 'Mr. Tambourine Man', which reached number 1 in the UK in July. The Byrds, a Californian group led by frontman Jim (later known as Roger) McGuinn, originally with a five-piece line-up, had first heard the song on a Dylan demo tape at Columbia Records Studios and subsequently recorded what Jonathan Gould has aptly described as 'a dreamily harmonized version', which, 'quite different from the weary transcendence of Dylan's acoustic version…sounded like surf music for the mind'.[31] Dylan heard The Bryds' cover, with the distinctive jangle of Roger McGuinn's twelve-string guitar, before it was released and liked it.[32]

With regard to Dylan's own view of the term 'folk-rock' as a description of the musical genre that The Byrds had served to generate, he told Nora Ephron and Susan Edmiston in their August 1965 interview that 'I've never even said that word. It has a hard gutter sound. Circusy atmosphere. It's nose-thumbing. Sound like you're looking down on what it is fantastic, great music.'[33] Nevertheless, he agreed with them when asked whether the definition of the term that they offered, namely, 'the combination of the electronic sound of rock 'n' roll with the meaningful lyrics of folk music', summed up what he was doing musically at that time.[34]

But although Dylan disavowed the term folk-rock as a descriptive label, Robert Shelton in his biography, first published in 1986, later credited Dylan with developing a form of music, increasingly categorised by that term, which marked a watershed in the maturation of popular music. 'Before 1965', Shelton wrote, 'many assumed that pop and rock were *supposed* to be about trivia, to be not only non-intellectual, but even *anti*-intellectual. This surface judgement belied a true understanding of popular music as popular expression. Folk-rock, after its fad phase cooled, effected a major improvement of popular music. For that, one must credit Dylan.'[35]

Paul Nelson, like Shelton a defender of Dylan's change of musical direction in the mid-1960s, later described folk-rock as historically 'a hastily assembled and transitory frontier junction to and from which several important musical roads were connected'. It was a musical hybrid 'with which many young urban folk musicians attempted to fuse revered teachings from the past…with an immediate and more personally relevant knowledge of the present'. In doing so, those young musicians were also 'rebelling against the anti-commercial snobbery of the folk/topical powers-that-be'.[36]

Folk-rock, which for Nelson was nascent in Dylan's transitional acoustic album *Another Side of Bob Dylan* and most clearly developed on his trilogy of 1965 and 1966, *Bringing It All Back Home*, *Highway 61 Revisited*, and *Blonde on Blonde*, thus influenced the musical development of American groups in the mid-1960s such as The Byrds, The Lovin' Spoonful, The Mamas and the Papas, and others, and in the late 1960s British electric-folk groups such as Fairport Convention and Steeleye Span.

For, then, an historically brief period Dylan was to be the leading, shaping influence on a style of music, labelled to his distaste as 'folk-rock', which appeared, as Keith Negus has observed, to be 'an intelligent genre addressed to adults, leaving behind the inarticulate rebellion of rock 'n' roll and the naïve romance of pop'.[37] Dylan's pioneering musical development in that respect would reach its controversial climax in 1966, after which he would return to more roots-oriented American music, drawing on folk, acoustic blues, and country-music traditions. Meanwhile, having moved away from topical songwriting in 1965, without, he pointed out, having turned his back on the folk-music tradition,[38] Dylan in his personal artistic re-creation now, in Gould's observation, 'embodied a literate and idiosyncratic style of cultural radicalism that harkened back to his bohemian forebears in San Francisco in the 1950s and Greenwich Village in the 1920s, to the Surrealists and Symbolist poets with whom new friends like Allen Ginsberg had begun to familiarize (and compare) him'.[39]

The spring 1965 British tour that had preceded such radical changes in Dylan's musical trajectory had itself taken place against the background of a significantly changed climate within the British, and specifically the London, folk-music scene. One of the most notable indicators of that change was the opening of the Les Cousins Club in Greek Street, Soho, London, in April 1965. Located in a small cellar under a restaurant, Les Cousins soon became established as the most vibrant and celebrated new folk club in London. Its resident performers, regulars, and visitors comprised, as Colin Harper has recalled, 'a virtual roll-call of folk music's contribution to the "Swinging Sixties"'. For among 'any number of extraordinary musicians' who regularly took the stage there during 1965 and the following year were:

> the three kings – [acoustic folk guitarists] Bert Jansch, John Renbourne and Davy Graham; the heirs to the thrones – Paul Simon, Al Stewart, Ralph McTell, Roy Harper, Jackson Frank, Dorris Henderson; the king and queen of 'pop-folk' – Donovan and Julie Felix; future legends of folk-rock taking floor spots – Sandy Denny, Trevor Lucas, Cat Stevens; emissaries from the living tradition – the Watersons, the Young Tradition, Anne Briggs, Dave and Toni Arthur; emissaries from Outer Space – the Incredible String Band; the godfathers – Alexis Korner and Alex Campbell;[40]

In addition, at Les Cousins during that period there were, Harper has noted, 'drop-in Americans of the quality of Doris Troy, Sandy Bull, Arlo Guthrie, Danny Kalb, "Spider" John Koerner, Derroll Adams, the Reverend Gary Davis and Bill Monroe', as well as 'once-only visitors of the mythic quality – Bob Dylan, John McLaughlin,

Eric Clapton and Jimi Hendrix'. Even unyielding traditionalists Ewan MacColl and Peggy Seeger came once, 'typically fearless in the very crucible of the new order'.[41]

Les Cousins did indeed at that time represent and epitomise the new order of musicians who used a traditional, acoustic folk-music format but combined it with a contemporary lyrical and musical style and resonance, thereby innovating rather than merely re-creating their song material. That approach had been evident in Bert Jansch's song 'Needle of Death', composed in memory of the young musician David 'Buck' Polley who had died of hard-drug overdosage. It was the only contemporary song regularly performed by the traditional folk duo Dave and Toni Arthur, and was also covered on record by the pop-folk singer, and popular television performer, Julie Felix on her *Second Album*.[42] Bert Jansch's own highly influential, eponymous first album had been released by Transatlantic Records on the very day that Les Cousins opened in April 1965.

The broader musical and cultural significance of what Les Cousins epitomised was later perceptively described by Karl Dallas, the leading British folk-music journalist, who wrote for *Melody Maker* from 1957 until 1981. Of the London folk scene in the mid-1960s, Dallas recalled:

> it was a time of polarisation when the young Turks were about to wrest the folk revival from the hands of the Old Left pioneers who ran the Singers' Club and *Sing* magazine, a schism which is remembered today, wrongly, in terms of attitudes to traditionalism and national culture but which was, in reality, more concerned with lifestyles and a reaction against the puritanical neo-Calvinism of Marxists like Bruce Dunnet and Ewan MacColl, for which the new band of what we were later to call singer-songwriters were to substitute something a great deal more hedonistic, instinctual, less rational.[43]

Among the contemporary folk singers who became residents at Les Cousins was Al Stewart, who also performed regularly at Bunjies coffee bar, not far away in Litchfield Street, just off Charing Cross Road in London. Formerly a lead guitarist in beat groups in his home town of Bournemouth, Stewart had moved to London in February 1965. He later recalled of his early years in London in the mid-1960s:

> I wasn't a folk singer at the time. I just happened to own a couple of Bob Dylan albums. But all these singer-songwriters I met in London seemed to be doing something very fresh, very exciting. And the folk scene seemed a little more intellectual than the rock'n'roll scene, and that was appealing. Wearing a corduroy jacket and living in a coffee bar when you're nineteen and discussing Sartre with like-minded people was a long way from being in Bournemouth talking about how the Surfaris got that great guitar sound.[44]

Al Stewart was by 1965, as his biographer Neville Judd has noted, 'becoming more and more in awe of Bob Dylan's songwriting'. Tracks on *Bringing It All Back Home* such as 'Subterranean Homesick Blues', 'Maggie's Farm', 'Mr. Tambourine Man', and 'It's All Over Now, Baby Blue' were all 'songs that Al may have admired but compositions which he none the less found impossible to match when it came to his own writing'.[45]

At Bunjies on Litchfield Street in late February 1965 Al Stewart, with his F-hole rock'n'roll-type guitar, had sung from the floor Dylan's 'The Times They Are A-Changin'' a few weeks before it had been released in the UK as a single, and did so, in Stewart's own words, 'with much spirit and very little finesse but to thunderous applause'.[46] That very night he was offered a weekly Friday night spot at Bunjies that would change the course of his musical career. He subsequently learnt the songs on Dylan's *The Freewheelin' Bob Dylan* and *The Times They A-Changin'* albums 'verbatim so I could return to Bunjies and sing every track off those LPs'.[47] Stewart's regular Friday night spot at Bunjies soon became a residency, singing Dylan covers as well as a few of his own original compositions, including the song 'Nothing At All', which was, on his own admission, 'totally Dylan'.[48]

Al Stewart later recalled that in London in early 1965: 'There was a very healthy Dylan cult but at the same time it was quite closed in – the world at large hadn't heard of Dylan but the inmates of Bunjies were very hip to Dylan and Dylan was the *aware* underground thing to be at the time'.[49] But Dylan's 1965 British tour clearly lifted him out of that relative obscurity, radically widening his popular appeal as a result both of his concert performances and of the quality and commercial success of his recorded albums and singles.

That in turn served to reinforce the steadily increasing boom in folk clubs and folk music, in both its traditional and contemporary forms, throughout Britain, and not just in London, during the course of 1965. An article in *Melody Maker* in February 1965 by Ray Coleman had provided the first detailed analysis of the British folk scene at that time. Coleman estimated that there were then about 300 folk clubs around Britain, with, according to the folk singer and folk-music organiser Roy Guest, about 40 of those clubs in London, at which about 20 professional musicians and about 100 semi-professionals regularly performed. But Coleman also noted that there was an in-built destruct mechanism within the British folk-music movement opposing commercial success. 'Immediately a folky record reaches the best sellers or gets mass exposure,' he wrote, 'purists often insist it is "not real folk music". Ironically, fervent folk fans seem concerned at the prospect of the music being discovered by too many.'[50] Musical and cultural snobbery, as well as factionalism, would thus place major obstacles in the path of any British folk boom on a large commercial scale. In a different way, Bob Dylan would begin to confront obstacles of that kind later in 1965, and more overtly during the following year.

In August 1965 The Beatles released the soundtrack album for their second feature film *Help*, which was premiered in London in late July. The album was recorded between February and June of that year. Its title track, with John Lennon as lead singer, was recorded in April and released as a single in July, reaching number 1 in the UK singles charts in early August. 'Help' provided further evidence of Bob

Dylan's growing influence on Lennon's approach to songwriting, with its greater emphasis on personal and emotionally direct lyrics. That was evident in the song's tone of honest and despondent self-appraisal, with lines such as 'Every now and then I feel so insecure' and 'Nowadays I'm not so self-assured'. Those were words and sentiments that simply did not appear in pop-music lyrics during the 1950s and early 1960s, with very few exceptions, such as, to some extent, Lennon's own 1963 song 'There's a Place' on *Please Please Me*.

On the personal nature of the background to 'Help', the album, and the making of the film, Lennon later commented, in the last major interview before his death, 'I was eating and drinking like a pig and I was fat as a pig, dissatisfied with myself, and subconsciously I was crying for help'.[51] In another earlier interview Lennon had expressed very similar sentiments, stating, with regard to the lyrical content of the song 'Help', that: 'I meant it. It's real! It's just me singing "Help", and I meant it.'[52]

Bob Dylan's influence on Lennon's songwriting was even more clearly apparent on another track on the *Help* album, 'You've Got to Hide Your Love Away', The Beatles' first entirely acoustic studio performance, recorded without overdubbing in February 1965. Later acknowledging that direct influence, Lennon stated that, as with 'I'm a Loser' on *Beatles for Sale*: 'That's me in my Dylan period again. I am like a chameleon, influenced by whatever is going on. If Elvis can do it, I can do it. If the Everly Brothers can do it, me and Paul can. Same with Dylan.'[53]

As for the personal tone of 'You've Got to Hide Your Love Away', Lennon also commented that: 'Instead of projecting myself into a situation, I would try to express what I felt about myself, which I had done in my books.[54] I think it was Dylan that helped me realise that.'[55] Dylan himself, however, was to do both those things in his songwriting during the 1960s and later, that is, to compose songs that were lyrical fictions which alluded to his own personal experience, thoughts, and feelings, thereby at the same time projecting himself into the situations that his songs' stories described.

Dylan's influence on Lennon's songwriting at that time was evident not just lyrically but also in the stark acoustic style and sound of 'You've Got to Hide Your Love Away', with its relatively simple chord pattern and progression. That development, replacing the much more unorthodox chord structures of many of The Beatles' earlier songs, what Dylan had called their 'outrageous chords' when he first heard 'I Want to Hold Your Hand' and others,[56] was to continue in their next studio album, *Rubber Soul*, released in December 1965. Paul McCartney certainly had no doubt about the extent of Dylan's influence on John Lennon, and specifically on his 'You've Got to Hide Your Love Away', in the mid-1960s. Dylan's own songwriting during that period, he later noted, contained 'masses of cluttered lyrics like John had written in his books'. It was thus to Lennon '…very appealing, it hit a chord in John; it was as if John felt, That should have been me'. Hence in McCartney's view 'You've Got to Hide Your Love Away' was 'virtually a Dylan impression'.[57]

Lennon biographer Philip Norman has thus underlined Dylan's dual influence, both lyrical and musical, on 'You've Got to Hide Your Love Away'. The song, 'a sombre ballad about rejection and alienation, couched in more "literary" language…than he'd [Lennon] ever previously tried', at the same time, Norman observed, was imbued with a tone that 'had taken on a Dylanesque quality: harder and more nasal than before, its phrasing more adventurous…laced with bitter irony as much as bleak self-pity'.[58] The Beatles' producer George Martin, at the time the song was recorded in February 1965, realising its strong underlying influence, had indeed later stated: 'I asked him [Lennon] not to sound too much like Dylan. He wasn't doing it deliberately, it was subconscious more than anything.'[59]

Keith Richards of The Rolling Stones later commented on Dylan's influence upon Lennon and, to a lesser extent, upon himself and Mick Jagger as songwriters:

> I'd say that Lennon felt a strong urge, not so much to compete with Dylan, but Bob did spur him to realize he could dig deeper. Mick and I felt that, too, although maybe we didn't feel it as strongly as John.[60]

With regard to Dylan's impact on The Rolling Stones' own songwriting, Richards cited 'Sympathy for the Devil', later released on their 1968 album *Beggars' Banquet*, as their most Dylanesque song. 'Mick wrote it', Richards recalled, 'almost as a Dylan song, but it ended up a rock'n'roll samba.'[61]

But there were also earlier signs of Dylan's influence, indirect or implicit, on other songs composed and recorded by The Rolling Stones in 1965, songs that were harsh or stringent in their mood and lyrical content. Most notable of these was '(I Can't Get No) Satisfaction', which reached number 1 in the UK singles charts in September 1965 and soon acquired the status of a rock classic, and 'Get off of My Cloud' which also reached number 1 (in November). They were both, as were subsequent Rolling Stones singles in 1966, expressions of social commentary, voicing dissatisfaction, dissent, and youthful rebelliousness directed in the face of what were perceived as the hypocritical, shallow, or restrictive aspects of contemporary society. Both songs, while to some extent departing from the musical constraints of purist rhythm and blues, The Rolling Stones' original source of artistic inspiration, were thus illustrations of Dylan's contemporary influence on British songwriting in so far as he had greatly expanded the range of lyrical concerns, themes, and subjects that could be addressed in modern popular music.

That was evident, too, in the work of Pete Townshend of The Who, who had been a Dylan-inspired apprentice songwriter in the early 1960s, in songs such as 'My Generation', released in October 1965 and also commercially successful, reaching number 2 in the UK singles charts, and 'Legal Matter', recorded in the same month for The Who's first album, *My Generation*. The former song forcefully expressed youthful unease at the generational gap of the 1960s, while the latter focused on the troubled issues of divorce and constraining domesticity. The Animals, too, released their own commercially successful single 'We Gotta Get out of This Place' in August 1965, reaching number 2 in the UK charts. Originally written by the American Brill Building songwriters Barry Mann and Cynthia Weil, The Animals' version of the song was lyrically revised in a manner that clearly voiced alienation from, and a desire to escape from, the harsh constraints of an industrial working-class city milieu, of the very kind from which the group itself had emerged.

All of those songs thus contained social observations or comments that were previously very rare in pop-music lyrics. In that respect they were implicitly manifestations of Bob Dylan's songwriting impact during that period. Social commentary and satire targeting English upper-middle-class snobbery and hypocrisy were also evident in 'A Well Respected Man' written by Ray Davies of The Kinks and released in September 1965. The song heralded the group's shift away from their early hard-rock, power-chord singles towards further reflections on aspects of contemporary British society in Ray Davies' 1966 songs, notably, 'A Dedicated Follower of Fashion', 'Sunny Afternoon', and 'Dead End Street'.

Yet paradoxically those were songs written by the one major British popular songwriter of the 1960s, among that relatively small grouping, who was probably least influenced by Bob Dylan. As Nick Hasted has observed of the highly British tone and content of 'A Well Respected Man', the song 'introduced British pop to the character study and satirical sketch. Owing nothing to Dylan's highly influential Ginsberg and acid-inspired style, it was more Noel Coward, Somerset Maugham or Peter Cook.'[62] Indeed, Ray Davies himself later wrote, in somewhat ambivalent terms, that: 'I had always distrusted Dylan as a songwriter, in the same way that at college I had distrusted Picasso as a painter. I had the feeling that both men were great artists but creative chameleons.' Davies conceded that Dylan and Picasso were 'two giants of twentieth-century art', but, in his view, they were at the same time 'both giving a new meaning to the expression "piss artist"...They were both masters of their art.' In Dylan's case, Davies thought that involved 'making fun of all the fashion victims who were calling him a great poet'.[63]

The most obvious example, however, of Dylan's direct influence on British popular music in 1965, apart from that provided by John Lennon and The Beatles, was evident in the work of Manfred Mann, who had started very much as a British R&B group, with Paul Jones on vocals. They covered Dylan's 'With God on Our Side', released on an EP in June 1965. Banned by the BBC from airplay because of what was considered its politically controversial lyrics, the group nonetheless performed the song live on ITV's highly popular programme *Ready Steady Go!* That in itself was a remarkable indicator of the changing lyrical content and approach of much of popular music by the mid-1960s, largely induced by Dylan. Manfred Mann also later covered Dylan's unreleased song 'If You Gotta Go, Go Now', which he had failed to complete at the disorganised and largely fruitless London recording session with John Mayall's Bluesbreakers in May 1965. Dylan himself stated in December 1965 that he considered that Manfred Mann were at that time the artists who in their cover versions of his songs did the most justice to his compositions, commenting: 'Each one of them has been right in context with what the song was all about'.[64]

In September 1965 Bob Dylan's *Highway 61 Revisited*, his sixth studio album, was released, having been recorded in late July and August of that year. Musically and lyrically groundbreaking in many ways, it was, in Michael Gray's description, 'Dylan's first fully fledged eagle-flight into rock'.[65] Widely regarded as one of Dylan's greatest albums, if not in the view of many his greatest, its significance and subsequent impact upon British popular music will be considered here later.

By autumn 1965 Dylan's popularity and commercial success in Britain had been clearly demonstrated. By then he had five entries in the UK top ten album charts, including *Highway 61 Revisited*, as well as, since March, 1965 five entries in the UK singles charts: 'The Times They Are A-Changin'', 'Subterranean Homesick Blues', 'Maggie's Farm', 'Like A Rolling Stone', and 'Positively Fourth Street'. In addition, other recording artists, mainly American, enjoyed major success in Britain during 1965 with their cover versions of Dylan's compositions, namely, The Byrds with 'Mr. Tambourine Man' and 'All I Really Want to Do', Cher also with the latter song, Joan Baez with 'It Ain't Me Babe', and Manfred Mann with 'If You Gotta Go, Go Now'. All of their recordings were, broadly speaking, examples of what by the mid-1960s was widely categorised in the popular-music business and the media as 'folk-rock', however much Dylan himself disliked the term. But the label was not without significance at that time, as the popularity of those cover versions confirmed. As Sean Egan later maintained: 'This was not a meaningless and pedantic designation of a sub-genre as happens frequently today in dance music but an acknowledgment that barriers between musical styles and audiences previously thought immovable were being torn asunder.'[66]

In Britain, however, Dylan's transition from acoustic folk music to electric folk-rock, which had been the catalyst in the breaking of those barriers, was certainly not without its critics. Ewan MacColl, the foremost and intransigent guardian of folk traditionalism in Britain, who had been distinctly unimpressed by Dylan ever since his appearance at the Singers' Club on his first visit to London in December 1962, made public in vehement and outspoken terms his view of Dylan's alleged shortcomings. In the November 1965 edition of the American folk-music magazine *Sing Out!* MacColl wrote: 'I am still unable to see in him anything other than a youth of mediocre talent. Only a completely non-critical audience nourished on the watery pap of pop music could have fallen for this tenth-rate drivel.'[67]

As had been the case with previous criticisms by folk traditionalists of Dylan's change of musical direction, he was defended in January 1966 by Robert Shelton in the *Sunday New York Times*, and later in its pages by Nat Hentoff and Paul Nelson.[68] In September 1965 MacColl had already attacked Dylan in *Melody Maker*, sparking a subsequent controversy in its editorials and correspondence columns that continued into the following month. 'Dylan', MacColl contended, 'is to me the perfect symbol of the anti-artist in our society. He is against everything – the last resort of someone who doesn't really want to change the world...I think his poetry is puerile. It's derivative and old hat.'[69]

In response, a *Melody Maker* editorial defended Dylan by maintaining that: 'He [MacColl] must be terribly upset that songs are being actually sung by people instead of being neatly parcelled on the shelves of his beloved folk museums.'[70] A later article, entitled 'Just Who Does Ewan MacColl Think He Is?', quoted a number of leading British recording artists in Dylan's defence, including Marianne Faithful, Manfred Mann, and Charlie MacKay of the New Faces. Paul Simon alone was quoted in defence of MacColl's criticism of Dylan's poetry, which, in Simon's view, was 'just rehashed Ginsberg'.[71] Simon, however, at the time, it has been claimed, nursed a longstanding grudge against Dylan dating from the time he talked through a Simon performance at Folk City in Greenwich Village.[72]

On the question of MacColl's strictures against Dylan, historian Gerard DeGroot later aptly described them as 'the predictable wail of a man enslaved by his own pieties' who 'sought purity in politics as much as in music'. Dylan's own response to such inflexibility, DeGroot added, had already been composed in his recantation 'My Back Pages' on his 1964 album *Another Side of Bob Dylan*, 'his stinging rebuke to those who discovered truth before the age of majority'.[73]

At the close of 1965, in December, The Beatles released their sixth studio album, *Rubber Soul*, which had been recorded against a tight deadline between mid-October and mid-November. Ian Inglis has maintained with considerable justification that: 'Of all the Beatles' LPs, it is *Rubber Soul* that provides the most unequivocal example of the manner in which their mid-1960s musical output derived from their contact with Dylan.'[74] Certainly a number of the album's songs displayed Dylan's song-writing influence in as much as they were not only lyrically more personal and emotionally direct, but also more reflective about relationships than had generally been the case in the pre-Dylan era of pop-music lyrics. Prominent examples on *Rubber Soul* were 'Norwegian Wood', 'Nowhere Man', 'Girl', and 'In My Life', all sung and largely composed by John Lennon, upon whom, among The Beatles, Dylan at that time exerted the greatest musical influence. Of these lyrical fictions that alluded to personal experience and feelings, 'Norwegian Wood' was thus, for instance, Lennon later recalled, 'about an affair I was having', about which he was 'very careful and paranoid', in view of his own marriage with Cynthia Lennon at the time.[75] Of 'Nowhere Man' Paul McCartney later recalled, years after Lennon's death, that it 'was really an anti-John song, written by John. He told me later, he didn't tell me then, he said he'd written about himself, feeling like he wasn't going anywhere.'[76]

As for the personal background of 'Girl' on *Rubber Soul*, Lennon recalled in 1980: 'That's me. Writing about this *dream* girl again – the one that hadn't come yet. It was Yoko.'[77] But, above all, probably most significant in terms of Lennon's song-writing on the album was 'In My Life'. He later considered that it was 'the first song that I wrote that was really consciously about my life'. It was originally 'sparked by a remark, a journalist and writer in England', almost certainly Kenneth Allsop, who asked Lennon after his book *In My Own Write* was published: 'Why don't you put some of the way you write in the book, as it were, in the songs? Or why don't you put something about your childhood into the songs?' All of that, Lennon pointed out, 'came out later as "Penny Lane" from Paul – although it was actually me who lived in Penny Lane – and "Strawberry Fields"'.[78]

'In My Life', one of The Beatles' and Lennon's finest and most poignant songs, was thus deeply suffused in its tone and content with, in Lennon's own words, 'a remembrance of friends and lovers of the past…And it was, I think, my first major piece of work. Up till then it had all been sort of glib and throwaway. And that was the first time I consciously put my literary part of myself into the lyric. Inspired by Kenneth Alsopf [sic] the British journalist and Bob Dylan.'[79]

Although not so obviously and directly influenced as Lennon by Dylan at that time, both Paul McCartney and George Harrison contributed to *Rubber Soul* songs that were either reflective about the mundane realities of everyday life, as in Harrison's 'Think for Yourself', or else provided realistic, even sceptical, observations about romantic relationships, as in McCartney's 'I'm Looking through You' and Harrison's 'If I Needed Someone'. Perhaps not as consciously as in Lennon's case, those songs reflected a greater desire to embrace a level of personal awareness that went beyond the conventional boy–girl romance lyrics of the pre-Dylan era, and which thus revealed, indirectly at least, the influence of Dylan's innovative song-writing. At the very least, the wider scope of the song content of *Rubber Soul* was a reflection of the fact that, as Ian MacDonald observed, The Beatles were 'gradually realising, from Dylan's example, that they didn't have to segregate their professional lives from their inner lives'.[80]

What Inglis has described as the synergy resulting from the interaction between the musical development of The Beatles and that of Bob Dylan during the mid-1960s was unquestionably the most striking and significant illustration of Dylan's influence on British popular music and musicians during that period. That influence was not, however, as we have seen, confined to being exerted on Lennon and The Beatles throughout the course of 1965. During the following year, and for the rest of the decade, it was to pervade much of what would soon be referred to as 'rock' music in Britain. Yet it was nonetheless, in the case of The Beatles, a process of *mutual* influence. As their road manager Neil Aspinall later pointed out: 'Dylan liked to say how much the Beatles learned from him. John [Lennon] used to mutter: "He learned a bit from us, too."'[81] That reciprocity, involving a combination of a widened range of lyrical themes with electric, often blues-based, rock'n'roll music, was to be vividly expressed, in Dylan's case in a highly controversial manner, in Britain during 1966.

Notes

1 Bob Dylan interview with Nat Hentoff, *Playboy*, March 1966; republished in Jonathan Cott (ed.), *Dylan on Dylan: The Essential Interviews* (London: Hodder & Stoughton, 2006), p. 97.
2 Bob Dylan interviewed by Marvin Bronstein, CCBC, Montreal, February 20, 1966, cited in Greil Marcus, *Like a Rolling Stone: Bob Dylan at the Crossroads* (London: Faber & Faber, 2005), p. 70.

3 Bob Dylan interviewed by Jules Siegel, *Saturday Evening Post*, July 30, 1966; cited in Howard Sounes, *Down the Highway: The Life of Bob Dylan* (London: Doubleday, 2011), p. 181.

4 Andy Gill, *Bob Dylan: The Stories behind the Songs 1962–1969* (London: Carlton Books, 2011), p. 116.

5 On 'Like a Rolling Stone', see Clinton Heylin, *Revolution in the Air: The Songs of Bob Dylan Vol. 1: 1957–73* (London: Constable, 2010), pp. 287–297; Gill, op. cit., pp. 116–117.

6 Gill, op. cit., p. 114.

7 *Mojo*, December 1993; cited in Sounes, op. cit., p. 183.

8 Bruce Springsteen speech at annual Rock and Roll Hall of Fame Induction dinner, New York City, January 20, 1988; reprinted in Elizabeth Thomson and David Gutman (eds.), *The Dylan Companion* (London: Macmillan, 1990), pp. 286–287.

9 Greil Marcus, *Like a Rolling Stone: Bob Dylan at the Crossroads* (London: Faber & Faber, 2005), p. 155.

10 For accounts of Bob Dylan's performance at the 1965 Newport Folk Festival, see Elijah Wald, *Dylan Goes Electric: Newport, Seeger and the Night That Split the Sixties* (New York: HarperCollins, 2015), passim; Clinton Heylin, *Behind the Shades: The 20th Anniversary Edition* (London: Faber & Faber, 2011), pp. 206–216; Anthony Scaduto, *Bob Dylan* (London: Helter Skelter, 2001), pp. 212–215; Robert Shelton, *No Direction Home: The Life and Music of Bob Dylan*, rev. and updated edn., ed. Elizabeth Thomson and Patrick Humphries (London: Omnibus, 2011), pp. 210–211; Sounes, op. cit., pp. 183–187; Marcus, op. cit., pp. 153–159. For an eyewitness account, see Joe Boyd, *White Bicycles: Making Music in the 1960s* (London: Serpent's Tail, 2006), pp. 92–108. For a concise summary of various interpretations of the occasion, see Nigel Williamson, *The Dead Straight Guide to Bob Dylan* (London: Red Planet, 2015), p. 52.

11 Scaduto, op. cit., p. 215.

12 Ibid., p. 214.

13 See Daniel Mark Epstein, *The Ballad of Bob Dylan: A Portrait* (London: Souvenir Press, 2011), p. 160.

14 Scaduto, op. cit., p. 215.

15 Shelton, op. cit., p. 211.

16 Bob Dylan, interview with Nat Hentoff, in Cott (ed.), op. cit., p. 99.

17 Ibid., p. 97.

18 Wald, op. cit., p. 301.

19 Joe Boyd quoted in Colin Irwin, *Bob Dylan: Highway 61 Revisited* (London: Flame Tree Publishing, 2008), p. 110.

20 Boyd, op. cit., pp. 106–107.

21 Paul Rothschild quoted in Irwin, op. cit., p. 110. On Newport 1965 in general, see, too, Irwin, op. cit., pp. 87–110.

22 Paul Williams, *Bob Dylan Performing Artist 1960–1973: The Early Years* (London: Omnibus, 2004 [first published 1990]), p. 157.

23 Shelton, op. cit., p. 189.

24 Ibid., pp. 182–183.

25 Scaduto, op. cit., p. 218.

26 Bob Dylan interview with Nat Hentoff, in Cott (ed.), op. cit., p. 98.

27 Ibid., p. 100.

28 Cited in Irwin, op. cit., p. 27.

29 Cited in John Hughes, *Invisible Now: Bob Dylan in the 1960s* (Farnham: Ashgate, 2013), p. 8.

30 See Scaduto, op. cit., p. 222; Heylin, *Behind the Shades*, p. 224.

31 Jonathan Gould, *Can't Buy Me Love: The Beatles, Britain and America* (London: Portrait, 2007), p. 287.

32 See Shelton, op. cit., p. 217.

33 Bob Dylan interview with Nora Ephron and Susan Edmiston, August 1965; cited in Cott (ed.), op. cit., p. 48.

34 Ibid.

35 Shelton, op. cit., p. 218.

36 Paul Nelson, 'Folk-rock', in Anthony De Curtis and James Henke (eds.), *The Rolling Stone Illustrated History of Rock and Roll* (London: Plexus, 1992), p. 313.

37 Keith Negus, *Bob Dylan* (London: Equinox, 2008), p. 41.

38 See Bob Dylan's interview with Ephron and Edmiston, in Cott (ed.), op. cit., p. 50.

39 Gould, op. cit., p. 288.

40 Colin Harper, *Dazzling Stranger: Bert Jansch and the British Folk and Blues Revival* (London: Bloomsbury, 2000), p. 176.

41 Ibid., p. 177.

42 Ibid., p. 156.

43 Karl Dallas, 'Roy Harper: One-Man Rock'n'Roll Band', *Acoustic Music*, July 1980; cited in Harper, op. cit., p. 177.

44 Al Stewart, *The Al Stewart Story*, BBC Radio 2, July 1999: cited in Harper, op. cit., pp. 181–182.

45 Neville Judd, *Al Stewart: The True Life Adventures of a Folk Song Troubadour* (London: Helter Skelter, 2005), p. 52.

46 Al Stewart quoted in Judd, op. cit., p. 59.

47 Ibid.

48 Ibid.

49 Ibid., p. 58.

50 Ray Coleman, 'Can There Ever Be a Boom in Folk?', *Melody Maker*, February 1965; cited in Harper, op. cit., p. 173.

51 John Lennon quoted in David Sheff (ed.), *Last Interview: All We Are Saying. John Lennon and Yoko Ono* (London: Pan Books, 2001), p. 176.

52 John Lennon quoted in Keith Batman, *The Beatles off the Record* (London: Omnibus, 2000), p. 162.

53 John Lennon quoted in Sheff (ed.), op. cit., p. 196.

54 Lennon was referring to his two published books, *In His Own Write* (1964) and *A Spaniard in the Works* (1965). They were collections of whimsical and deliberately non-sensical word-play.

55 John Lennon quoted in Batman, op. cit., p. 165.

56 For an often-cited musicological analysis of such songs, specifically on The Beatles' second album, *With The Beatles*, see the *The Times'* music critic William Mann's comment in his favourable review that 'they think simultaneously of harmony and melody, so firmly are the major tonic sevenths and ninths built into their tunes, and the flat-submedianth key switches, so natural is the Aeolian cadence at the end of "Not a Second Time"'; cited in Ian Inglis, 'Synergies and Reciprocities: The Dynamics of Musical and Professional Interaction between The Beatles and Bob Dylan', *Popular Music and Society*, 20 (4), 1996, p. 57.

57 Paul McCartney quoted in Barry Miles, *Paul McCartney: Many Years from Now* (London: Secker & Warburg, 1997), p. 195.

58 Philip Norman, *John Lennon: The Life* (New York: Ecco, 2009), p. 398.

59 George Martin quoted in Batman, op. cit., p. 165.

60 Keith Richards quoted in Sean Egan, *Keith Richards on Keith Richards: Interviews and Encounters* (London: Omnibus, 2013), p. 147.

61 Ibid.

62 Nick Hasted, *The Story of the Kinks: You Really Got Me*, rev. edn. (London: Omnibus, 2013), p. 65.

63 Ray Davies, *X-Ray* (London: Penguin, 1995), pp. 350–351.

64 Bob Dylan interviewed at a television press conference (KQED), San Francisco, December 3, 1965; quoted in Cott (ed.), op. cit., p. 65.

65 Michael Gray, *Song and Dance Man III: The Art of Bob Dylan* (London: Continuum, 2000), p. 5.

66 Sean Egan, 'Highway 61 Revisited', in Sean Egan (ed.), *The Mammoth Book of Bob Dylan* (London: Constable & Robinson, 2011), p. 84.

67 Cited in C.P. Lee, 'The Geography of Innocence', in Derek Barker (ed.), *Isis: A Bob Dylan Anthology*, rev. edn. (London: Helter Skelter, 2004), pp. 111–112.

68 See Shelton, op. cit., p. 219.

69 Cited in Lee, op. cit., p. 111.

70 *Melody Maker*, September 25, 1965; cited in Bob Spitz, *Dylan: A Biography* (London: Michael Joseph, 1989), p. 577, notes.

71 *Melody Maker*, October 2, 1965; cited in ibid.

72 See Spitz, op. cit., pp. 312–313.

73 Gerard DeGroot, *The 60s Unplugged: A Kaleidoscopic History of a Disorderly Decade* (London: Macmillan, 2008), p. 231.

74 Inglis, op. cit., p. 66.

75 John Lennon quoted in Sheff (ed.), op. cit., p. 178.

76 Paul McCartney quoted in Miles, op. cit., p. 272.

77 John Lennon quoted in Sheff (ed.), op. cit., p. 197.

78 Ibid., p. 152. John Lennon had lived in Newcastle Road in the Penny Lane district of Liverpool until he was aged four.

79 Ibid., p. 179.

80 Ian MacDonald, *Revolution in the Head: The Beatles' Records and the Sixties* (London: Pimlico, 1995), p. 145.

81 Neil Aspinall quoted in Norman, op. cit., p. 415.

6

1965–66 REVISITED

Bob Dylan's radical and controversial change of musical direction throughout 1965 – in March on the non-acoustic side of *Another Side of Bob Dylan*, released that month, and in June with the release of 'Like a Rolling Stone' a few days before his appearance at the Newport Folk Festival – found its most brilliant and innovative expression to date on his sixth studio album, *Highway 61 Revisited*.[1] Recorded between mid-June and early August, and produced by Bob Johnston, after Tom Wilson had been producer on its initial, iconic track 'Like a Rolling Stone', the album, released in September 1965, was an immediate commercial success, reaching a top-five spot in the album charts in both the United States and the UK.

Al Kooper, organist on the recording sessions, as, by fortuitous circumstance, he had been for 'Like a Rolling Stone', later said of those sessions: 'I can't tell you how disorganised it was. *Highway 61* has a very raw edge to it, because half the people involved were studio musicians, and half weren't, so it's got that rough thing which Dylan loves.'[2] The creative outcome was a remarkable musical achievement, a milestone in the course of what would soon become known as rock music. On its ten songs Dylan grafted surrealistic, often absurdist, lyrics, which at that time, as Michael Gray has justly observed, 'were light years ahead of anyone else's',[3] on to driving, exhilarating blues-based rock'n'roll as the band provided the sound for his own song-pictures. That, he later stated, had been a major reason for his playing with an electric band in the first place.[4] Moreover, in presenting those 'song-pictures' in performance, Dylan did so with clear and compelling phrasing and delivery, punctuated by outstanding guitar work by Mike Bloomfield, notably, for instance, on 'Tombstone Blues'.

In terms of the lyrical content of *Highway 61 Revisited*, Dylan as a songwriter was, as Nigel Williamson has noted, 'adopting the position of the artist as an outsider looking in on an increasingly absurdist world', in the face of which 'his weapons are no longer protest and righteousness but mockery and wit'.[5] In that respect *Highway 61 Revisited* thus exemplified, as did the earlier 'Subterranean Homesick Blues' and 'It's Alright, Ma (I'm Only Bleeding)', what his friend and biographer Robert Shelton later aptly called Dylan's 'street existentialism' during the mid-1960s, that is, an outlook concerned with the assertion of personal freedom and the search for authenticity in the face of both the absurdities of contemporary society and the inescapable existential realities of the human condition. Yet for the traditionalist opponents of Dylan's new music, that was a source of harsh criticism rather than commendation. Irwin Silver, editor of *Sing Out!* magazine, who had originally criticised the more subjective, inner-directed songs of *Another Side of Bob Dylan* not long after it was released in August 1964, thus, referring to the 'essentially existentialist philosophy' of *Highway 61 Revisited*, wrote:

> Song after song adds up to the same basic statement. Life is an absurd con-
> glomeration of meaningless events capsuled into the unnatural vacuum
> created by birth and completed by death; we are all living under a perpetual
> sentence of death and to seek meaning or purpose in life is as unrewarding as
> it is pointless; all your modern civilization does is further alienate man from
> his fellow man and from nature.[6]

As, however, John Hughes and others have observed, it is this broadly existentialist position in *Highway 61 Revisited*, evident in its pervasive recognition of apparent absurdity and meaninglessness, that in fact provides the source of its songs' palpable vitality and liberating sense of freedom from illusion and self-deception. As Hughes has written in general of Dylan's work during that period:

> The great discovery of this mid-'60s music…was of the energy and joy that
> inhabit the expression of disillusion. Acknowledging one's illusions and con-
> fusion is the mainspring of stepping beyond fateful self-captivity, as—for
> Thoreau and Emerson—the American mind must acknowledge desperation
> or dejection. This is both what the mid-60s songs are about, in some form or
> other, and the hidden source of their own powers.[7]

It should be added, nonetheless, that that sense of liberation from life's illusions was combined in the lyrics of *Highway 61 Revisited* with the expressed need to evade society's various traps. Keith Negus' perceptive description of Dylan's 'It's Alright, Ma (I'm Only Bleeding)', as a song that condensed 'social critique and existential anxiety' into its memorable, aphoristic lines,[8] applies, too, to the song content of *Highway 61 Revisited*. The album thus provides a surreal journey across the America of his time, exposing through satire and allegory its widespread absurdities and hyp-ocrisies. As Andrew Gamble has commented:

> The starting point is that the lunatics have taken over the asylum, and that
> sane people, or those that want to remain sane, had better watch out. In this

way…Dylan provides a series of commentaries and notes on how to survive in modern America.[9]

As well as being a milestone in the course of modern popular music, *Highway 61 Revisited* also broke new ground in other ways. With a running time of just over 51 minutes, it was about ten minutes longer than most 1960s albums. In addition, Dylan, in making it, was creating completely new and unprecedented techniques of both songwriting and recording, which were to continue on his next studio album, *Blonde on Blonde*. As Colin Irwin observed, that process involved and included:

> The inordinate length of many of the songs, the unconventional mode of recording, the minimal rehearsals, the free-form improvisational approach, the sessions creeping long into the night, the songs written and re-written in the studio, the lack of instructions to studio musicians…all these things went against the grain of how records were made at the time.[10]

Yet in spite of such unorthodox recording methods, the sessions, lasting from July 29 until early August 1965, appear to have proceeded fluently and highly productively.[11]

In terms of songwriting, what was groundbreaking, too, about *Highway 61 Revisited* was the innovative nature of its lyrical content. Often expressed in, as has been noted, surrealistic and absurdist imagery, and using satire and allegory, as well as biblical, literary, and possibly political allusions,[12] the lyrics conveyed the strong impression of having something significant to say, albeit laced with sardonic humour, about the individual's position both within contemporary American society and in the face of the human condition. The overall artistic effect, the lyrics and the sound, the aural pictures, were thus widely perceived by their audience at the time as having a seriousness of purpose that transcended mere pop-music entertainment.

Dylan himself, so often an implacable critic of his own work, also appeared impressed by the end-result of *Highway 61 Revisited*. 'I'm not gonna be able to make a record better than that one', he declared. 'There's a lot of stuff on there that I would listen to!'[13] Reminiscing, too, 13 years later about the album's historical context as far as he was concerned, he stated: 'Those were exciting times. We were doing it [the transition from folk to rock] before anybody we knew would—or could…It was the sound of the streets. It still is. I symbolically hear that sound wherever I am'.[14]

Soon after recording *Highway 61 Revisited*, Bob Dylan, acting on a recommendation, made contact with Robbie Robertson, the guitarist of Canadian rock'n'roll band Levon and The Hawks, who had originally backed a rockabilly singer, Ronnie Hawkins. After hearing them play in Toronto, Dylan, highly impressed, hired Robertson and their drummer Levon Helm to join Al Kooper and Harvey

Brooks, both of whom had played on the *Highway 61* sessions, and back him at a concert in late August 1965 at the Forest Hills Stadium in New York City, where their electric set received a mixed, often hostile reception. The following month, in late September, Dylan began an autumn tour of the United States with Robertson, Helm, and the other members of The Hawks. A similar audience response to that encountered at Forest Hills was often replicated.

In early October 1965, Dylan and The Hawks, together with Al Kooper and Bobby Gregg on some sessions, began recording Dylan's next studio album in New York. The sessions stretched on until late January 1966, in a manner that was less than satisfactory, producing only two finished songs. At the suggestion of his producer Bob Johnston, which proved to be an inspired one, Dylan in February 1966 went down to Nashville, Tennessee, the crucible of American country music, accompanied by Robbie Robertson and Al Kooper, to record with a crew of crack session musicians, who were generally used to working with leading country-music singers. This unlikely development led to the recording in February and March, in harmonious sessions that once again demonstrated Dylan's highly unorthodox recording and songwriting techniques,[15] of another of Dylan's greatest albums. Entitled *Blonde on Blonde*, it was released, as rock music's first double album, in the United States in May 1966 and in August of that year in the UK.

Because of Dylan's practice of declining to rehearse or to follow studio charts, the recording sessions took only about 40 studio hours to complete, and assumed a largely improvisatory character. As for the resulting musical sound, created by the instrumental blend of guitar, bass guitar, drums, piano, organ, and harmonica that Dylan had earlier employed on *Highway 61 Revisited*, and to some extent on *Bringing It All Back Home*, he stated 12 years later, in an often-quoted comment, that 'the closest I ever got to the sound I hear in my mind was on individual bands in the *Blonde on Blonde* album. It's that thin, that wild mercury sound. It's metallic and bright gold, with whatever that conjures up. That's my particular sound.'[16]

Al Kooper has recalled, with regard to the highly improbable recording venue, Nashville, and the regionally diverse composition of the musicians on the *Blonde on Blonde* Nashville sessions, that in musical terms it amounted to a cultural fusion. He thus explained that:

> It's an amazing record, like taking two cultures and smashing them together with a huge explosion...Because it was a very bizarre move at the time for Dylan to go to Nashville to record that album...He was the quintessential New York hipster—what was he doing in Nashville? It didn't make any sense whatsoever. But you take those two elements, pour them into a test-tube, and it just exploded.[17]

The individually distinctive songs on *Blonde on Blonde* were more directly personal than those on *Highway 61 Revisited*. Lyrically, they were, as Bob Spitz observed, 'full of wit, passion, rich and poetic language, vitriol, double entendre, bravado, high and low camp, chutzpah, and charm'.[18] But in addition, Dylan's wit, in Robert

Shelton's words, 'alternates with a dominant theme of entrapment by circumstance, love, society, illusions, and unrealized hopes',[19] a theme exemplified most vividly in 'Visions of Joanna' and 'Stuck Inside of Mobile with the Memphis Blues Again'.[20]

One particular track on the album, 'Fourth Time Around', appeared to be a pastiche, even a parody, of the Beatles' 'Norwegian Wood (This Bird Has Flown)', sung and largely written by John Lennon and recorded in October 1965 for the *Rubber Soul* album, released in December of that year. Recorded by Dylan in Nashville in mid-February 1966, 'Fourth Time Around', an at times surreal and rather dark portrayal of a romantic encounter, is similar certainly in its melody, structure, and subject matter to Lennon's song about a clandestine affair.[21] There is some evidence to suggest, however, that Dylan's own song was conceived before Lennon's. In view of the similarities between the two songs, Al Kooper had at the time asked Dylan about The Beatles' reaction to 'Fourth Time Around'. Dylan had replied: 'Well, actually "Norwegian Wood" sounds a lot like *this*! I'm afraid they took it from me, and I feel that I have to, y'know, record it.'[22] To reinforce that point, he had told Kooper that: 'When I played it to them [The Beatles], there was no "Norwegian Wood".'[23] Irrespective of the precise accuracy of the chronological sequence of the two songs, Dylan nonetheless performed 'Fourth Time Around' on the final night of his 1966 world tour, at the second Royal Albert Hall concert on May 27, attended, among many others, by The Beatles.

Commercially, *Blonde on Blonde*, like its predecessor, was another major success for Dylan, reaching the top ten in the US album charts soon after its release in May 1966, and the top three in the UK album charts in August of that year. Artistically, it was the culmination of a remarkable period of musical creativity, stretching over barely 14 months, with the recording of what has been called the 'amphetamine trilogy', beginning in January 1965 with the first sessions for *Bringing It All Back Home*, through June to August of that year with *Highway 61 Revisited*, and concluding in January to March 1966 with *Blonde on Blonde*, with the latter two seminal albums released in the United States during a similar 14-month period, between March 1965 and May 1966. In those intensely fruitful months, Dylan had thus radically changed the whole course of a major part of modern popular music.

On June 11, 1965, a large-scale poetry reading was held at London's Royal Albert Hall. It has been viewed in retrospect by social and cultural historians as the first formal occasion in which the 'counter-culture' in Britain became aware of itself collectively. Some 7,000 people turned up to hear poets such as Allen Ginsberg, Lawrence Ferlinghetti, Gregory Corso, Michael Horovitz, Adrian Mitchell, and others recite their poems. It was filmed by the British filmmaker Peter Whitehead as a short documentary entitled *Wholly Communion*, which appeared that year. In the view of Barry Miles, who was among those who helped to organise the event, the poetry reading was historically imbued with great cultural significance since 'for the youth of London it was a catalyst: the birth of the London underground'.[24] In its wake emerged, he pointed out, several manifestations of the 'counter-culture' in London, including the underground press, exemplified by *International Times* and later *Oz* and others, the UFO Club, and the Roundhouse as a venue in Chalk Farm, north London.[25]

The terms 'counter-culture', or, as it was also often called, 'the Underground' or 'alternative society', were, as Jonathon Green later noted, widely used throughout the second half of the 1960s 'to denote a primarily cultural rather than political alternative to establishment society'.[26] Originating in the United States during the mid-1960s, particularly on the West Coast, the counter-culture had its deeper roots in a long Western tradition of rebellion against the prevailing social and cultural norms of established society, a tradition stretching from the Romantic movement of the 18th and 19th centuries through to the Beat writers – poets and novelists – in America during the 1950s, including Jack Kerouac, John Clellon Holmes, William Burroughs, and Allen Ginsberg.

In the late 1960s the counter-culture was defined in more stark ideological terms following the publication in 1969 in the United States of a collection of essays by Theodore Roszack entitled *The Making of a Counter-Culture: Reflections on the Technocratic Society and Its Youthful Opposition*.[27] A year earlier Roszack had defined the counter-culture in overtly leftist, even Marxisant, political terms. It was in his view:

> the embryonic cultural base of New Left politics, the effort to discover new types of community, new family patterns, new sexual mores, new kinds of livelihood, new aesthetic forms, new personal identities, on the far side of power politics, the bourgeois home, and the Protestant work ethic.[28]

But in Britain from the mid-1960s onwards the counter-culture was, Green had pointed out, a predominantly cultural development, though in some cases it was certainly not devoid of the kind of political implications that Roszack had outlined. In demographic terms, most of the participants in the counter-culture were those who had been born either during the Second World War or just after it, the so-called 'baby boomers'. It was thus rooted in the emergence of a popular-music-based youth culture in the late 1950s and early 1960s. That demographic reality, and the related collective desire of that age group for alternative values and lifestyles compared to those prevalent in established Western societies, meant that in reality the counter-culture functioned in Britain, from about 1965 into the early 1970s, as, in Mark Donnelly's words, 'a kind of short-lived, utopian parallel universe for the disaffected young middle class'.[29]

Moreover, in Britain the alternative society and culture that many of those young people embraced was made more appealing and accessible both economically by the combination of the post-war boom during the 1950s and 1960s and politically by the absence, unlike in the United States, of a major and controversial war for the young to contend with and oppose. As Jenny Diski later recalled, from the perspective of someone who had been at that time a young, left-wing political activist:

'Perhaps it was simply that a fortunate set of political and economic circumstances gave us the longest gap year in history'.[30]

The counter-culture emerging in Britain in the mid-1960s was not, however, a cohesive or unified cultural movement. Rather, it was a broad cultural network based on attitude, lifestyle, music, and, in many cases, the use of psychoactive drugs. Essentially individualist and libertarian, its central creed rested on the assumption that individual liberation was the precondition of social and cultural change. In London, the most conspicuous heart of that network in the 1960s, the counter-culture was, Green also observed, geographically 'split between the West End and the West, from Notting Hill Gate itself to the two groves, Westbourne and Ladbroke, and stretching at its furthest limits to Bayswater in the West and Kensal Rise in the East', with the Harrow Road as its 'effective northern boundary'.[31]

Embraced by a significant minority of young people in Britain, as well as in the United States and continental Western Europe, the counter-culture was to develop further during the rest of the 1960s and into the early 1970s. Arthur Marwick later even argued that 'it is reasonable…to apply the term "cultural revolution" to this period, but only if we evacuate from both adjective and noun any Marxist implications of violent confrontation or of one discrete and integrated culture replacing another'. He added, however, that a preference for 'the route of linguistic caution' might result in the use of the phrase 'social and cultural transformation' as a satisfactory alternative.[32]

The counter-culture, however loose, amorphous, and, so it was to prove, transient, did indeed help at least to shape some of the significant social and cultural developments that changed British society during the second half of the 1960s. But it was also the case, as Marwick pointed out, that 'most of the movements, subcultures, and new institutions which are at the heart of the Sixties change were thoroughly imbued with the entrepreneurial profit-making ethic'.[33] In that respect the 'counter-culture' or 'alternative society' in many cases replicated in a different guise the consumerist ethos of the parent culture. As Gerard DeGroot later observed: 'Thus, in common with the "straight" world, the counterculture had its own restaurants, bookshops, record stores, newspapers, art galleries, theatres, concert halls, cinemas, travel agencies, and people ripping each other off.'[34] That economic development was certainly true of popular music, which, in spite of the partial democratisation within it that The Beatles, The Rolling Stones, and other leading British groups had helped to foster since the early 1960s, still constituted in many respects, in Marwick's description, 'the perfect paradigm of culture as commodity constructed by the modern capitalist market'.[35] Yet it was also apparent that a highly significant indicator of cultural change in Britain during the mid-1960s was the greater importance attached to popular music, both in the media and in British society at large. In the years before, during the 1950s and early 1960s, as Dominic Sandbrook has commented, 'pop music had been widely criticised as hollow, trivial, even corrupt; but now, in the eyes of the press, it had suddenly become an example of cultural creativity and a source of national pride'.[36]

This wider public recognition in Britain of the importance of much of popular music, which Bob Dylan, and the influence he exerted on The Beatles and other prominent British rock musicians, had done so much to generate through his song-writing, was later to lead to a widening gulf, and musical distinction, from about 1966–67 onwards between pop, on the one hand, and what was by then widely called rock, on the other. Pop music, as Sandbrook also noted:

> was catchy and commercial, designed for the radio and the singles charts, but its detractors saw it as trivial and insubstantial. Rock, on the other hand, was meant to be authentic and artistic, and appeared on albums, not singles. Rock was worthy but difficult; pop was cheerful but trite. Rock appealed to adults, pop to teenagers.[37]

Such a stark distinction was in some cases simplistic and overstated; yet it did reflect a divergence in popular-music tastes during the second half of the 1960s. Bob Dylan's three albums of 1965 and 1966 demonstrably fostered that distinction and divergence, as did The Beatles' *Rubber Soul* in 1965, and in 1966 and 1967 their more overtly artistic albums *Revolver* and *Sergeant Pepper's Lonely Hearts Club Band*, as well as The Rolling Stones' *Aftermath*, released in April 1966 and consisting wholly of original Jagger/Richards compositions.

Along with those developments there developed a new seriousness of ambition and purpose ascribed to that strand of popular music, rock, by both musicians and their audiences. As Jon Savage has observed, popular music in that form 'had become the focus not just of youth consumerism but a way of seeing, the prism through which the world was interpreted'. As a genre of music it was thus 'connected to events outside the pop bubble and was understood to do so by many of its listeners;…there was something more than image and sales at stake'.[38] As John Lennon had said, on more than one occasion, of the new kind of music that The Beatles and others were developing: 'This is not show business. This is something else.'[39]

That view was confirmed at the time, at the end of 1966, by Bob Dylan's friend Robert Shelton, who wrote:

> The level of our pop music has changed profoundly in 20 years, no in five years, from pop art to juke-box poetry. Today's music is talking about unvarnished reality, not about the fantasy that pop-song-writers were so deeply mired in.[40]

The epicentre of this new order of popular music and culture in Britain during 1966, and for the rest of the 1960s, was unquestionably London. That reality, albeit one that also disguised a fair measure of fantasy, was epitomised by a celebrated American article in *Time* magazine. Published on April 15, 1966, the same day that The Rolling Stones' *Aftermath* was released, the cover of the magazine bore the strapline 'London: The Swinging City'. The article itself, written by Piri Halasz, was entitled 'You Can Walk Across It on the Grass', a reference to the capital's many urban parks. It declared that: 'In a once sedate world of faded splendour, everything new, uninhibited and kinky is blooming at the top of London life.' The capital's new-found cultural vitality, it further maintained, was 'the result of the simple friction of a young population on an old seasoned culture that has lost its drive'.[41] The demographic reality was indeed that at that time, in the spring of 1966, 30 per cent of London's population, amounting to 2.4 million people, were in the 15 to 34 age group.

Andrea Adam, one of the *Time* team that originally assembled the article, later pointed out that the expression 'Swinging London' 'just came out of the blue. One of the editors used it jokingly…Then it became a working title…and then it was used for the cover.' As for the inspiration behind the article, she stated that: 'We knew that there actually was a phenomenon going on in London which kind of differed from what was going on in the States, and the London Sixties had this mystique.'[42]

Certainly it was the case that much of London's apparent vitality at that time derived from occupations that were previously regarded within the British class system as clearly downmarket – namely, photography, fashion design, hairdressing, interior design, advertising, journalism, and, above all, popular music. The individuals and groups within them now acquired an elevated socio-cultural status, which in turn was inflated by the recently created colour supplements of national newspapers.

That there was, however, an element of fantasy underlying the portrayed reality of 'Swinging London' in 1966 seems hard to deny. Savage has maintained that its portrayal by the media was indeed:

> a seductive and well-presented fantasy that had some basis in truth. Even if the swinging lifestyle was not available to the mass of teenagers, it was there as an ideal propagated by a sophisticated national media, and it could be seen and bought in cities around the country…each with their own youth enclaves: boutiques, coffee bars, clubs[43]

Even more unfavourably, arguably too harshly, Brenda Polan described 'Swinging London' 25 years later as 'the first example of the instant media myth, a combination of a new pop-sociology and that old propagandist's favourite, the big lie based on a small truth'.[44] Moreover, even if such a dismissal seemed overstated, the fact that the broader image of the 'Swinging Sixties' was so much focused on London was itself an inherent shortcoming. As DeGroot has written: 'in London, where the beautiful people congregated, it was easy to feel part of something. But the hip crowd was a small group from whom fantasy radiated outward and flattery inward.'[45] Miles from London, he added, in provincial Britain, 'the great seismic shifts were felt as tiny tremors. An awareness of what was happening came only from reading newspapers and watching television, not from taking part.'[46] As C.P. Lee, too, later observed with regard to his own native city of Manchester: 'The reality of living in a provincial town was significantly different from the images of "Swinging" London and the Poptastic world of Carnaby Street, Modesty Blaise and David Bailey that loomed out at us from the (newly created) Sunday Newspapers' colour supplements.'[47]

The degree of fantasy inherent in the image of 'Swinging London' was itself well-understood by Londoner rock musicians such as The Kinks and The Rolling Stones. That was evident in songs of theirs that offered satirical or cynical social observations, such as Ray Davies of The Kinks' 'Dedicated Follower of Fashion', released in February 1966, and The Rolling Stones' '19th Nervous Breakdown' and 'Mother's Little Helper', released in February and June of that year respectively.

Part of the mythologising element embedded in the portrayal of 'Swinging London' was also the notion that Britain's traditional class-bound society was dissolving, that class stratification was being eroded. That was at best only a partial truth. As Ray Davies later wrote:

> Although the Sixties had been revolutionary in lots of ways, resulting in many class barriers being broken down, there was still a dividing line between the City [of London], where all the 'old' money was handled by established stockbrokers and merchant banks, and the West End, where the 'new' money was being made, mainly through the entertainment and fashion industries, the standard bearers for the new pop culture.[48]

But in spite of all that, and the subsequent debunking of 'Swinging London' and the British Sixties, significantly often by younger historians who did not personally experience those times, there was manifestly something vibrant and creatively energetic occurring at that time in the field of popular music certainly, but also in what had become conspicuously high-profile areas such as high-street fashion design, interior design,[49] photography, and film. The manner in which Jonathon Green later looked back on the counter-culture in London and Britain, in the face of the subsequent demythologising, applied, at least to some extent, to the broader picture of the era as a whole when he maintained:

> So much for the hindsight. The contemporary reality was very different. Had it not been, whence all those agonised newspaper features, those earnest discussions on late-night television, those celebrations and denunciations of 'the counter-culture' or the 'alternative society'? Something, as Bob Dylan admonished his 'straight' everyman 'Mr. Jones', was definitely happening,[50] and if it wasn't as clear-cut, as black-and-white as might have been proclaimed, then that in no way diminished the overall event.[51]

The continuing vitality of much of British popular music in 1966 was certainly a major factor contributing to the palpable energy evident in London at that time. Bob Dylan's influence on British songwriting, whether direct or indirect, in terms both of broadening the range of themes and subjects beyond boy–girl romance and of expressing something significant to say, had become apparent in songs such as those by The Rolling Stones and The Kinks, whose reflective social commentaries, in the latter case, also included 'Sunny Afternoon' and 'Dead End Street', released in June and November 1966. Dylan's influence was felt, too, elsewhere, in songs, for instance, by The Yardbirds, a group which, as Savage has observed, 'had started out in the same west London blues scene – centred around Ealing, Twickenham and Richmond – as the Rolling Stones' and 'had struggled with the same problems of authenticity as the Stones: whether to stick with the ever-diminishing repertoire of purist R&B or to go pop'.[52] In making that transition, The Yardbirds produced singles such as, in particular, 'Shapes of Things', a song containing 'a complex, contradictory mixture of idealism, contempt and shame' that clearly diverged from the norms of pre-Dylan pop lyrics, as did its flip side 'You're a Better Man Than I', written by Mike Hugg of Manfred Mann, 'a finger-pointing classic, tackling racism, militarism and intolerance in three short verses'.[53]

Highly significant, too, at that time within British popular music was the increasing market prominence and emerging ascendancy of LPs (by then termed, as in the United States, albums) compared with singles. That development was conducive to the recording of much longer tracks than songs recorded on the customary 2½ to 3 minute single. Dylan's 'Like a Rolling Stone' and 'Desolation Row' on *Highway 61 Revisited*, at just over six and just over 11 minutes respectively, and later his 'Visions of Johanna' and 'Sad-Eyed Lady of the Lowlands' on *Blonde on Blonde*, at just over seven and just over 11 minutes, the latter track occupying an entire side of the album, were clearly important influences on British rock musicians during that period. As Keith Richards of The Rolling Stones later recalled:

> If LPs hadn't existed, probably the Beatles and ourselves wouldn't have lasted more than two and a half years. You had to keep condensing, reducing what you wanted to say [on singles] to please the distributor. Otherwise radio stations wouldn't play it. Dylan's 'Visions of Johanna' was the breakthrough. 'Going Home' [on *Aftermath*] was eleven minutes long…We said, you can't edit this shit. It either goes out like it is or you're done with it. I've no doubt Dylan felt the same about 'Sad-Eyed Lady of the Lowlands', or 'Visions of Johanna'…The Beatles and ourselves probably made the album *the* vehicle for recording and hastening the demise of the single.[54]

As for Dylan's influence in changing the thematic range of popular songwriting at that time, Richards added:

> The fact you could get that kind of tasty bite into the lyrics by mixing in contemporary stories or narrative was so far away from pop music and also from Cole Porter or Hoagy Carmichael…The Beatles and Bob Dylan to a great extent changed songwriting in that way.[55]

The Rolling Stones' release of *Aftermath* in April 1966, and, later that year, even more significantly (for the Stones' greatest albums were yet to come) The Beatles'

Revolver, recorded in April and June 1966 and eventually released in August of that year, were major expressions of the musical developments that Richards described. Such innovations were nonetheless accompanied throughout 1966, it is true, by the continuing commercial success in the UK singles charts of mainstream pop songs by Jim Reeves, Cliff Richard, Ken Dodd, and others, all with decidedly pre-Dylan pop lyrics. More broadly, there was also, as previously noted, a marked difference, experienced or perceived, between London's cultural vitality and everyday life in the British provinces, suburbs, and small towns, and a similar distance, too, between the hip participants in the 'Swinging Sixties' and the voyeurs or onlookers of that fabled scene. Yet for all that, something distinctive and exceptional appeared to have emerged, musically and culturally, in the Britain of 1966. Such was the climate in which the UK part of Dylan's world tour began in May 1966, and developed in a highly controversial, overtly confrontational manner.

Notes

1 On this point, see Andy Gill, *Bob Dylan: The Stories behind the Songs, 1962–69* (London: Carlton Books, 2011), pp. 116–117.

2 Al Kooper quoted in ibid., p. 112. On the line-up of the musicians on the recording sessions, which included Mike Bloomfield, who had accompanied Dylan at Newport, on lead guitar, see Brian Hinton, *Bob Dylan: Album File and Complete Discography* (London: Cassell Illustrated, 2006), p. 47.

3 Michael Gray, *Song and Dance Man III: The Art of Bob Dylan* (London: Continuum, 2000), p. 5.

4 On this point, see Bob Dylan, interview with Nat Hentoff, *Playboy*, March 1966; republished in Jonathan Cott (ed.), *Dylan on Dylan: The Essential Interviews* (London: Hodder & Stoughton, 2006), p. 97.

5 Nigel Williamson, *The Dead Straight Guide to Bob Dylan* (London: Red Planet, 2015), p. 182.

6 Cited in Gill, op. cit., p. 113.

7 John Hughes, *Invisible Now: Bob Dylan in the 1960s* (Farnham: Ashgate, 2013), p. 120.

8 Keith Negus, *Bob Dylan* (London: Equinox, 2008), p. 37.

9 Andrew Gamble, 'The Drifter's Escape', in David Boucher and Gary Browning (eds.), *The Political Art of Bob Dylan*, rev. and expanded second edn. (Exeter: Imprint Academic, 2009), p. 38.

10 Colin Irwin, *Bob Dylan: Highway 61 Revisited* (London: Flame Tree Publishing, 2008), p. 232.

11 See Hinton, op. cit., pp. 47, 49. For a detailed and insightful analysis of each of the songs on *Highway 61 Revisited*, with regard to both their content and their recording, see Clinton Heylin, *Revolution in the Air: The Songs of Bob Dylan Vol. 1: 1957–73* (London: Constable, 2010), pp. 281–285, 287–297, 298–300, 300–305, 306, 311–325.

12 Robert Shelton and others have maintained that lines from 'Tombstone Blues', for instance, contain allegorical allusions to the Vietnam War. See Robert Shelton, *No Direction Home: The Life and Music of Bob Dylan*, rev. and updated edn., ed. Elizabeth Thomson and Patrick Humphries (London: Omnibus, 2011), p. 197.

13 Cited in Gill, op. cit., p. 209.

14 Bob Dylan, interview with Ron Rosenbaum, *Playboy*, March 1978; republished in Cott (ed.), op. cit., p. 209.

15 On the harmonious and productive relations, both musical and personal, during the recording sessions between Dylan, Robertson, Kooper, and the Nashville musicians, see Al Kooper quoted in Gill, op. cit., pp. 133, 135; Robbie Robertson, *Testimony* (London: William Heinemann, 2016), pp. 212–214. On Dylan's recording methods during the Nashville sessions for *Blonde on Blonde*, see Hinton, op. cit., p. 55; Gill, op. cit., pp. 133–135.

16 Bob Dylan, interview with Ron Rosenbaum, *Playboy*, March 1978; republished in Cott (ed.), op. cit., p. 208.

17 Al Kooper quoted in Gill, op. cit., p. 135.

18 Bob Spitz, *Dylan: A Biography* (New York and London: W.W. Norton & Co., 1991), p. 341.

19 Shelton, op. cit., p. 224.

20 On the nature and scope of the song content of *Blonde on Blonde*, see Gill, op. cit., pp. 135–143; Hinton, op. cit., pp. 56–59; Gray, op. cit., p. 5.

21 On 'Fourth Time Around', see Heylin, op. cit., pp. 355–358; on 'Norwegian Wood', see above Ch. 5 n. 75.

22 Al Kooper quoted in Gill, op. cit., p. 150.

23 Al Kooper quoted in Johnny Black, 'Vinyl Icon: *Blonde on Blonde*', in Sean Egan (ed.), *The Mammoth Book of Bob Dylan* (London: Constable & Robinson, 2011), p. 95. (Black's article was first published in *HiFi News*, January 2010.)

24 See Barry Miles, *London Calling: A Countercultural History of London since 1945* (London: Atlantic Books, 2011), p. 151. On the poetry reading itself as an event, see ibid., pp. 144–151.

25 Ibid., p. 151.

26 Jonathon Green, *All Dressed Up: The Sixties and the Counterculture* (London: Pimlico, 1999), p. 113.

27 Theodore Roszack, *The Making of a Counter-Culture: Reflections on the Technocratic Society and Its Youthful Opposition* (New York: Doubleday, 1969).

28 Theodore Roszack, 'Youth and the Great Refusal', *The Nation*, March 25, 1968; cited in Arthur Marwick, *The Sixties: Cultural Revolution in Britain, France, Italy and the United States* (Oxford: Oxford University Press, 1998), p. 11.

29 Mark Donnelly, *Sixties Britain: Culture, Society and Politics* (Harlow: Pearson Longman, 2005), p. 124.

30 Jenny Diski, *The Sixties* (London: Profile Books, 2009), p. 4.

31 Green, op. cit., p. 160.

32 Marwick, op. cit., p. 801.

33 Ibid., p. 13.

34 Gerard DeGroot, *The 60s Unplugged: A Kaleidoscopic History of a Disorderly Decade* (London: Macmillan, 2008), p. 249.

35 Arthur Marwick, *Culture in Britain since 1945* (Oxford: Basil Blackwell, 1991), p. 93.

36 Dominic Sandbrook, *White Heat: A History of Britain in the Swinging Sixties* (London: Little, Brown, 2006), p. 113.

37 Ibid., p. 528.

38 Jon Savage, *1966: The Year the Decade Exploded* (London: Faber & Faber, 2015), pp. ix, xi.

39 Cited in Jonathan Gould, *Can't Buy Me Love: The Beatles, Britain and America* (London: Portrait, 2007), p. 331.

40 Robert Shelton, 'Orpheus Plugs In', *Aspen*, 1 (3) (the 'Fab' issue), December 1966; cited in Savage, op. cit., p. viii.

41 Cited in Savage, op. cit., pp. 73–74.

42 Cited in Green, op. cit., pp. 71–72.

43 Savage, op. cit., p. 74.

44 Brenda Polan, 'Fab, Gear and Very Groovy', *RA* magazine, no. 3, autumn 1991; cited in Green, op. cit., pp. 85–86.

45 DeGroot, op. cit., p. 252.

46 Ibid., p. 253.

47 C.P. Lee, *Like the Night: Bob Dylan and the Road to the Manchester Free Trade Hall* (London: Helter Skelter, 1998), p. 88.

48 Ray Davies, *X-Ray* (London: Penguin, 1995), p. 263.

49 Innovation in the field of interior design was epitomised by the opening of Terence Conran's Habitat stores in May 1964.

50 Green was referring to the lyrics of Dylan's 'Ballad of a Thin Man' on *Highway 61 Revisited* (1965).

51 Green, op. cit., p. 114.

52 Savage, op. cit., p. 58.

53 Ibid., p. 59.

54 Keith Richards with James Fox, *Life* (London: Weidenfeld & Nicolson, 2010), p. 182.

55 Ibid., p. 268.

7

'JUDAS'

The 1966 British tour

After completing the recording of *Blonde on Blonde* in Nashville in March 1966, the album being released in May of that year, Bob Dylan and The Hawks headed off on a world tour, which began in Australia in April.

The tour was to be an intensive one, comprising 24 concerts over the course of 50 days, with 13 shows later planned in Britain and Ireland. During the tour Dylan was accompanied by all members of The Hawks except Levon Helm, namely, Robbie Robertson on lead guitar, Rick Danko on bass guitar, Garth Hudson on organ, and Richard Manuel on piano. Levon Helm, their original drummer, had pulled out of Dylan's earlier autumn 1965 tour of the United States at the end of November 1965. Demoralised by the frequently hostile audience reaction to the electric sets of the US concerts, Helm later recalled: 'I began to think it was a ridiculous way to make a living: flying to concerts in Bob's thirteen seat Lodestar, jumping in and out of limousines, and then getting booed.'[1] Faced with the prospect of similar hostility in Europe, and specifically in Britain, Helm at the time told Hawks pianist Richard Manuel: 'Richard, it seems a long way around – England – to get where I wanna go. I can take getting booed here; this is my country. But I can't see taking it to Europe and hearing this shit.'[2] Mickey Jones, from the New York band The First Edition, was therefore hired to deputise for Levon Helm as drummer for the subsequent 1966 world tour. Robbie Robertson, The Hawks' lead guitarist, has observed that, while less demoralised than Levon Helm by the hostile audiences encountered in several US concert appearances, he, too, nonetheless shared his colleague's sense of deep unease about the concert at Forest Hills Stadium in New York City in August 1965, which had provided the first real tour experience of that hostility:

> I thought, *what's the big deal? Let the man play his music how he wants.* This was such a strange situation, and Levon and I had nothing to compare to; these

folk traditionalists were rabid. We felt like we were on a desolate island where cannibalism hadn't been outlawed yet.[3]

Robbie Robertson's reaction on that occasion was to be replicated just as strongly during Dylan's 1966 world tour, and in the British part of the tour in particular. In Australia, in April 1966, the start of the tour, there were already mass walkouts during the second, electric half of Dylan's concerts.

Eating and sleeping little during the tour as it progressed, Dylan himself clearly appeared, under the pressure, to be using a cocktail of drugs, prescribed or otherwise, including amphetamines of various kinds.[4] That was evident, for instance, in what Nigel Williamson has described as 'a wasted but inspired Dylan' during the acoustic set of his, later bootlegged, Melbourne concert.[5] A month earlier Dylan had told his friend Robert Shelton that: 'It takes a lot of medicine to keep up this pace.'[6]

The European part of the world tour began in late April in Sweden, in Stockholm, where the touring party met Donn Pennebaker, the American filmmaker who had directed the groundbreaking documentary *Don't Look Back*, which covered Dylan's 1965 British tour. Pennebaker was hired as cinematographer for another, hour-long, documentary, *Eat the Document*, to cover the European part of the 1966 tour, and originally scheduled for ABC television.[7]

The British and Irish leg of the European part of Dylan's 1966 world tour began in Dublin on May 5. The second, electric segment of that concert was greeted with slow hand-claps and hostile shouts from the audience. A *Melody Maker* reporter wrote unfavourably: 'It was unbelievable to see a hip, swinging Dylan trying to look and sound like Mick Jagger and to realize after the first few minutes that it wasn't a take-off.'[8] The first concert in Britain was on May 10 at the Colston Hall in Bristol. The audience reaction to the electric half of the concerts was once more unfavourable, with walkouts and subsequent poor reviews. One traditionally inclined member of that audience wrote to the *Bristol Evening Post*, lamenting the fact that: 'I have just attended a funeral…They buried…Dylan…In a grave of guitars…and deafening drums…The only consolation, Woody Guthrie wasn't there to witness it.'[9]

By that stage of Dylan's world tour, Robbie Robertson has recalled that to him it had become 'obvious that Bob was maintaining his performance level with the help of amphetamines'. Robertson himself, moreover, had 'started feeling protective of Bob' since, with the tour running 'at a gruelling pace', the harsh reality was that 'every day I saw him getting a little more run-down'.[10]

The night after the British concert Dylan received a better reaction in the Welsh capital Cardiff on May 11. But three days later in Birmingham what became the established pattern of audience response throughout the British tour – respect for the acoustic solo part of the concert, hostility to the electric segment – became palpably clear. In Liverpool, very much The Beatles' turf, on May 14 Dylan responded to one heckler's shout of 'what's happened to your conscience?' by retorting: 'There's a guy up there looking for a saint.'[11] Following a further hostile reaction to the electric set in Leicester on May 15, Dylan was nonetheless defended by a reviewer in the *Illustrated Leicester Chronicle*, David Sandison, who wrote that 'Dylan has a great band to support him', and that, as 'probably one of the greatest young poets alive', 'he was doing what…Ginsberg and Corso have been doing in free verse…Perhaps those who spoiled…the concert will also mature…and realise…their prejudice is almost as great as the prejudices Dylan used to campaign against.'[12]

On May 16 in Sheffield a hoax bomb scare resulted in the fire brigade and police searching the Gaumont theatre for two hours. The tension continued at another British concert hall where, with its stage barely higher than the seating of the audience, a girl rushed the stage with scissors in her hand, but was grabbed just in time by security. At that moment Robbie Robertson was unable to tell 'whether she wanted to give Bob a trim or stab him'.[13]

With the hostility of audiences appearing to mount with each successive concert, it seemed to Robertson that:

> A kind of madness was percolating. We had to be constantly on alert. The whole atmosphere was heightened. I adjusted the strap on my Telecaster so I could release it with a quick thumb movement and use the guitar as a weapon. The concerts were starting to feel *that* unpredictable.[14]

Yet, in his view, 'at the same time, the band was getting better and better', with the rhythm section of Rick Danko and Mickey Jones establishing 'a strong footing and a solid foundation' that 'allowed the rest of us to dance on top.'[15]

The most overtly confrontational, and historically the most notorious, concert of the British tour was at the Manchester Free Trade Hall on May 17. Erroneously known later as 'the Royal Albert Hall concert', a live recording of the Manchester gig was officially released by Columbia as an album 32 years after the event, in October 1998. Robbie Robertson has recalled that at Manchester:

> Between songs the crowd would yell and holler insults, and Bob would murmur and mumble into the microphone. I looked at Rick [Danko] and was surprised to see him laughing, either out of embarrassment or simply because everything was so strange that all you could do was laugh.[16]

By that stage of the British tour it certainly did seem to both Dylan and the Hawks, as well as to that section of the audiences sympathetic to the folk-rock segment of the performances, that, in Robert Shelton's description, 'the rude part of the press and the audience was a conformist mob with reactionary views and Neanderthal aesthetics'.[17] Yet with regard to their purist expectations of Dylan, at Bristol, Manchester, and elsewhere in May 1966, Robbie Robertson has stressed that: 'We did not see what was wrong musically. We were treating the songs with great respect.'[18]

At the Manchester Free Trade Hall, however, amid mounting hostility, expressed in heckling and slow hand-clapping from a substantial section of the audience, someone shouted out 'Judas!', to which Dylan responded: 'I don't believe you. You're a liar', and called out to The Hawks: 'Play fucking loud!' They then launched into a memorable and electrifying version of 'Like a Rolling Stone'.[19] In spite of the intensely confrontational atmosphere in Manchester that evening, Robbie Robertson has nonetheless recalled that: 'I don't know why, but that particular night I especially enjoyed playing. You never know when that muse is going to sneak up on you and spread her wings.'[20]

The indignant audience member who had insultingly shouted 'Judas!' at Dylan, namely, Keith Butler, a student at Keele University in 1966, claimed 32 years later, after Columbia's release of the live recording, to have been responsible for the insult and participated in a BBC Radio 1 documentary about the concert, presented by Andy Kershaw.[21] Another audience member, however, John Cordwell, also later claimed to have been the perpetrator of the insult, and his testimony was added in Kershaw's documentary. Of the second, electric segment of the concert, Cordwell recalled:

> It wasn't simply that it was electric music, and that it was loud. That wasn't the problem…Although the sound quality in the hall was dreadful, nothing like the live recording [taken from the soundboard] The sense of betrayal I felt, shared by many in the audience, came from the way that Dylan threw away those precious lyrics. We simply couldn't hear the words. And – perhaps the last straw – the man just simply didn't seem to care![22]

Hostile reactions to the electric half of Dylan's concerts continued at other British cities in May 1966 – in Scotland, at both Glasgow and Edinburgh, and in Newcastle in north-east England. C.P. Lee has observed, in recollection of Dylan's experience throughout the British tour, that:

> The audience confrontations can be amusing from the perspective of hindsight, yet also deeply disturbing. I'm hard pressed to think of many other artists who have had to suffer that kind of humiliation night after night. That Dylan and the Hawks could put up with it and carry on is a remarkable testimony to the vision of Dylan.[23]

Lee has added, however, with regard to those British concerts:

> With reflection and hindsight it does not appear to have been an act of incredible masochism, this nightly act of humiliation and pain. But these are the very things that drive the music along, creating the unique power of those electric performances.[24]

'Perhaps', in his view, 'there existed on Dylan's part a subconscious desire for confrontation – to face the enemy head on'.[25] Certainly that was reflected, in the recollection of another attendee of the Manchester concert, 'in the lengthy tune-ups between the songs in Dylan's performance, which appeared to be sheer defiance. Very calculated. He was such a cool guy.'[26]

Another vivid illustration of such apparent defiance was Dylan's introduction to 'I Don't Believe You', the second song on the Manchester electric set, and which had originally been on his transitional 1964 acoustic album *Another Side of Bob Dylan*. In introducing his live electric version, Dylan said: 'It used to be like that, and now it goes like this.' That night may have been a deliberate attempt to provoke, even antagonise, his audience. As Michael Jones has observed of that spoken intro-duction, Dylan expressed it:

> in a kind of uninflected monotone unlike natural speech but with an unnat-ural extension of the second syllable of 'believe.' This is Dylan exercising 'cool' authority (or the authority of cool). He expects trouble and his apparently unemotional delivery (matter-of-fact to the point of disengagement) is in its disrespect for the audience, a symbol of defiance.[27]

In relation to Dylan's rearrangement of songs from his acoustic albums into an electric format in his 1966 concert, Andrea Cossu has made the interesting obser-vation that it was usually 'Baby, Let Me Follow You Down' and 'One Too Many Mornings', from his first and third albums respectively, 'that sparked the most bitter confrontation during the electric set'. His transformation of these songs in that manner provided the first instances of a process of rearrangement that was to be reproduced many times in the years ahead. Yet, in the context of the 1966 electric sets, 'those changes seemed to many nothing less than open betrayal, the attempt to make profane that which was viewed as pure – sacred, traditional folk and the old Dylan'.[28]

After the Scottish concerts on the British tour Dylan and The Hawks played L'Olympia in Paris on May 24, Dylan's 25th birthday, again to a generally hostile audience. Their reaction had been provoked, too, in part by the unfurling of a huge Stars and Stripes flag at the back of the stage. It was a time, after all, of major escal-ation in the Vietnam War, one that was generating a large-scale protest movement throughout the United States and Western Europe. A year after the 1966 tour, about 550,000 US combat troops were to be involved in the conflict in the former French colony.

After Paris, the British tour moved to London for its finale, with two concerts at the Royal Albert Hall on May 26 and 27. During his time in London, Bob Dylan stayed at the May Fair Hotel, in Stratton Street, Mayfair. Among his visitors were The Beatles. Robbie Robertson has recalled how they turned up with their road manager Mal Evans, 'full of humour and high spirits'. On meeting them, Dylan had asked them 'about playing for screaming girls' and whether that was 'still going well'. In response, John Lennon had asked: 'What about you, Bobby? The girls still screaming for you?', to which Dylan had replied: 'Oh yeah, the girls and the boys are still screaming at what we're doing, but not in the same way as for you.'[29] Paul McCartney later recalled of that meeting:

> It was a bit like An Audience with Dylan in those days. You went round to the May Fair Hotel and waited in an outer room while Bob was, you know, in the other room, in the bedroom, and we were getting ushered in one by one.[30]

The Beatles were particularly keen to play Dylan and The Hawks an early copy of their latest studio album, *Revolver*, recorded between April and June 1966 and to be released later that year, in August. Robbie Robertson remembered how, on hearing it, 'what caught my ear immediately was the use of the recording studio as a musical instrument…incredible experimentation with sounds and effects, quite the opposite of a Bob Dylan record'.[31] An example of that was 'Tomorrow Never Knows' with its backward tapes, and with John Lennon's vocals recorded, according to George Harrison, through a Hammond organ Leslie speaker.[32]

With regard to the impact of Dylan's encounter with The Beatles at the May Fair Hotel that May in 1966, his producer Bob Johnston, who had flown into London to assist in the recording of the concerts, in retrospect considered it to have been profound. He recalled:

> All four of the Beatles were in his hotel room and he talked to them all night long…When (they) came out the next morning they were John Lennon, George Harrison and Paul McCartney. They weren't the Beatles (any more).[33]

The culmination of the tense and confrontational British part of Dylan's 1966 world tour was its final concerts at London's Royal Albert Hall on May 26 and 27. (George Harrison had told Dylan at the May Fair Hotel that he and the other Beatles would be attending the second of those concerts.) But in what had been promoted as the climactic finale of the British tour the already established pattern of audience response – rapt, highly favourable attention to the acoustic set, and widespread hostility to the electric set – once again became apparent. During the electric set there was much heckling, together with numerous walkouts among the 9,000 strong audience. But Dylan this time responded more directly to hecklers than in the previous concerts. To those in the audience demanding more 'protest songs', he replied: 'Oh, come on, these are all protest songs.'[34] Moreover, during the acoustic set he stated:

> I'm not going to play any more concerts in England. So I'd just like to say the next song is what your English musical papers would call a 'drug song'. I never have and never will write a 'drug song' and don't know how to. It's not a drug song: it's just vulgar. I like my old songs. I never said they were 'rubbish'. That's not in my vocabulary…Folk music was just an interruption, which was very useful…This is not English music you are listening to. You really haven't heard American music before. I want now to say what you're hearing is just songs. You're not hearing anything else but words and sounds. You can take it or leave it.[35]

At the first Royal Albert Hall concert on May 26, Robbie Robertson has recalled that during the electric set:

> the hostility truly spewed towards the stage. We stood our ground and played with a 'here it is, take it or leave it' attitude. Bob poured his soul out in those songs. A couple of times his balance wavered a bit. I didn't know where he was pulling the energy from, and I kept a watchful eye in his direction during the show. As thick as our skins had become throughout the tour, the negative reaction at the Albert Hall made us angry. Sometimes we'd been able to let it roll off our backs like a joke, but it wasn't funny any more.[36]

By the time of the second Albert Hall concert on May 27, the last one of the entire 1966 world tour, The Hawks were, in Robertson's words, 'feeling a sense of relief and survival'.[37] Furthermore, Robertson recalled how, as he watched Dylan's last acoustic set from the wings, he thought of the many occasions when he had been dismayed and hurt to hear music-business people telling Dylan and Albert Grossman to get rid of The Hawks, saying that they were ruining Dylan's music and reputation. Yet in the face of those exchanges Dylan had never wavered in his support for the band. 'Commendable, I thought,' Robertson added, 'that Bob stood by us in the face of all those naysayers.'[38]

As, for the final concert of the tour, The Hawks walked out on to the stage for the electric set, amid 'catcalls, hooting, cheering and booing', Robertson's recollection of that moment was that it was highly charged and confrontational: 'Fire and ice, that's what it felt like as we charged into "Tell Me, Momma". The tempo and attitude were aggressive. We had nothing to give back but a cold shoulder.'[39] In view, too, of the fact that the hall was filled with British rock stars, including The Beatles in their balcony box, it struck him at the time 'as odd, playing in front of all these famous musicians from the British Isles – our peers, our brethren. *Bet you guys have never been through anything like this*, I thought.'[40]

But The Beatles and The Rolling Stones, and many other audience members at those London concerts, were nonetheless full of praise for the performances, including the electric sets. Bill Wyman, for example, then bass guitarist of The Rolling Stones, recalled that all of the Stones and their girlfriends shared a balcony box at one of the Albert Hall concerts, an occasion 'that helped to unite the great rock audience and alienate a lot of purists', and one in which its second, electric set was 'historically shaping the course of folk-rock'.[41] The Rolling Stones entourage enjoyed the concert and adjourned afterwards for food and drinks at one of their favoured haunts, the Scotch of St James' Club, 'the epicentre of rock musicians in the mid-sixties',[42] situated in a basement off Masons Yard, not far from the Fortnum and Mason store on Piccadilly. The Beatles who attended the final concert also enjoyed that show, and had shouted back from their box at those booing the electric set.[43] They sent a message to Dylan and The Hawks at the end of the concert that stated 'The booing didn't matter, the music did', and announced that they were coming over later to Dylan's suite at the May Fair Hotel. Dylan himself by the time of the concert's final number, 'Like a Rolling Stone', had, in Robbie Robertson's recollection, 'looked like Jake La Motta. He'd gone fifteen hard rounds, but he never went down', and in response to The Beatles' message had 'nodded his head slowly, tiredly, taking in the encouragement'.[44]

George Harrison later strongly defended Dylan's artistic right to use an electric band, at the Royal Albert Hall and throughout the 1966 tour, stating that:

> The people who walked out must have been idiots and they couldn't have known the real Dylan. It was all still pure Dylan, and he has to find his own directions. If he felt he wanted electrification, that's the way he had to do it. Who's laying down rules?[45]

What, then, were the explanations for the continuing hostility that Dylan and The Hawks faced throughout the 1966 British tour, a reaction that in retrospect seems so inflated. Part of that hostility undoubtedly derived from the fact that the angry response of folk traditionalists and purists in Britain was more overtly political in nature than in the United States. Many of those British traditionalists held attitudes towards popular music that were shared by Ewan MacColl, Bert Lloyd, and their colleagues, who were, or had been, politically affiliated with, or highly sympathetic to, the Far Left in terms of their principles and beliefs. They were thus driven in their disdain for electric rock and pop music, and its perceived commercialisation, by considerations of ideological purity. As Gerard DeGroot has observed of the politico-cultural climate at the time:

> British folkies, cultural Stalinists, believed that music was an extension of class and that groups like the Beatles were capitalist – or, worse, fascist – plots. They were Luddites who believed that by shouting long enough they could smash the machine of pop music.[46]

In their eyes, pop music was thus, along with Hollywood films, pulp fiction, and popular magazines, a conspicuous manifestation of American, or American-influenced, capitalist mass society and culture. Folk music, in contrast, was revered as the collective expression of industrial or rural working-class experience.

Indeed, it has even been claimed that people were actually recruited from many traditionalist British folk clubs to break up or disrupt Dylan's 1966 concerts, with demonstrations in Scotland allegedly organised by the Communist Party of Great Britain. Protesters were therefore 'strategically spread out in pockets throughout the concert theatres' and 'disgusted departures were carefully choreographed'.[47] 'Whether or not they really were', DeGroot added, 'is beside the point, since the allegation demonstrates that some people genuinely believed that Dylan had sold out to capitalism.'[48] 'That was why', C.P. Lee noted, Dylan was in their eyes 'a "traitor", a "Judas"! He had sold out the sanctity of Folk for his thirty pieces of silver.'[49]

Among those, therefore, who denounced Dylan's decision to transform his music during the 1966 British tour were, as Michael Jones observed, politically 'a broad constituency within the British folk revival…Communist members, along with those other Marxists in far smaller organisations, together with young, left-wing trade unionists, left Labour Party members and "non aligned" individuals in and around the central "campaigns" of the day (notably, but not solely, CND)'.[50]

Yet, as Jones justifiably maintained, 'Bob Dylan truly "betrayed" no one – whether at the Albert Hall, the Manchester Free Trade Hall, Forest Hills or Newport. As a songwriter and a performer, Bob Dylan was not responsible for the "world views" of members of his audience.'[51]

There was also, however, another less politically engaged or ideologically driven section of Dylan's audiences, including people like John Cordwell or Keith Butler, that responded in a hostile manner to Dylan's new electric music. It comprised folk-music enthusiasts who resented the fact that the often poor sound quality in British concert halls, as at Manchester, prevented them from hearing the outstanding lyrics of Dylan's now heavily amplified songs. They were young people who cherished his early topical songs of 1962–63 which dealt with contemporary social and political issues, albeit addressed from the standpoint of particular individuals. But they were young people, too, who greatly appreciated songs such as 'One Too Many Mornings' and those on *Another Side of Bob Dylan* that were much more personally reflective in nature and tone. They were in fact people who, in Britain as in the United States, constituted an important part of what Al Aronowitz had earlier recognised as Dylan's core audience. In Jonathan Gould's broad but essentially accurate description, they were generally well-educated 'with artistic or intellectual learnings, a dawning political and social idealism, and a mildly bohemian style', and Dylan's music 'appealed to their maturity, their sensitivity, their morality, and their verbal sophistication'.[52]

Dylan was thus perceived by that section of his British audience in 1966 as unquestionably liberal on the social and political issues of the day, and admired as the pre-eminent 'protest singer' of that time, however much he disliked, and was to repudiate, that label, with all its implications for him both as an individual and as a singer-songwriter. There was also no denying his great personal appeal to that audience. C.P. Lee recalled that to young people in provincial Britain, and elsewhere, Dylan seemed to offer 'a cornucopia of influences that went beyond anything experienced before. He became a guide, guru, and mentor for a whole generation of people who hungered for change', and 'who were inspired by his creations to go out and look for more than was being offered them by society'.[53]

At a time, too, when the 'counter-culture', or 'alternative society', was increasingly manifesting itself in Britain, it appeared to many young people that 'of all the standard bearers Dylan was the primary signifier of the changes about to be wrought'. To them his individuality and his songwriting 'represented an alternative escape route that defied the dictates of society', one 'that existed through the liberation of one's own head'.[54] In that respect, as DeGroot has pointed out: 'Whether he liked it or not, Dylan was the voice of a generation, though not perhaps in the way that people imagined.'[55] Dylan's own disavowal of that widespread popular perception of his identity and role was to become more clearly apparent during the rest of the 1960s.

To that substantial section of Dylan's audience his appeal, too, in more overtly personal terms was, as Lee also noted, that:

> In the mid-sixties Dylan was the epitome of hip: he oozed cool from every pore in his body. The enigmatic liner notes and photographs. The fact that so little information about the man was ever forthcoming. The Beatles were too cuddly ever to be totally hip, the Stones too obviously trying for hipdom. Only Dylan was ever truly, solidly, honest to goodness, laid-down, freaky hip.[56]

Apart from that broader popular appeal, it should also be stressed that, distinct from those varied opponents of Dylan's new electric music, both the hard-line, politically committed folk traditionalists and the gentler, idealistic, 'mildly bohemian' folk enthusiasts, there were many in Dylan's concert audiences who had been strongly drawn to the revitalised rock'n'roll and rhythm and blues which British groups had performed since the early 1960s, and who recognised the unprecedented qualities of the music that Dylan had pioneered throughout 1965 and 1966 – on the electric side of *Bringing It All Back Home*, on the innovative singles 'Subterranean Homesick Blues' and 'Like a Rolling Stone', and on the remarkable, pulsating *Highway 61 Revisited*.

That appreciative part of Dylan's British audiences in 1966 most conspicuously included The Beatles and The Rolling Stones, and others directly responsible for the revitalisation of rock music in Britain. But it also included contemporary folk musicians such as Al Stewart and many others, who since 1964 had been developing an innovative form of acoustic music, at Les Cousins in London and elsewhere, that was distinct in certain respects, in particular lyrically, from traditional folk music. Such musicians were thus also clearly sympathetic to Dylan's electric concert sets, which were, in Bill Wyman's words, 'historically shaping the course of folk-rock'. Indeed, recalling Dylan's 1966 British tour 33 years later, Paul Du Noyer observed that it was historically ironic that, while at the Royal Albert Hall and elsewhere Dylan had been 'heckled by folk's hard-liners for betraying the true faith in favour of electric rock surrealism', it was nonetheless discernible at that time, since 'as usual in folk circles there was a political dimension', that 'it was the leftists who were the conservatives, and that the pop audience was open to experiment'.[57] Moreover, while throughout Dylan's 1966 British concerts there had regularly been 'opposed factions of "freaks" and "folkies" – the former in favour of his new electric incarnation and the latter disapproving', in Du Noyer's view it was the case that, 'in London, the freaks now seemed to be a majority'.[58]

By the end of the final concert of his 1966 world tour at the Royal Albert Hall, Bob Dylan was exhausted and, secluded in his hotel suite at the May Fair Hotel, incapable of meeting any visitors, including The Beatles, who were excluded by Albert Grossman from seeing him.[59] More seriously, by the end of the world tour as a whole Dylan was, in David Hajdu's description, 'overworked and overdrugged, overexploited and overindulged' and 'had nearly succumbed to the demons that assault every rock and roll king'.[60] It might well have been the case, too, that Dylan's experience of the 1966 British tour reinforced at that time his own sense of personal alienation or displacement. For as Tim Riley has suggested: 'Confronting the folk faithful with the electric rock he knew they would have trouble accepting, and touring to hostile audiences in England, Dylan must have felt even more like an outsider than he had to begin with.'[61] Indeed, self-awareness of that kind was already, according to his first biographer Anthony Scaduto, firmly rooted in Dylan's own personal history.[62] Musically, in the mid-1960s that sense of alienation was itself memorably evoked in his 'elaborate escape fantasies',[63] embodied in song masterpieces such as 'Mr. Tambourine Man' and 'Stuck Inside of Mobile with the Memphis Blues Again'.

In June 1966 The Hawks returned to the United States, in Robert Shelton's words, 'dispirited, exhausted and angry'.[64] Dylan and Sara Lowndes, whom he had married in a private ceremony in late November 1965, briefly recuperated on a short holiday in Spain. Just over a month later, on July 29, Dylan had an accident while riding his motorcycle on a back road near his home in Woodstock, upstate New York. The extent of his injuries has since been a subject of some controversy and conjecture.[65] But under pressure both to complete *Tarantula*, his experimental novel, for the publishers Macmillan, and to finish editing with Howard Alk a final version for ABC Television of the film *Eat the Document*,[66] and with Albert Grossman also having set up a punishing schedule of 64 concerts starting in early August 1966 and continuing into 1967, the motorcycle accident did allow much-needed relief from the intolerably intense pace at which Dylan had been working and living over the past months. His friend Robert Shelton later observed that, while details of the accident 'were not easy to ascertain', it was nonetheless 'widely reported that Dylan nearly lost his life. To me it seems more likely that his mishap *saved* his life. The locking of the back wheel of Dylan's Triumph 500 started a chain of redemptive events that allowed him to slow down.'[67] The aftermath of the accident was indeed a lengthy period of seclusion in Woodstock, with only three public musical appearances, in 1968 and 1969, and a nearly eight-year interval before Dylan's resumption of major touring in 1974. That period also heralded, however, another significant change in his musical development, involving a return, backed by The Hawks, who soon became known simply as The Band, to American roots-tinged music. That change was once more to shape the course of the development of much of modern popular music, both in America and in Britain.

Notes

1 Levon Helm with Stephen Davis, *This Wheel's On Fire: Levon Helm and the Story of the Band* (London: Plexus, 1994), p. 138.

2 Ibid., p. 139.

3 Robbie Robertson, *Testimony* (London: William Heinemann, 2016), p. 172.

4 On this point, see Nigel Williamson, *The Dead Straight Guide to Bob Dylan* (London: Red Planet, 2015), pp. 62–63; Robertson, op. cit., p. 230; Daniel Mark Epstein, *The Ballad of Bob Dylan: A Portrait* (London: Souvenir Press, 2011), pp. 176–179.

5 Williamson, op. cit., p. 64.

6 Cited in ibid., p. 62.

7 On the making of *Eat the Document*, see Epstein, op. cit., pp. 175–179; C.P. Lee, *Like the Night: Bob Dylan and the Road to the Manchester Free Trade Hall* (London: Helter Skelter, 1998), pp. 167–168.

8 Vincent Doyle, review of Dylan's concert at the Adelphi, Dublin, *Melody Maker*, May 14, 1966; cited in Howard Sounes, *Down the Highway: The Life of Bob Dylan*, rev. and updated edn. (London: Doubleday, 2011), p. 214.

9 Cited in Robert Shelton, *No Direction Home: The Life and Music of Bob Dylan*, rev. and updated edn., ed. Elizabeth Thomson and Patrick Humphries (London: Omnibus, 2011), p. 253.

10 Robertson, op. cit., p. 230.

11 Cited in Shelton, op. cit., p. 254.

12 Ibid.

13 Robertson, op. cit., p. 231.

14 Ibid.

15 Ibid.

16 Ibid., p. 232.

17 Shelton, op. cit., p. 254. On the 1966 British tour as a whole, see ibid., pp. 253–256.

18 Robbie Robertson quoted in Johny Black, 'Dylan in 1966', in Sean Egan (ed.), *The Mammoth Book of Bob Dylan* (London: Constable and Robinson, 2011), p. 211. (Black's article was originally published in *Mojo*, October 1988.)

19 See Robertson, op. cit., p. 232.

20 Ibid.

21 See Williamson, op. cit., p. 65.

22 John Cordwell quoted in *The Ghost of Electricity*, BBC Radio 1, 1999; cited in Ian MacDonald, *The People's Music* (London: Pimlico, 2003), p. 8. On the Manchester Free Trade concert as a whole, see in particular C.P. Lee, op. cit., pp. 85–159.

23 C.P. Lee, 'The Geography of Innocence', in Derek Barker (ed.), *Isis: A Bob Dylan Anthology*, rev. edn. (London: Helter Shelter, 2004), pp. 116–117.

24 Lee, *Like the Night*, p. 148.

25 Ibid., p. 149.

26 Rick Saunders quoted in ibid., p. 147.

27 Michael Jones, 'Judas and the Many "Betrayals" of Bob Dylan', in David Boucher and Gary Browning (eds.), *The Political Art of Bob Dylan*, 2nd enlarged edn. (Exeter: Imprint Academic, 2009), pp. 92–93.

28 Andrea Cossu, *It Ain't Me, Babe: Bob Dylan and the Performance of Authenticity* (Boulder, CO: Paradigm Publishers, 2012), p. 63.

29 Robertson, op. cit., pp. 237–238.

30 Paul McCartney quoted in Black, 'Dylan in 1966', in Egan (ed.), op. cit., p. 109.

31 Robertson, op. cit., p. 238.

32 Ibid., p. 239.

33 Bob Johnston quoted in Sounes, op. cit., p. 215.

34 Cited in Shelton, op. cit., p. 256.

35 As reported in *Melody Maker*, May 1966; cited in Shelton, op. cit., p. 256.

36 Robertson, op. cit., p. 240.

37 Ibid., p. 241.

38 Ibid. On this point, see, too, ibid., pp. 187, 196.

39 Ibid., p. 241.

40 Ibid.

41 Bill Wyman with Ray Coleman, *Stone Alone: The Story of a Rock 'n' Roll Band* (London: Viking, 1990), p. 379.

42 Ibid.

43 Shelton, op. cit., p. 253.

44 Robertson, op. cit., p. 241.

45 Cited in Shelton, op. cit., p. 255.

46 Gerard DeGroot, *The 60s Unplugged: A Kaleidoscopic History of a Disorderly Decade* (London: Macmillan, 2008), p. 230.

47 On this point, see Greil Marcus, *Like a Rolling Stone: Bob Dylan at the Crossroads* (London: Faber & Faber, 2005), p. 180; DeGroot, op. cit., p. 230.

48 DeGroot, op. cit., p. 230.

49 Lee, 'The Geography of Innocence', in Barker (ed.), op. cit., p. 116.

50 Michael Jones, 'Judas and the Many "Betrayals" of Bob Dylan', in Boucher and Browning (eds.), op. cit., p. 89.

51 Ibid., p. 91.

52 Jonathan Gould, *Can't Buy Me Love: The Beatles, Britain and America* (London: Portrait, 2007), p. 253.

53 Lee, *Like the Night*, pp. 36–37.

54 Ibid., pp. 88–89.

55 DeGroot, op. cit., p. 236.

56 Lee, *Like the Night*, pp. 150–151.

57 Paul Du Noyer, *In the City: A Celebration of London Music* (London: Virgin Books, 2009), p. 156.

58 Ibid., p. 175.

59 See Robertson, op. cit., pp. 241–243.

60 David Hajdu, *Positively Fourth Street: The Lives and Times of Bob Dylan, Joan Baez, Mimi Baez Farina and Richard Farina* (London: Bloomsbury, 2001), p. 294.

61 Tim Riley, *Hard Rain: A Dylan Commentary*, updated edn. (New York: Da Capo Press, 1999), p. 157.

62 Anthony Scaduto, *Bob Dylan* (London: Helter Skelter, 2001), p. 17.

63 Riley, op. cit., p. 157.

64 Shelton, op. cit., p. 256.

65 On Dylan's motorcycle accident in July 1966, see, for a concise summary of the available evidence, Williamson, op. cit., p. 68. For more detailed accounts, see Epstein, op. cit., pp. 180–181; Clinton Heylin, *Behind the Shades: The 20th Anniversary Edition* (London: Faber & Faber, 2011), pp. 266–269; Shelton, op. cit., pp. 256, 259; Sounes, op. cit., pp. 219–221.

66 *Eat the Document*, edited jointly by Bob Dylan and Donn Pennebaker's cameraman/editor Howard Alk, was eventually rejected by ABC Television on the ground that it was too unorthodox and obscure in its content for a mainstream television audience. It has subsequently never been officially released in DVD format. Some of the film's footage appeared, however, in Martin Scorsese's excellent 2005 documentary *No Direction Home*. On *Eat the Document*, see Williamson, op. cit., pp. 291–293; on *No Direction Home*, see ibid., pp. 301–303.

67 Shelton, op. cit., p. 259.

8

BACK TO THE COUNTRY

1967–68

Seeking stability in his life as a married, family man, Bob Dylan was living, during the course of 1967, in Byrdcliffe near Woodstock, upstate New York, with his wife Sara, her five-year-old daughter by her first marriage, and their own one-year-old son Jesse. It had not been until ten months after his motorcycle accident in July 1966 that a journalist had broken into Dylan's public seclusion by visiting and interviewing him at his home, in May 1967.[1] Of that period, and the following year, Dylan later recalled: 'What I was fantasising about was a nine-to-five existence, a house on a tree-lined block with a white picket fence, pink roses in the backyard. That would have been nice.'[2]

Looking back at that time of their musical and personal association near Woodstock from early 1967 onwards, Robbie Robertson has observed that Dylan 'looked different and sounded different. I'd never seen him in a more relaxed, contented state…We were off the manic treadmill of fame and madness, and it might have been lifesaving.'[3] Robertson has recalled, too, that Dylan:

> was a very special friend and co-conspirator. We were already survivors from our year of living dangerously on one of the craziest tours in history. Now we had our feet back on the ground and sanity reigned – some of the time.[4]

In spite, however, of that newly discovered, shared stability, the period from early 1967 was for Dylan one of sustained musical creativity during which over 100 songs, at least about a third of which were his own compositions, were recorded with The Band during the summer and autumn of 1967, with numerous copyrights taken out by Dylan's musical publisher Dwarf Music. An acetate, that is, publishing demo tapes, of some of those songs had been circulated among recording artists wishing to cover original Dylan song material. Towards the end of 1967 cover versions of his own compositions were being recorded. These included Peter, Paul and Mary with 'Too Much of Nothing' and The Byrds with 'You Ain't Going Nowhere', and in Britain Manfred Mann with 'Quinn the Eskimo', a UK singles number 1 in January 1968, and July Driscoll, Brian Auger and The Trinity with 'This Wheel's on Fire', which much later became the soundtrack for the 1990s British TV situation comedy series *Absolutely Fabulous*, about two London 1960s-survivors.

The end-result of all the original, informal music-making by Bob Dylan and The Band was the recording between June and October 1967 of about 50 songs that were initially bootlegged, of which 24 were eventually released officially in June 1975 as an edited double album entitled *The Basement Tapes*.[5] The extent to which Dylan had introduced The Band to roots-tinged American music also became clearly apparent on their own highly influential 1968 album *Music from Big Pink*, released in July of that year.

The songs comprising *The Basement Tapes* are, in Andy Gill's description, 'songs of departure, but rarely arrival; of the search for salvation; and of nonsense as the coin of hidden meaning'.[6] Within the historical context of their composition, 'the summer of love' of 1967 with the widespread prevalence of the mass hippie movement and psychedelic rock music, presenting 'mostly facile paeans to universal love draped in interminable guitar solos of dubious quality',[7] *The Basement Tapes*, drawing on strands of country music, blues, and gospel, and performed instrumentally on mandolin and accordion, as well as on guitars, drums, and keyboards, clearly went against the musical current of the times.

Back in Britain at that time *Melody Maker*, in an exclusive by Nick Jones in November 1967, announced that it had listened to seven new Dylan recordings, three of which eventually appeared over seven years later on *The Basement Tapes* – namely, 'Please Mrs Henry', 'This Wheel's on Fire', and 'Tears of Rage'. On the seven tracks Jones commented:

> The group is still there and sounding good and Dylan is sounding beautiful. The tapes we heard were rough and unbalanced, although musically good enough to be finished products…there has been quite a lot of change in Dylan's musical outlook…They don't really sound like anything much Bob has done before. Overall Dylan has lost some of the cruelty and cynicism from his voice – the hard edge sounds as though it has been gently rounded off.[8]

That substantial 'change in Dylan's musical outlook', noted by Jones, in what were to become *The Basement Tapes*, was thus really a return to more traditional forms of American music. In terms of The Band's own musical evolution, Robbie Robertson has later recalled of that period their transition, since first working with Dylan in the mid-1960s, from 'our explosive, "electric" sacrilege with Bob' to 'our loose-as-a-goose, devil-may-care style of the basement tapes'.[9]

That musical transition was evident on The Band's *Music from Big Pink*, which in itself heralded a new, back-to-the-roots direction in American popular music, with both the advent of country-rock and the further development, on both sides of the Atlantic, of folk-rock. In Britain Eric Clapton, for example, once he had got hold of the acetate of *The Basement Tapes*, thought 'that's where I'd like to be musically', and, when later he heard *Music from Big Pink*, the album 'bowled me over cause I thought that's where everything should be going', whereas his own rock super-group Cream 'were nowhere near it'.[10] Clapton visited Dylan and The Band in upstate New York in autumn 1968 and was impressed by their informal, sparse, and understated approach to making music. Whereas, he noted, in appearance The Band 'looked like characters from the Hole in the Wall Gang', Cream had in contrast become 'psychedelic loonies'.[11] Meeting and hearing The Band, and being so impressed by their music, were in fact significant factors underlying Clapton's eventual decision to part from Cream in November 1968.

The Band's *Music from Big Pink* really reinforced the earlier appearance of Bob Dylan's eighth studio album, *John Wesley Harding*, which was recorded between October and November 1967. It seemed that, in returning to traditional musical modes, symbols, and images, The Band, in Dylan's support at that time, had, Tim Riley later observed, thereby 'created an imaginary past for rock while everybody else was chasing an empty psychedelic future'.[12]

When Bob Dylan began work on *John Wesley Harding* in mid-October 1967, he did so with Bob Johnston as producer in Nashville, as on *Blonde on Blonde*, with just drummer Kenny Buttrey and bassist Charlie McCoy retained from those earlier sessions, and with Pete Drake's pedal steel guitar added on two tracks. The album, consisting of 12 songs, was completed in mid-November 1967 in recording sessions stretching over only three days and lasting in total just over six hours.

Kenny Buttrey later recalled of the *John Wesley Harding* recording sessions:

> I ran into George Harrison some time after the record was out, and he told me that the album was one of his all-time favourites, but he imagined it must have been a bitch to record. He wanted to know how long it took to do the damn thing. So I looked at my watch and said 'About six hours.' Then he said, 'Well, how long did it take to mix?' and I said, 'That *was* mixed! We just put it down and Columbia threw it out. Nobody ever went into the studio to mix a note.'[13]

In early December 1967 Dylan asked Robbie Robertson if he and Garth Hudson, on organ, might overdub the sparse original tracks of *John Wesley Harding*. Robertson later recalled that at the time he thought: 'They sounded complete to me in their bold, minimalist way', and he told Dylan 'how much I enjoyed the record just as it was'. Two days later he was pleased when Dylan told him that 'he was going to leave his new songs just the way they were'.[14]

John Wesley Harding was released by Columbia at the very end of December 1967 and, at Dylan's request, as he later stated, 'with no publicity and no hype because this was the season of hype'.[15] In spite of that, the album sold 250,000 copies in the first week of its release and reached number 2 in the US charts. It was also twice at number 1 in the UK album charts in the first quarter of 1968. Like *The Basement Tapes* it clearly ran against the musical current of the times. But it was less jovial and whimsical than *The Basement Tapes*, and more stark and austere in mood and tone. In Nigel Williamson's description, in *John Wesley Harding* Dylan 'married the outlaw mythology of the Old West to Old Testament allegory and came up with a fearful portrait of human dread in the face of eternity'.[16]

In its lyrical content *John Wesley Harding* provided, too, a stark illustration of one of the major themes of Dylan's entire musical output: the individual's endless search for salvation and redemption in a world of pain, sorrow, and unfulfilment. What Keith Negus has written of Dylan's songwriting in general thus pertains in particular to much of *John Wesley Harding*, and to some of *The Basement Tapes*, when he observed that:

> Time and again in Dylan's lyrical imagery there is no feeling of personal ful-
> filment, no redemption from a world of strife, estrangement, alienation and
> disaffection. There are temporary moments of reprieve in the arms of women
> or, for a very brief period, in the teachings of Jesus.[17]

Lyrically the songs on *John Wesley Harding* were also more concise and pared-down than before, as Dylan himself told Allen Ginsberg at the time, and designed to advance the terse stories, parables, or allegories that the songs contained with functional rather than elaborate or surrealistic imagery.[18] Overall, then, the album comprised a new style of composition on Dylan's part. Yet it presented nonetheless, in Michael Gray's words, 'a most serious, darkly visionary exploration of the myths and extinct strengths of America', one that was suffused with an 'eerie power' that was drawn from 'mixing the severely biblical with a surreal nineteenth-century American pioneer ethos'.[19] In Gray's view, too, *John Wesley Harding* 'was to be Dylan's last masterpiece of the 1960s – and in its spirit it was markedly not a part of the 1960s world at all'.[20]

Underlining that point in terms of the album's highly unorthodox and minim-alist musical nature at the time of its release, Dylan's producer Bob Johnston later recalled that in 1967: 'Every artist in the world was in the studio trying to make the biggest-sounding record they possibly could. So what does he do? He comes to Nashville and tells me he wants to record with a bass, drum, and guitar.'[21]

Certainly, while not marking an explicit reaffirmation of Dylan's earlier use of traditional folk-music modes and melodies, *John Wesley Harding* did display a return to both the acoustic simplicity and the symbols and narrative structure of traditional American music. Confirming that point shortly after the album's release, Dylan stated in a *Newsweek* interview: 'I was always with the traditional song. I just used electricity to wrap it up in. Probably I wasn't ready yet to make it simple.'[22]

In relation to Dylan's enduring attachment to traditional musical forms, Michael Jones has perceptively suggested that:

> Perhaps it was the case that the unceasing hostility vented at Dylan during
> 1965 and 1966 in the name of tradition caused him to consider tradition
> more fully, to confront it more nakedly and to mine it more deeply than in his

first encounter with it when, to an extent, he had used it fortuitously rather than opportunistically to *become* Bob Dylan.[23]

At any rate, *John Wesley Harding* clearly, as Bob Johnston had noted, ran against the prevailing climate of rock music during late 1967 and 1968, a period that had seen the release of albums such as The Beatles' *Sergeant Pepper's Lonely Hearts Club Band*, The Rolling Stones' *Their Satanic Majesties Request*, Jefferson Airplane's *After Bathing at Baxters*, and many others that featured electronic overdubbing, multi-tracking and various other studio techniques, and, in some cases, sheer overproduc-tion. To have released, therefore, a virtually acoustic album in that musical climate was itself a testimony to Dylan's own artistic confidence, influence, and independ-ence, as well as to his ability to stand apart from the dominant trends in rock music at that time, characterised as they often were, admittedly amid much music of energy and quality, by several examples of pretension, bombast, and self-indulgence.

Politically, too, *John Wesley Harding*, in its form, content, and spirit, indicated a detachment from the increasing contemporary interaction between rock music and culture and radical politics, and seemed to underline Dylan's ostensibly apolitical stance at a time of political and social turmoil in America. It was, after all, a period marked by the presence, by 1967, of half a million US troops in Vietnam and a rising death toll there, and in 1968 by the assassinations of Robert Kennedy and Martin Luther King, together with large-scale demonstrations against the Vietnam War in both the United States and Western Europe, growing student unrest on univer-sity campuses, urban riots in black American neighbourhoods, and 'les événements' in Paris.

In related, personal terms, *John Wesley Harding* also marked, as Riley later noted, 'the beginning of Dylan's detachment from his audience as a generational hero, as somebody listeners identify with as a spokesperson for their age group'.[24] The song 'The Wicked Messenger' on the album has thus often been plausibly interpreted as referring obliquely to Dylan's own disavowal of the role that was being thrust on him as a guru or prophet, as the eloquent voice of dissident Western youth, as, in his own later description, 'the Big Bubba of Rebellion, High Priest of Protest, the Czar of Dissent'.[25]

––––––––

In spite of Dylan's detachment in the late 1960s from the dominant popular musical and cultural climate, his influence on other rock musicians in Britain and the United States remained far-reaching. Specifically, that had become apparent in a widespread return to roots-tinged music, with the further development of folk-rock and the emergence of country-rock, as those forms became labelled. In the case of the two leading and most popular British rock bands of the day, The Beatles and The Rolling Stones, Dylan's influence, whether direct or indirect, was clearly evident.

George Harrison had visited Bob Dylan and The Band in Woodstock a few months after the release of *Music from Big Pink* in July 1968, and soon after, too, Eric Clapton's earlier visit. Robbie Robertson has recalled that Harrison then seemed to be 'the biggest fan among the Beatles of Bob's writing', and that, during his visit, he had also spoken 'incredibly candidly about the problems with the Beatles at that time'.[26]

Inspired by the music of *Music from Big Pink* and *John Wesley Harding*, Harrison returned to London to take part in the troubled recording sessions for The Beatles' next studio album, *Let It Be*, in early 1969. The sessions were an attempt, strongly advocated by John Lennon, to move away from the overdubbed recording techniques of their most recent albums, most conspicuously evident on the five-month-long production of *Sergeant Pepper's Lonely Hearts Club Band*, and instead to play their new album live in the studio. George Martin, their producer, later recalled:

> John said there was to be no echoes, no overdubbing, and none of my jiggery-pokery. It was to be an 'honest' album in that if they didn't get it right the first time they would record it again and again until they did. It was awful, we did take after take. And John would be asking if Take Sixty-Seven was better than Take Thirty-Nine.[27]

Eventually Billy Preston, the American organist, was recruited to fill out the sound of the album, which was deemed to be too thin without multi-tracking and overdubs. Later, in March 1970, the renowned American producer Phil Spector was invited to begin the task of remixing and overdubbing the often inadequately recorded material, to Lennon's eventual approval, but not to McCartney's, and the album was finally released in May 1970.[28]

Bob Dylan, who in recording *John Wesley Harding* had clearly distanced himself from the excesses of psychedelic rock during the 'Summer of Love' of 1967, or the 'Season of Hype' as he preferred to call it, had also thereby stepped away from the prevailing recording climate of studio trickery and, in many cases, overproduction of the kind that The Beatles had initially tried to jettison on *Let It Be*. In a 1968 interview in *Sing Out!*, while comparing his own recording methods with those of The Beatles, Dylan had simply stated that: 'they work much more with studio equipment, they take advantage of the new sound inventions of the past year or two. Whereas I don't know anything about it. I just do the songs, and sing them and that's all.'[29] Ten years later, however, he was more openly critical of the recording methods employed on *Sergeant Pepper*, stating that it was an album 'which I didn't like at all…I thought it was a very indulgent album, though the songs on it were real good. I didn't think all that production was necessary 'cause The Beatles had never done that before.'[30]

A desire for a looser, more understated, and roots-oriented musical style which The Beatles had originally favoured on *Let It Be*, and which Dylan and The Band had demonstrated in Woodstock, was expressed, too, in The Rolling Stones' artistic transition from the psychedelic bombast of their 1967 album *Their Satanic Majesties Request* to *Beggars Banquet*, their seventh British studio album, recorded between March and July 1968 and released in December of that year. With regard to that overt transition, Keith Richards has recalled that, while *Their Satanic Majesties*

Request had been 'all a bit of flimflam to me' and had heralded 'a period where we could have floundered – a natural end to a hit-making band', nonetheless, with the advent of new producer Jimmy Miller, 'out of this drift we extracted *Beggars Banquet* and helped to take the Stones to a different level'.[31] A return to The Rolling Stones' musical roots in blues and blues-based rock'n'roll was that 'different level'. Earlier, too, Richards had stated that during the late 1960s he had 'grown sick to death of the whole Maharishi guru shit and the beads and bells'[32] of that psychedelic rock and hippie era, and that the back-to-the-roots approach of *Beggars Banquet* was thus to a large extent part of a musical backlash against that cultural climate.

Most of the tracks on *Beggars Banquet* were either blues, including 'Stray Cat Blues' and 'Prodigal Son', a cover of a Robert Wilkins blues spiritual, or country music. In Richards' view, only 'Sympathy for the Devil', which he also later recalled had, in its early composition, begun as a Dylan-influenced song,[33] and 'Street Fighting Man' could really be broadly classified as rock'n'roll.[34]

Paul Cable later suggested that Dylan's lyrical influence could be detected on another track on *Beggars Banquet*, 'Jigsaw Puzzle', since, in his view, 'lyrically it's a poor man's "Desolation Row", with a mass of characters engaging in incongruous activities and generally evoking chaos…Then at the height of the chaos… the whole thing turns (apparently) into a spoof.'[35]

In addition, the influence of American country music, and of Gram Parsons, a leading pioneer of country-rock, in particular,[36] was evident on the sessions for *Beggars Banquet*, as well as in 'Honky Tonk Woman' on The Rolling Stones' next, their eighth, studio album, *Let It Bleed*, released in December 1969, and in, for instance, the use of pedal guitar on 'Wild Horses' on their ninth album, *Sticky Fingers*, recorded at Muscle Shoals studio, Sheffield, Alabama, and released in April 1971. Those three albums, together with The Rolling Stones' tenth, *Exile on Main Street* (1972), all amounted, in their different ways, to a return to their musical roots, and also constituted, in the view of many, The Rolling Stones' greatest recorded musical achievement.

In November 1968 Van Morrison, formerly lead singer of the Belfast-based R&B group Them, released his second solo album, *Astral Weeks*, which also appeared, in both its musical approach and the concentrated nature of its recording, to evoke at least the spirit of Dylan's *John Wesley Harding* and The Band's *Music from Big Pink*. With its musical blend of blues, folk, and jazz, *Astral Weeks* was recorded in New York City in three sessions covering barely 48 hours, in September and October 1968. Van Morrison had been a longstanding admirer of Bob Dylan ever since he first heard *The Freewheelin' Bob Dylan*. As Morrison later recalled:

> I think I first heard it in a record shop in Smith Street [in Belfast]. And I thought it was incredible that this guy's not singing about 'moon in June' and he's getting away with it. That's what I thought at the time. The subject matter wasn't pop songs, ya know, and I thought this kind of opens the whole thing up…Dylan put it into the mainstream that this could be done.[37]

Morrison later recorded his own version of Dylan's 'It's All Over Now, Baby Blue', on his Belfast group's second album, *Them Again* (1966). In its 'delicately understated rendition', it remains, in Clinton Heylin's view, 'that genuine rarity, a Dylan cover to match the original'.[38]

Eighteen months before the release of *Astral Weeks*, a single was released in Britain, in May 1967, by Procol Harum, a group that had originally been formed for the very purpose of recording it. Entitled 'A Whiter Shade of Pale', it had at first been widely regarded within the popular-music industry as lyrically too abstract and surrealistic. Eventually, however, it reached number 1 in the UK singles charts in June 1967, and subsequently sold over 10 million copies worldwide, becoming an enduring classic in modern popular music. An outstanding, powerful, and memorable single, its lyrics appeared to have been highly influenced by Bob Dylan's poetic imagery, though at the time, as with many other instances of radical change in the nature of contemporary songwriting, which Dylan had done so much to instigate, his influence was not always openly acknowledged. Of 'A Whiter Shade of Pale', Paul Cable later observed:

> lyrically, it owed everything to Dylan. This didn't extend only to the employ-
> ment of disconnected, surrealistic, incongruous semantics and allusion to a
> character from classic literature – the Miller; in one place it involved lifting,
> and only nominally revamping, an *entire* scene from a Dylan song. Compare
> 'while sixteen vestal virgins were leaving from the coast' with 'And picking
> up Angel who just arrived from the coast' (from 'Just Like Tom Thumb's
> Blues. [on *Highway 61 Revisited*]. The 'sixteen' is the only thing that doesn't
> tally there, and you only have to look as far as 'Obviously Five Believers' [on
> *Blonde on Blonde*] for 'fifteen jugglers' to complete the picture.'[39]

Whether or not Keith Reid, the songwriter of 'A Whiter Shade of Pale', owed a lyrical debt to Dylan as explicit as Cable maintained, Dylan's underlying influence on its lyrics, in terms of style, tone, and imagery, as well as on the lyrics of other songs of the late 1960s, seems hard to dispute. Cable noted, too, for instance, Dylan's influence, direct or indirect, on songs by the progressive rock band Pink Floyd such as 'Arnold Layne' and 'See Emily Play', released as singles in March and June 1967. While lacking Dylan's depth, they were 'musically not that outrageous, but lyric-ally distinctly strange and distinctly post-Dylan'[40] A similar lyrical style, it could be added, was evident in the lyrics of some of the compositions of the blues-rock group Cream, notably in 'White Room', written by Peter Brown and sung by Jack Bruce, Cream's bass guitarist. Brown had earlier been prominent in the early 1960s in London in promoting the fusion of poetry and jazz.

Bob Dylan's influence was more overtly and directly apparent, too, in the music of the most prominent British electric-folk groups of the late 1960s, Fairport Convention and later Steeleye Span. Ashley Hutchings, founder member and bass guitarist of Fairport Convention, had been introduced by his girlfriend Ann Shaftel to The Band's *Music from Big Pink*, and was already at that time, in his words, 'a great, great, Dylan fan' who 'sought out the most obscure Dylan stuff'.⁴¹

By the summer of 1967 Fairport Convention were performing live versions of Dylan songs such as 'Chimes of Freedom', 'My Back Pages', 'Lay Down Your Weary Tune', and 'It Takes a Lot to Laugh, It Takes a Train to Cry'. The group also played with Jimi Hendrix their version of Dylan's 'Absolutely Sweet Marie' at the Speakeasy Club in London, where Hendrix and Fairport Convention's lead guitarist Richard Thompson jammed on what must have been a memorable, exploratory 30-minute version of 'Like a Rolling Stone'.⁴²

Through producer Joe Boyd, Fairport Convention were later invited to Bob Dylan's London music publishers, to hear on demo tapes then-unreleased tracks from *The Basement Tapes* sessions in Woodstock.⁴³ Highly impressed, the group recorded their version of one of those songs, 'Million Dollar Bash', on their third studio album, *Unhalfbricking*, released in July 1969, although they would like to have recorded versions of far more of the tracks. On their second album, *What We Did on Our Holidays*, released in January 1969, they had recorded their version of Dylan's early song 'I'll Keep It with Mine', while *Unhalfbricking* included, as well as 'Million Dollar Bash', their rendition of Dylan's early 'Percy's Song' and their French language version of 'If You Gotta Go, Go Now', 'Si Tu Dois Partir'. A later CD reissue of *Unhalfbricking* added as a bonus track their cover of 'Dear Landlord', from *John Wesley Harding*. Ashley Hutchings left Fairport Convention in 1969 and joined another British electric-folk band, Steeleye Span, whose members later included Dylan's friend Martin Carthy, whom he had originally met in London in the winter of 1962–63.

The largely acoustic Scottish folk duo The Incredible String Band, consisting of Robin Williamson and Mike Heron, also released as a single in July 1967 a highly unusual song, 'Way Back in the 1960s', written by Williamson, which subsequently appeared on their second album *The 5000 Spirits or the Layers of the Onion*, released a month later. What was striking about the song was the way in which, in the summer of 1967, Williamson's lyric, in a humorous yet wistful, almost Kierkegaardian manner, sought to remember the future, looking back at that decade, 70 or more years later:

> I was a young man back in the 1960s ...
> There was one fellow singing in those days
> And he was quite good, and I mean to say that
> His name was Bob Dylan, and I used to do gigs too,
> Before I made my first million.

Dylan's influence, however, on The Hollies, the popular Manchester beat/R&B group since the early 1960s, was, in its musical result, far less satisfactory than in those more folk-oriented renditions during the late 1960s. That was certainly the view of Graham Nash, founder member of The Hollies, when the group decided to record an album of Dylan covers, *The Hollies Sing Dylan*, in November 1968 that was released in 1969. As Nash later recalled:

once we got into the studio, everything went wrong. The guys decided to make Dylan swing. The arrangements whitewashed the songs, giving them a slick, saccharine, Las Vegasy feel. They emasculated them, obliterated their power. We did a version of 'Blowing in the Wind' that sounded like a Nelson Riddle affair. It was a hatchet job, just awful.[44]

In the aftermath of their recording the album, Nash, who from the very outset, whilst agreeing to the project, had felt that 'something about it sounded cheesy', became 'convinced that The Hollies had lost their focus'.[45] The experience was a major factor underlying his decision to leave the group in December 1968. He subsequently joined David Crosby and Stephen Stills to form the American folk-rock group that bore their surnames, Crosby, Stills and Nash, whose influential eponymous album was released in 1969.

A black American rock guitarist of exceptional talent, Jimi Hendrix, had earlier demonstrated Dylan's influence more effectively than The Hollies in terms of a combination of electric instrumentation, in the form of blues-rock innovations and traditional blues, with, in some cases, reflective lyrics. Having moved to London from the United States in September 1966, Hendrix formed a blues-rock trio, The Jimi Hendrix Experience, with Noel Redding on bass guitar and Mitch Mitchell on drums. Their musical and commercial success was reflected in three UK top ten singles in the first quarter of 1967 – namely, 'Hey Joe', 'Purple Haze', and 'The Wind Cries Mary'. The last of those clearly displayed Bob Dylan's lyrical influence. Indeed, Dylan himself later stated that it was his favourite Hendrix song.[46]

Furthermore, in early 1968, Jimi Hendrix recorded his own cover version of Dylan's 'All Along the Watchtower', which has since been widely regarded as one of very few Dylan covers to equal, or even surpass, the original. Hendrix's version was released in the UK in October 1968 both as a track on the Jimi Hendrix Experience's album *Electric Ladyland* and as a single that reached number 5 in the UK singles charts.

Dylan later stated that: 'I liked Jimi Hendrix's record of this and ever since he died I've been doing it that way. Strange how when I sing it, I always feel like it's a tribute to him in some kind of way.'[47] That tribute was notably expressed in Dylan's live recording of the song with The Band in Los Angeles in February 1974, which appeared on their album of that year *Before the Flood*. In a 1995 interview Dylan again lavishly praised Hendrix's version, recalling that:

It overwhelmed me really. He had such talent, he could find things inside a song and vigorously develop them. He could find things that other people wouldn't think of finding in there. He probably improved upon it by the spaces he was using.[48]

In early 1967 Mick Jagger, Keith Richards, and Brian Jones of The Rolling Stones, together with other prominent British rock musicians, found themselves increasingly hounded by both the British press and the police in connection with allegations about their recreational use of psychoactive drugs. Following articles in the *News of the World* national newspaper, in mid-February the West Sussex Police raided Keith Richards' home Redlands near the village of West Wittering, not far from Chichester. Later that year, in May, Mick Jagger and Keith Richards, along with their art dealer friend Robert Fraser, were accused of drugs offences at the Chichester police court under the Dangerous Drugs (Prevention of Misuse) Act (1964). On the very same day, May 10, the Scotland Yard Drug Squad of the Metropolitan Police raided Brian Jones' London flat and charged him under the same Act with possession of cocaine, methedrine, and cannabis.

The Rolling Stones' biographer Philip Norman later commented on the significance of the historical coincidence of those two events in the following terms:

> The exquisitely neat alignment of Brian's bust with Mick and Keith's committal for trial proved beyond any doubt that the Rolling Stones, through their three most prominent and notorious members, were under systematic attack by the establishment whose sensibilities they had so long carelessly flouted. Not for their own misdemeanours only, but for all the pampered arrogance of Britain's pop generation, they had been marked down for a retribution which, in the ensuing weeks, despite all its judicial pomp and deliberateness, bore marked similarities to a medieval hue-and-cry.[49]

Following their subsequent trial in late June 1967 at the West Sussex Quarter Sessions court in Chichester, Mick Jagger was sentenced to three months' imprisonment for possession of four amphetamine tablets, while Keith Richards was found guilty of permitting the smoking of cannabis on his Sussex property, with a sentence of one year's imprisonment.

For the prosecution at the Chichester trial Malcolm Morris QC had asked Richards, during part of his cross-examination, to respond to a question framed in words that crystallised the widespread cultural and generational, and in this case social class, differences in attitude and lifestyle that had appeared in Britain during the mid-to-late 1960s. Morris thus asked:

> There was, as we know, a young woman sitting on a settee, wearing only a fur rug. Would you agree that, in the ordinary course of events, you would expect a young woman to be embarrassed if she had nothing on but a fur rug in the company of eight men, two of whom were hangers-on and another a Moroccan servant?[50]

To which Richards replied, 'Not at all', and, finally, in Norman's words, showing a 'flicker of contempt for the proceedings', added: 'We are not old men. We're not worried about petty morals.'[51]

The day after the Chichester trial, however, on July 1, 1967, an unexpected intervention occurred. William Rees-Mogg, the editor of *The Times* newspaper, very much at the time a pillar of the British establishment, whose advertising strapline in the early 1960s had been 'Top people take *The Times*', wrote a much publicised, and later widely cited, editorial. Entitled 'Who breaks a butterfly on a wheel', a literary allusion to a line from a poem by Alexander Pope,[52] Rees-Mogg maintained that Mick Jagger had been treated far more harshly for a relatively minor first offence than 'any purely anonymous young man', thereby implying that Jagger, as a leading youth-culture celebrity, had been made an example of by the law-enforcement authorities – both the Chichester court and the West Sussex Police.

At the end of July 1967 the Court of Criminal Appeal in London, headed by Lord Chief Justice Parker, overturned Keith Richards' conviction, and, while upholding Mick Jagger's, quashed his sentence, reducing it to a 12-month conditional discharge. All three Appeal judges agreed that they themselves would have disallowed a large section, the more lurid part, of the prosecution's evidence at Chichester, and that Richards could not possibly be convicted, on the evidence, of 'knowingly permitting' something which the prosecution in that trial had failed to prove ever happened in the first place.[53]

Later, on the same day as the hearing of Jagger and Richards' successful appeals, a televised discussion, for Granada TV's *World in Action* programme, took place between Jagger and four members of the British establishment, namely, William Rees-Mogg; Dr Mervyn Stockwood, the Bishop of Woolwich; a Jesuit priest, Father Thomas Corbishley; and Lord Stow Hill, Sir Frank Soskice, formerly Home Secretary in the Labour government between October 1964 and December 1965. The four men were thus leading representatives from Britain's churches, journalism, and government.

The televised discussion, which assumed the appearance, as Norman put it, of 'a summit conference…between the generations in conflict',[54] was thus imbued with considerable social and cultural significance at that time. It was organised by the young Liverpudlian television producer John Birt, who was later, ironically, to become Director-General of the BBC.

Keith Richards later recalled that 'the dark side' of the developments of that five-month period in 1967, as they affected Jagger and himself, 'was discovering that we'd become the focal point of a nervous establishment'. Of the four representatives at that meeting with Jagger, it seemed to Richards in retrospect that:

> They'd been sent out as a scouting party, waving a white flag, to discover whether the new youth culture was a threat to the established order. Trying to bridge the unbridgeable gap between the generations…They were trying to make peace with us, like Chamberlain.[55]

The year 1967 in Britain was also, however, one in which a liberal, reforming politician, Roy Jenkins, operating within a bastion of the British establishment, the Home Office, one which had been represented in that symbolically significant Granada TV discussion, was responsible for the passage of a number of ground-breaking progressive legal reforms in British government and society. Jenkins, Home

Secretary in Harold Wilson's Labour government, succeeding Sir Frank Soskice, served in that office for only 23 months, between December 1965 and November 1967. Yet during that brief period he was effective in assisting and securing into law in the British Parliament Private Members' bills concerning the decriminalisation of homosexuality between consenting adults, easier access to legal abortion, and the removal of flogging from the penal and prison discipline codes. Jenkins, during his tenure at the Home Office, also paved the way for the later removal of theatre censorship in Britain, and for more effective race relations legislation that outlawed, in the Race Relations Act (1968), discrimination against ethnic minority people in the fields of employment and housing as well as previously, as in the 1965 Act, discrimination in public places.

Roy Jenkins had earlier set out his personal manifesto in his book *The Labour Case*, written for the British 1959 general election, in which he advocated the achievement of a more civilised society in Britain. In a chapter of the book which was itself headed 'Is Britain civilized?' he had stressed 'the need for the State to do less to restrict personal freedom', as well as 'the need, independently of the State, to create a climate of opinion which is favourable to gaiety, tolerance, and beauty, and unfavourable to puritanical restriction, to petty-minded disapproval, to hypocrisy and to a dreary, ugly pattern of life'.[56]

Jonathon Green, in his cultural history of the 1960s, published in 1999, in praising Jenkins' achievements at the British Home Office, concluded that:

> It may ultimately have been thanks not to some cabal of toking [*sic*] hippies, but to a Home Secretary whose own taste ran rather to vintage claret, that the great legacy of the Sixties is the huge expansion of personal choice... Aided by a visionary Home Secretary, who turned his office's usual function – repression, narrow-mindedness, conservatism – on its head, the country gained a level of freedom that had never been vouchsafed before.[57]

In similar vein, Roy Jenkins' biographer John Campbell has observed that Jenkins was 'far more in tune with the times than most Home Secretaries. He was openly on the side of the youth revolution, not against it, and if a forty-five-year-old balding politician could hardly be its patron saint, he was certainly its benevolent sponsor'.[58]

The finding of the Court of Criminal Appeal in London in favour of Mick Jagger and Keith Richards at the end of July 1967 did thus, at least in part, reflect the changing social climate that Jenkins had done much to promote. Indeed, a junior minister at the Home Office during Jenkins' tenure, the Labour MP Dick Taverne QC, had at the time been sympathetic to The Rolling Stones' legal position, having pointed out shortly after their committal for trial that unrestricted reporting of the committal proceedings at Chichester would inevitably create prejudice against the accused before they had yet spoken in their own defence.[59]

Taverne's intervention, together with the subsequent judgement of Lord Justice Parker and his two fellow Appeal judges, and more broadly Roy Jenkins' record at the Home Office, were all illustrations of what Arthur Marwick later described as a 'vital factor' during the 1960s, namely, 'the existence, and expansion, of the liberal and progressive element within the structures of authority, who practised measured judgement'. That factor, in Marwick's view, was 'what gave the societies of the Sixties much of their unique quality', in sharp contrast with 'the stuffy conservatism of previous decades'.[60]

The sympathetic and balanced attitudes of that 'liberal and progressive element' within British public life during the mid-to-late 1960s with regard to the developing youth culture, with popular music at its heart, had thus been manifested in the outcome of the Redlands court case, as well as in that of Brian Jones' later appeal against an original prison sentence.[61] Throughout 1967 The Rolling Stones and The Beatles were unquestionably perceived as the dominant figures in rock music in Britain, and hence appeared as the leading representatives of its associated popular youth culture.

Meanwhile, the third, coeval creative force in modern popular music at that time, Bob Dylan, remained an absent yet constant underlying musical influence. Secluded but musically productive in rural upstate New York, and detached, too, from the contemporary counter-culture, Dylan was to return to Britain, after an absence of over three years, in the late summer of 1969.

Notes

1 See Nigel Williamson, *The Dead Straight Guide to Bob Dylan* (London: Red Planet, 2015), pp. 69, 70–71.

2 Bob Dylan, *Chronicles Volume One* (London: Simon & Schuster, 2004), p. 117.

3 Robbie Robertson, *Testimony* (London: William Heinemann, 2016), p. 276.

4 Ibid., p. 272.

5 On *The Basement Tapes*, see Brian Hinton, *Bob Dylan Album File and Complete Discography* (London: Cassell Illustrated, 2006), pp. 130–138; Andy Gill, *Bob Dylan: The Stories behind the Songs 1962–1969* (London: Carlton Books, 2011), pp. 157–175; Williamson, op. cit., pp. 69–73, 185–188.

6 Gill, op. cit., p. 159.

7 Ibid., p. 160.

8 Nick Jones, 'Bob Dylan Today', *Melody Maker*, November 4, 1967, p. 5.

9 Robertson, op. cit., p. 296.

10 Eric Clapton quoted in Michael Schumacher, *Eric Clapton* (London: Sphere, 2008), pp. 105, 106.

11 Ibid., p. 113.

12 Tim Riley, *Hard Rain: A Dylan Commentary* (New York: Da Capo Press, 1999), p. 158.

13 Kenny Buttrey quoted in Bob Spitz, *Dylan: A Biography* (New York and London: W.W. Norton & Co., 1989), p. 389.

14 Robertson, op. cit., p. 295.

15 Dylan cited in Williamson, op. cit., p. 74.

16 Williamson, op. cit., p. 188. On *John Wesley Harding*, see ibid., pp. 73–75, 188–189; Gill, op. cit., pp. 177–193; Riley, op. cit., pp. 171–185.

17 Keith Negus, *Bob Dylan* (London: Equinox, 2008), p. 111.

18 See Clinton Heylin, *Behind the Shades: The 20th Anniversary Edition* (London: Faber & Faber, 2011), p. 287.

19 Michael Gray, *Song and Dance Man III: The Art of Bob Dylan* (London: Continuum, 2000), p. 6. On the biblical aspect of *John Wesley Harding*, Heylin notes that Bert Cartwright, in his study *The Bible in the Lyrics of Bob Dylan*, cited 61 biblical allusions on the album. Heylin, op. cit., pp. 285–286.

20 Ibid.

21 Bob Johnston quoted in Howard Sounes, *Down the Highway: The Life of Bob Dylan*, rev. and updated edn. (London: Doubleday, 2011), p. 229.

22 Bob Dylan, interview in *Newsweek*, February 26, 1968; cited in Robert Shelton, *No Direction Home: The Life and Music of Bob Dylan*, rev. and updated edn., ed. Elizabeth Thomson and Patrick Humphries (London: Omnibus, 2011), p. 267.

23 Michael Jones, 'Judas and the Many "Betrayals" of Bob Dylan', in David Boucher and Gary Browning (eds.), *The Political Art of Bob Dylan*, 2nd enlarged edn. (Exeter: Imprint Academic, 2009), p. 100.

24 Riley, op. cit., p. 176.

25 Dylan, op. cit., p. 120; on this point, see, too, ibid., pp. 109, 113–124.

26 Robertson, op. cit., pp. 323–324.

27 George Martin quoted in Barry Miles, *Paul McCartney: Many Years from Now* (London: Secker & Warburg, 1997), p. 534.

28 On *Let It Be*, see ibid., pp. 534–539.

29 Bob Dylan, interview with John Cohen and Happy Traum, *Sing Out!*, October/November 1968; cited in Jonathan Cott (ed.), *Dylan on Dylan: The Essential Interviews* (London: Hodder & Stoughton, 2006), p. 120.

30 Cited in Heylin, op. cit., p. 284.

31 Keith Richards with James Fox, *Life* (London: Weidenfeld & Nicolson, 2010), p. 235.

32 Keith Richards quoted in Mick Jagger, Keith Richards, Charlie Watts, and Ronnie Wood, *According to the Rolling Stones* (San Francisco, CA: Chronicle Books, 2003), p. 114.

33 See above, Ch. 5, n. 61.

34 See Richards, *Life*, p. 328.

35 Paul Cable, 'A Savage Gift on a Wayward Bus: The Influence of Bob Dylan on Popular Music', in Elizabeth M. Thomson (ed.), *Conclusions on the Wall: New Essays on Bob Dylan* (Manchester: Thin Man, 1980), p. 93.

36 On Gram Parsons' musical influence during the late 1960s and early 1970s, see Peter Doggett, *Are You Ready for the Country? Elvis, Dylan, Parsons and the Roots of Country Rock* (London: Viking, 2000), pp. 79–85.

37 Van Morrison quoted in Clinton Heylin, *Can You Feel the Silence? Van Morrison: A New Biography* (London: Viking, 2002), p. 184.

38 Heylin, *Can You Feel the Silence?*, p. 177.

39 Cable in Thomson (ed.), op. cit., p. 92.

40 Ibid., p. 93.

41 Ashley Hutchings quoted in Brian Hinton and Geoff Wall, *Ashley Hutchings: The Guvnor and the Rise of Folk Rock* (London: Helter Skelter, 2002), p. 44. On Fairport Convention, see, too, Patrick Humphries, *Meet on the Ledge. Fairport Convention: The Classic Years* (London: Virgin Books, 1997).

42 Hinton and Wall, op. cit., p. 59.

43 Ibid., p. 44.

44 Graham Nash, *Wild Tales: A Rock & Roll Life* (London: Viking/Penguin, 2013), p. 119.

45 Ibid.

46 Bob Dylan quoted in Cameron Crowe, liner notes for *Biograph* (Special Rider Music/ Columbia Records, 1985).

47 Ibid.

48 John Dolen, 'A Midnight Chat with Bob Dylan', *Fort Lauderdale Sun Sentinel*, September 29, 1995; cited in Carl Benson, *The Bob Dylan Companion: Four Decades of Commentary* (New York: Schirmer Books, 1998), p. 228.

49 Philip Norman, *The Stones*, updated edn. (London: Sidgwick & Jackson, 2001), p. 246.

50 Ibid., p. 261.

51 Ibid., pp. 261–262.

52 Alexander Pope's *Epistle to Dr. Arbuthnot* (1735).

53 On The Rolling Stones' drugs busts and subsequent trials, see Norman, op. cit., pp. 222–232, 243–276.

54 Ibid., p. 271.

55 Richards, op. cit., pp. 227, 229. On Mick Jagger's own recollection of the episode 50 years later, see his interview with Ben Macintyre, *The Times*, July 1, 2017.

56 Roy Jenkins, *The Labour Case* (London: Penguin, 1959), p. 135. On these points, see, too, ibid., p. 146.

57 Jonathon Green, *All Dressed Up: The Sixties and the Counterculture* (London: Pimlico, 1999), pp. 446, 447. On Roy Jenkins' promotion of what he himself referred to as 'the civilised society', see, too, Green, op. cit., pp. 55–58.

58 John Campbell, *Roy Jenkins: A Well-Rounded Life* (London: Jonathan Cape, 2014), p. 260.

59 See Norman, op. cit., p. 247.

60 Arthur Marwick, *The Sixties: Cultural Revolution in Britain, France, Italy and the United States, c. 1958–c. 1974* (Oxford: Oxford University Press, 1998), p. 806.

61 Following Brian Jones' trial in late October 1967 and his subsequent appeal against a nine-month prison sentence, he was fined and put on three months' probation. See Norman, op. cit., pp. 290–292, 294.

9

FROM WOODSTOCK TO THE ISLE OF WIGHT 1968–69

Two weeks before Bob Dylan began recording *John Wesley Harding* in October 1967 Woody Guthrie, his first musical mentor, died of Huntington's chorea disease. Soon afterwards Dylan offered his services to Guthrie's long-time friend and agent Harold Leventhal at any planned memorial concert. Dylan subsequently performed, along with Arlo Guthrie, Judy Collins, Odetta and Ramblin' Jack Elliot, at Carnegie Hall, New York City, on January 20, 1968. That was Dylan's first concert appearance, backed on that occasion by The Band, since his performance at the Royal Albert Hall in London on May 27, 1966. At the Carnegie Hall Dylan and The Band played three of Woody Guthrie's songs: 'Grand Coulie Dam', 'Dear Mrs. Roosevelt', and 'I Ain't Got No Home'.

The following month, February 1968, Dylan was back in Nashville to record his ninth studio album, *Nashville Skyline*, which was released in May 1969. The recording musicians included the core rhythm section of Charlie McCoy and Kenny Buttrey who had played on the previous sessions for *Blonde on Blonde* and *John Wesley Harding*.

In *Chronicles Volume One* Bob Dylan strongly suggested that he had recorded and released *Nashville Skyline*, at least in part, to neutralise the role of generational spokesman that was still being thrust upon him. He thus recalled that:

> I quickly recorded what appeared to be a country-western record and made sure it sounded pretty bridled and house-broken. The music press didn't know what to make of it. I used a different voice, too. People scratched their heads.[1]

Dylan at the same time appeared to hope that, once released, *Nashville Skyline* would provide for him a pathway to greater obscurity. He hoped that 'when the critics dismissed my work', as, he pointed out, they had done with Herman

Melville's literary work after *Moby Dick*, then 'the same thing would happen to me…the public would forget about me'.[2]

The mixed reviews of *Nashville Skyline* did to some extent confirm Dylan's expectations. Ed Ochs, *Billboard*'s reviewer, for example, at the time wrote dismissively: 'Dylan, the satisfied man, speaks in cliches and blushes as if every day were Valentine's Day…So goodbye, Bob Dylan. I'm glad you're happy though you meant more to me when you were…confused like everybody else.'[3] Over 40 years later, John Hughes' broadly similar, if more measured, judgement was that 'it is hard not to feel there is something forced or willful in the album's affirmations of pastoral harmony, and something inherently unstable and temporary in its valorisation of the present'.[4]

Commercially, *Nashville Skyline* was nonetheless a great success. The album was a big seller in both the UK and US album charts, reaching number 1 in the UK and number 3 in the US. One of its tracks, 'Lay, Lady, Lay', released as a single, reached number 5 in the UK singles charts, Dylan's first UK charts single since 'Rainy Day Women #12 & 35'. He had, however, at first been opposed to its release, since he 'never felt close to the song or thought it was representative of anything I do'. The view of Clive Davis, then president of Columbia Records, that it would be a hit single, prevailed.[5]

In spite of Dylan's originally low-key expectations of the impact of *Nashville Skyline*, its influence on popular musicians from 1969 onwards was considerable. Since his early youth he had greatly admired country-music singers such as Hank Williams, George Jones, and more latterly Johnny Cash. In the second half of the 1960s Gram Parsons had already, as has been noted, been a key influence underlying the fusion of rock and country music ever since he joined The Byrds in 1967, most clearly evident in their 1968 album *Sweetheart of the Rodeo*, which had included their versions of Dylan's 'You Ain't Going Nowhere' and 'Nothing Was Delivered'. The original renditions of those two songs later appeared on *The Basement Tapes*, when that album was eventually released in 1975.

Dylan's own musical influence in the wake of *Nashville Skyline* was later apparent in the emergence from the late 1960s onwards of Creedence Clearwater Revival, as well as in the work of Crosby, Stills, Nash and Young, Kris Kristofferson, and The Eagles. Dylan's increasing interest, too, in country-music performers was later demonstrated in the appearance of Emmylou Harris as backing vocalist on his 1976 studio album *Desire*.

Elements and examples of country music had previously existed within both American and British rock and pop music. In Britain that had been evident on The Beatles' albums of 1964 and 1965, *Beatles for Sale* and *Help*, and later on The Rolling Stones' four great albums of 1968–72. But as Robert Shelton wrote eight years after the release of *Nashville Skyline*: 'Dylan provided the strap that began to link pop closer to country, with *Skyline* as the buckle'.[6]

At any rate, *Nashville Skyline* represented another change in Dylan's musical style and direction. As Michael Gray has commented: 'Again a massive contrast to the previous album: down-home instead of visionary, warm instead of severely ascetic, optimistic instead of dark…It offered a complete change of language – away from the impressionistic and the allegorical; away from the complexity of his previous work'.[7] Apart from the pop-music attractiveness of 'Lay, Lady, Lay', some critics maintained that the album contained only two or three other tracks of, by Dylan's high standards, real musical substance, most notably 'I'll Be Staying Here with You' and 'I Threw It All Away'. Yet within its historical context the impact of *Nashville Skyline* was musically significant. As Gray pointed out:

> Country music was despised hick music when Dylan took it up. People were divided into the hip and the non-hip. The counter-culture was in full swing and riddled with its own self-importance and snobbery. *Nashville Skyline* was a hard pill to swallow but it did 'em good.[8]

Shortly after its release in May 1969, in an interview with *Rolling* Stone magazine, Dylan surprisingly stated that the material on *Nashville Skyline* consisted of 'the types of songs that I always felt like writing when I've been alone to do so'; they 'reflect more of the inner me than the songs of the past'.[9] Yet 'I Threw It All Away' was probably the only song on the album that clearly displayed self-revelation or self-appraisal.

Nine years later Dylan felt differently about the effect of the experience of recording the album, stating that

> on *Nashville Skyline* you had to read between the lines…I was trying to grasp something that would lead me on to where I should be, and it didn't go nowhere…it just went down, down, down. I couldn't be anybody but myself, and at that point I didn't know it or want to know it.[10]

A month after the release of *Nashville Skyline*, Dylan appeared on ABC TV's *The Johnny Cash Show* on June 7, 1969, singing some of his own songs and duetting with Cash on 'Girl from the North Country'. On the night before the show Dylan attended a dinner at Johnny and June Cash's house outside Nashville, along with other guests who included Joni Mitchell, Kris Kristofferson, and Graham Nash. Following Johnny Cash's request that their guests should 'sing for their supper', Graham Nash years later recalled that Dylan:

> got up and did 'Lay, Lady, Lay', 'Don't Think Twice', and a few other songs. His performance that night was overwhelming. Everyone was in tears. This was *Bob Dylan*, for God's sake. No one had known if he'd ever sing again. It was an incredible moment, especially for me, I revered Bob, but I was pretty confident too. The *Crosby, Stills and Nash* album was about to be released, and I knew how special it was, even in front of this crowd.[11]

Two months later the Woodstock Festival was held in mid–August 1969, not actually in Woodstock itself but 43 miles away in the small town of Bethel in upstate

New York. The very name of the festival implicitly signalled, at least in part, that it was hoped to lure Bob Dylan out of his rural seclusion to headline there. But in the event he declined to perform. As he much later put it tersely: 'I missed out on Woodstock – just wasn't there.'[12] Yet as Tim Riley observed 20 years after the festival: 'Dylan was the absent guest at the counterculture's biggest party, a figure who loomed over the proceedings even more than the Beatles and the Stones.'[13]

Dylan himself later explained the nature of the suffocating climate that he endured in Woodstock at that time, with the continuing invasion of his, and his family's, privacy in what had been his rural, even once idyllic, retreat. He recalled that:

> it was like a wave of insanity breakin' loose around the house day and night. You'd come in the house and find people there, people coming through the woods, at all hours of the day and night, knockin' on your door. It was really dark and depressing...
>
> This was just about the time of the Woodstock Festival, which was the sum total of all this bullshit. And it seemed to have something to do with *me*, this Woodstock Nation, and everything it represented. So we couldn't *breathe*. I couldn't get any space for myself and my family, and there was no help, nowhere. I got very resentful about the whole thing, and we got outta there.[14]

Before a huge gathering of, at its peak, about 450,000 people, among those musicians who subsequently played at the Woodstock Festival were The Band, Crosby, Stills and Nash, Jefferson Airplane, The Who, and, at the very end, Jimi Hendrix. In broader counter-cultural terms, as an event, Jonathon Green noted 30 years later:

> It encouraged hyperbolic assessments, not least of which was the characterisation of 'Woodstock Nation', a generic for the love and peace tribe, and much embraced by their members...Woodstock represented all that, in hippie eyes, seemed right about their fantasies of an alternative culture...It combined the requisite ingredients of dope and sex and rock 'n' roll, of love and peace, of self-sufficiency and vegetarian cooking. It was the supreme counter-cultural feelgood event and unsurprisingly spawned a number of clones.[15]

Underlining Bob Dylan's detachment at that time from all those trappings of hippiedom, Hugh Romney, popularly known as 'Wavy Gravy', a New York alternative comedian, whom Dylan had first met and befriended in Greenwich Village in 1961, and who was Master of Ceremonies at Woodstock, was someone who, as Dylan biographer Howard Sounes later pointed out, 'never perceived Bob as part of the world of beads, tie-dyed T-shirts, and incense sticks'. Indeed, Wavy Gravy himself stated of Dylan: 'I don't think he was ever [a hippy], never maintained he was that and always turned away from that.'[16]

Instead of appearing at the Woodstock Festival, Bob Dylan signed a contract to play at the Isle of Wight Festival of Music in southern England, where he was to perform on August 31, 1969. The invasion of his privacy at his home in Woodstock had certainly been a major factor underlying both his deciding to perform there rather than at the Woodstock Festival, and later his decision to move back to live in New York City, one that he was shortly to regret. For after buying a house on MacDougal Street in Greenwich Village, of which he had fond memories, towards the end of 1969, his privacy was soon once more to be regularly invaded, with crowds gathering outside his house. 'The Woodstock Nation', as he later put it, 'had overtaken MacDougal Street also.'[17]

Of the counter-culture in the late 1960s, epitomised by that 'Woodstock Nation', and the turbulent developments which provided its historical backdrop, Dylan later wrote:

> The events of the day, all the cultural mumbojumbo were imprisoning my soul – nauseating me…I was determined to put myself beyond the reach of it all. I was a family man now and didn't want to be part of that group portrait.[18]

Yet even in his rural seclusion in Woodstock over the course of three years, it seemed nonetheless to Dylan that:

> the big bugs in the press kept promoting me as the mouthpiece, spokesman, or even conscience of a generation. That was funny. All I'd ever done was sing songs that were dead straight and expressed powerful new realities. I had very little in common with and knew even less about a generation that I was supposed to be the voice of…Being true to yourself, that was the thing. I was more a cowpuncher than a Pied Piper.[19]

Moreover, he recalled that 'whatever the counterculture was, I'd seen enough of it. I was sick of the way my lyrics had been extrapolated, their meanings subverted into polemics.'[20] As the years passed, however, he found that:

> The old image slowly faded and in time I found myself no longer under the canopy of some malignant influence. Eventually different anachronisms were thrust upon me…Legend, Icon, Enigma (Buddha in European clothes was my favourite) – stuff like that, but that was all right. These titles were placid and harmless, threadbare, easy to get around with them. Prophet, Messiah, Savior – those are tough ones.[21]

Dylan's earlier description of 'the summer of love' of 1967 as 'the Season of Hype'[22] had seemed to underline both those stated feelings of detachment from the counter-culture and his related sense of revulsion at the role of generational spokesman that was consistently being imposed on him. As an American bohemian, and even in some ways an outsider, he was instinctively suspicious of the prevailing alternative mass culture represented by psychedelia and hippiedom. He had probably foreseen, too, that what might once have been the challenging or authentic aspects of the counter-culture would soon be neutralised and commodified by commercial forces. Certainly the individualist thrust of his songwriting indicated a sensibility and perspective that were out of line with any mass movement during the 1960s, whether it was the British and American folk-music movement of the early 1960s or the counter-culture of the late 1960s. With his strong sense of individuality, he recoiled from any notion of the individual's will being subordinated to the collective will of any group, organisation, or mass movement. After all, he had sung in 'It's Alright Ma (I'm Only Bleeding)', on his 1965 album *Bringing It All Back Home*, of the urgent need: 'To keep it in your mind and not forget / that it is not he or she or them or it / that you belong to'.

In any case, Dylan's artistic outlook contained a notion of personal emancipation – from conformist social pressures, from counter-cultural fantasies, and from self-deception in its various forms – that was at odds with much of mass counter-cultural sentiment. As Hughes has perceptively written:

> Emancipation for him is always a matter of an on-going resistance to the culture that claims us: more a case of escapology – an obscure grappling with social chains and restraints in an underwater sack – than easy riding or the sunny nirvana of Haight Ashbury fantasy.[23]

That form of 'escapology' had, after all, already been powerfully and vividly expressed in what Tim Riley later described as Dylan's 'elaborate escape fantasies' embodied in songs such as 'Mr. Tambourine Man' and 'Stuck Inside of Mobile (with the Memphis Blues Again)'.[24]

When Bob Dylan appeared at the Isle of Wight Festival of Music on August 31, 1969, it was his first concert appearance in Britain for over three years, his last British tour having ended in late May 1966. It was also his only fully public live performance during that period, apart from his 15-minute appearance with The Band at the Woody Guthrie Memorial Concert in January 1968, his TV appearance on the *Johnny Cash Show* in June 1969, and his impromptu guest appearance with The Band in Edwardsville, Illinois, in mid-July 1969.

The Isle of Wight Festival of Music was organised by two young Englishmen, Ray and Ron Foulk. It was their second such festival, the previous one having been held in 1968. Bob Dylan was to headline their 1969 festival for a fee of $50,000, plus expenses, backed by The Band, who would receive $20,000. Other prominent rock and folk musicians who would perform included, from the United States, Richie Havens, Tom Paxton, and American-born Martha Hunt, and, from Britain, The Who, Joe Cocker, Nice, Pentangle, and Julie Felix, among others. The festival site surrounded Woodside Bay near the village of Wooton Bridge on the Isle of Wight.

During their time on the Island Bob Dylan and his wife Sara stayed at Forelands Farm, a 16th century farmhouse near Bembridge. Dylan had expressed his desire to see the former home of the poet Alfred Lord Tennyson, Farringford House, as a major reason for his coming to perform at the Isle of Wight. He made that point at the pre-concert press conference held at the Halland Hotel on the island on August 27.[25] Dylan also stated elsewhere that the loyalty of his British admirers was another factor underlying his decision to play in England again after an absence of over three years. In spite of the mixed reception he had received during much of his confrontational 1966 British tour, he maintained that: 'They are the most loyal fans I have and that was one of the reasons to…come to England to make my comeback.'[26]

About 150,000 people attended the 1969 Isle of Wight Festival, which was at that time the largest paying audience in the history of British rock and pop music. Their number included much of the elite of British rock: three of The Beatles, John Lennon, George Harrison, and Ringo Starr (Paul McCartney was absent since his daughter Mary had been born only three days earlier); three of The Rolling Stones, Keith Richards, Bill Wyman, and Charlie Watts; Eric Clapton; Jack Bruce; Elton John; and many others.

Bob Dylan eventually came on late, on August 31, at 11 p.m., following The Band's 50-minute set. The delay, for which Dylan was in no way responsible, was caused by a lengthy period of setting up equipment, on behalf of CBS, for his performance, with a view to a live album release, as arranged under the concert contract with Dylan.[27] This delay occurred before The Band appeared. Their set-list included nine songs, two of which were Dylan compositions: 'Don't Ya Tell Henry' and 'I Shall Be Released'. Six of those songs were taken from their 1968 album *Music from Big Pink*.[28]

Dylan's eventual appearance before this huge audience, the largest in his musical career, heralded an hour-long performance consisting of 17 songs, 14 of which were drawn from seven of his previous nine studio albums. Nine of the songs on Dylan's set-list were for him concert debuts. Four of them were also acoustic solos, namely 'Wild Mountain Thyme', 'It Ain't Me Babe', 'To Ramona', memorably performed, and 'Mr. Tambourine Man'. Among the remaining songs, accompanied by The Band, was a version of 'Like a Rolling Stone' which, in its arrangement and delivery, clearly differed markedly from the famous original 1965 studio track. Some critics later judged that live performance unfavourably. For Dylan biographer Soames it 'was the antithesis of the screaming brilliance of his last British appearance' in 1966, while for Stephen Scobie it was 'to put it mildly, a mess. A genial mess though'. More harshly, in Donald Brown's view: 'There, Dylan flails his own legacy alive. It would be hard to imagine someone performing the song with less feel for its dynamic.'[29] In the face of such judgements, it should nevertheless be noted that Dylan's rendition of 'Like a Rolling Stone' at the Isle of Wight Festival was among the first examples of his subsequent practice of rearranging and reinterpreting his song material in terms of their melodies, their lyrics, and their vocal delivery – and as such can be regarded as an assertion of his artistic independence.

Towards the end of his set, before his performance of 'Quinn the Eskimo (The Mighty Quinn)', Dylan praised the performers of the cover version of his song, the

British group Manfred Mann, with the words: 'This is a song that was a big hit in England for Manfred Mann – a great group, great group.' That was further confirmation of his view, expressed in an earlier 1965 interview, that they were at that time the best interpreters of his songs.[30]

The overall reaction to Dylan's Isle of Wight performance was generally favourable without being enthusiastic. Co-organiser Ray Foulk's judgement, over 40 years later, was that it was 'for the most part confident, certainly accomplished, but very different…My first reaction [in 1969] was that it was somehow utterly tamer than the Dylan I knew from albums.' But in terms of song content, he recalled, 'the Isle of Wight audience was treated to a remarkable selection' of songs which 'had profound things to say or issues to be challenged by – whether of love and loss, life and death or God and human frailty'.[31] Foulk also noted, however, the absence from Dylan's set of any of the early, celebrated 'protest songs' from his second and third albums.

Some in the audience felt that the length of Dylan's performance was shorter than they had expected. (He played for one hour according to the original contract.) But such expectations had in large part been fuelled by false press rumours of a much longer, three-hour performance, with Dylan even jamming with The Beatles or The Rolling Stones.[32] Among The Beatles who attended, John Lennon was quoted as saying of Dylan that: 'He gave a reasonable, albeit slightly flat, performance, but everyone was expecting Godot, Jesus, to appear.'[33] But in contrast George Harrison stated more effusively that: 'The concert was marvellous…He gave a brilliant performance.'[34] Another rock music celebrity attendee, Eric Clapton, later stated that Dylan 'was Hank Williams…That's the way he was. He was fantastic. He changed everything. He used to have a blues voice but he changed voices, and then suddenly he was a country and western singer with a white suit on.' After *Nashville Skyline*, Clapton added, Dylan had 'tapped the roots going back to Hank Williams, George Jones, and all those great country singers'.[35]

Al Aronowitz, journalist, friend, and personal road manager of Dylan on that major occasion, later recalled, too, that, in spite of mixed reactions there to the nature and length of Dylan's performance, and even to his style of musical approach, 'afterwards, I for one would remember only the monster's loud, throaty, exultant and cheering roar of approval…only the loud roar of the crowd calling Dylan back'.[36]

George Harrison, who, with his then wife Pattie Boyd, had been houseguests at Forelands Farm on the Isle of Wight, had earlier visited Dylan at Woodstock in November 1968 and had, as we have seen, been increasingly drawn at that time to the more organic, roots-tinged musical styles that Dylan and The Band were then developing. While staying at Forelands Farm, or shortly afterwards, Harrison wrote 'Behind That Locked Door', a highly personal, country-style song directly addressed to Dylan and designed to draw him out of what was perceived as his introspective withdrawal. The desired effect of the song was the closer personal and musical interaction between the two of them.[37] On one occasion, for example, Ray Foulk later recalled walking into the sitting room at Forelands Farm to see them singing in close harmony on acoustic guitars 'an astonishingly beautiful rendition' of The Everly Brothers song 'All I Have to Do Is Dream'.[38] While he was in Woodstock in November 1968, Harrison had also co-written with Dylan another country-style song, 'I'll Have You Any Time', which, along with 'Behind That Locked Door', later appeared on Harrison's solo triple album *All Things Must Pass*, released in November 1970. At Woodstock he also wrote that album's title track, 'seeking out', in the words of his biographer Graeme Thomson, 'the simple, soulful spirit that informed "The Weight"', The Band's song which, as Harrison himself put it, 'had a religious and a country feeling to it, and I wanted that'.[39]

During his stay at Forelands Farm George Harrison unveiled a freshly pressed acetate of The Beatles' recently recorded studio album *Abbey Road*, which was released, a month later, in September 1969. At the farmhouse he candidly expressed to Ray Foulk his disappointment that John Lennon and Paul McCartney generally did not allow more than two of Harrison's own compositions on The Beatles' studio albums. While at first Foulk was hardly surprised at that, in view of Lennon and McCartney's stature as songwriters, he soon realised that Harrison's two compositions in question on the *Abbey Road* album, namely, 'Something', which Frank Sinatra was later to describe as 'the greatest love song ever written', and 'Here Comes the Sun', were both songs that were 'among the greatest in the Beatles oeuvre'.[40] Harrison played *Abbey Road* through the rehearsal barn speakers at Forelands Farm for the assembled company there, including Dylan and The Band. Al Aronowitz later recalled of that occasion: 'Although my own mind was blown by the album, I don't remember Bob and the boys lifting George on their shoulders to tell him how much they loved it. In fact, if I detected any sentiment at all, it was envy.'[41]

Following his performance at the Isle of Wight Festival of Music, Bob Dylan went to stay with George Harrison and Pattie Boyd at their home in Esher, Surrey, about 15 miles south of London, after first visiting John Lennon and Yoko Ono at their home not far away in Weybridge. When Dylan eventually returned to the United States, he stated that he had no wish to return to Britain in the foreseeable future. Possibly influenced by some negative stories about his Isle of Wight performance in some of the British popular press, he declared: 'They make too much of singers over there. Singers are front-page news.'[42] According to Robert Shelton, Dylan had left England 'in a very disappointed mood',[43] in spite of the favourable view of his performance held both by concertgoers at the Isle of Wight and by large sections of the British press. In Shelton's view, too, Dylan's experience there 'had a great deal to do with his holding off further live performances until early 1974',[44] apart, that is, from his appearance at George Harrison's concert for Bangladesh at Madison Square Garden in New York City in August 1971.[45] That period of nearly four years before Dylan resumed touring again was contrary to what he had told British journalist Don Short of the *Daily Mirror* and *Melody Maker* shortly before he appeared at the Isle of Wight, when he stated that he envisaged his concert there as the prelude to a major city tour by himself and The Band, and thus as 'the start of a new life for me'.[46] In the event, his performance at the Isle of Wight was to be his only full concert performance in the course of a period of nearly seven and a half years.

The aftermath of that performance was also, in Shelton's judgement, 'the beginning of a low period for Dylan professionally'.[47] There were several unfavourable factors, quite separate from his experience at the Isle of Wight, that underlay at the time that condition of artistic lassitude. First, during the months preceding and immediately following his Isle of Wight concert there were considerable pressures exerted on himself and his family. In particular there were the incursions into their privacy and security, first in Woodstock and later, from 1970 onwards, in Greenwich Village, where 'the Woodstock nation' had decamped. In addition, when Dylan's seven-year contract with his manager Albert Grossman expired in August 1969, Dylan declined to renew it and their business relationship was formally dissolved in July 1970. Relations between them at that time were thus very strained, and at the Isle of Wight Bert Block, Grossman's associate, acted in effect as Dylan's manager. During the aftermath, too, of Dylan's Isle of Wight concert, his tenth studio album, *Self-Portrait*, recorded from April 1969 onwards and released in June 1970, received damning reviews, although the reasons for his recording and releasing the album have remained a matter of some controversy.[48]

A further debilitating factor affecting Dylan as the 1960s ended and the 1970s began was that he appeared to face a predicament, what he himself described as one of 'amnesia', in respect of his own songwriting. It has already been noted that later, in a 1978 interview, Dylan admitted that his 1969 album *Nashville Skyline* represented for him a musical cul-de-sac, one that marked a path that 'just went down, down, down'.[49] In that same interview he had also stated with regard to his songwriting that:

> Right through the time of *Blonde on Blonde* I was doing it unconsciously. Then one day I was half-stepping and the lights went out. And since that point, I more or less had amnesia. Now, you can take that statement as literally or metaphysically as you need to, but that's what happened to me. It took me a long time to get to do consciously what I used to be able to do unconsciously.[50]

As his biographer Clinton Heylin later wrote, Dylan at that time thus 'forgot not only how to write, but who he was'.[51] But in that 1978 interview Dylan added that later:

> I had the good fortune to meet a man in New York City who taught me how to see. He put my mind and my hand and my eye together in a way that allowed me to do consciously what I unconsciously felt. And I didn't know how to pull it off. I wasn't sure it could be done in songs because I'd never written a song like that. But when I started doing it, the first album I made

was *Blood on the Tracks.* Everybody agrees that that was pretty different, and what's different about it is that there's a code in the lyrics and also there's no sense of time. There's no respect for it: you've got yesterday, today and tomorrow in the same room, and there's very little you can't imagine not happening.[52]

In an earlier interview in 1978 Dylan had also stated, in relation to that source of his regeneration as a songwriter, while citing only the first name of the person who had inspired him, that:

A lot of the ideas I have were influenced by an old man who had definite ideas on life and the universe and nature – all that matters…He came to this country in the twenties, started out as a boxer, and ended up painting portraits of women…His first name was Norman. Every time I mention somebody's [full] name, it's like they get a tremendous amount of distraction and irrelevancy in their lives.[53]

The 'man in New York City' was the 73-year-old painter Norman Raeben, with whom Dylan attended painting classes in the summer of 1974.[54] Dylan's great album *Blood on the Tracks*, widely regarded as one of his finest, recorded between September and December of 1974 and released in January 1975, was thus the first artistic product of the songwriting techniques that he had learned to develop under Raeben's influence.

———————

Bob Dylan's performance at the Isle of Wight Festival at the end of August 1969, while judged low-key and anticlimactic by some, had nonetheless been in many ways a musical and commercial success, and one which effectively reaffirmed his artistic autonomy. As Ray Foulk has maintained in retrospect, Dylan:

was an artist who didn't need to look back, he had everything he needed. Unlike one-hit wonders he could afford to change and progress. He was not going to replicate tired song formats, and, as supreme risk-taker, he was not going to be a slave to his back catalogue.[55]

Dylan's performance at the Isle of Wight underlined the fact that those creative patterns would continue to stretch into his future musical development. His continuing influence and popularity in Britain were reflected in the fact that *Melody Maker*, which remained at that time Britain's most substantial popular-music paper, placed him top of its International Pop Poll on September 20, 1969 as leading international male singer.[56] His towering status had been reflected, too, in the presence at the Isle of Wight of many of the luminaries of British rock music at the time.

It has nonetheless been maintained that Dylan's alleged dissatisfaction with his performance at the Isle of Wight Festival, which was consistent, it should be added, with his often critical attitude towards his own studio recordings, before and ever since, was evident specifically in his acquiescence in the shelving of an official Columbia live album of the event,[57] which was only officially released 44 years later on *Bob Dylan: The Bootleg Series Vol. 10: Another Self-Portrait* (2013).[58] For the Foulk brothers, however, it had been 'gratifying' at least that four songs from Dylan's Isle of Wight concert, intended for the planned live album, for which they were paid on a pro rata basis according to the original Grossman contract, were released soon afterwards on the much-reviled original *Self-Portrait* album in June 1970. The tracks in question were: 'She Belongs to Me', 'Like a Rolling Stone', 'The Mighty Quinn (Quinn the Eskimo)', and 'Minstrel Boy'.[59]

At any rate, in spite of differing views of Bob Dylan's performance at the 1969 Isle of Wight Festival of Music and, more broadly, different perceptions of his recent changes of musical style, approach, and direction, his high artistic reputation in Britain at that time had clearly been confirmed by both the unprecedented size and the diverse character of his audience at the event. As the British Sixties came to an end, his dominant influence, too, upon popular music in Britain, even after his absence from its shores for over three years, remained undiminished and unchallenged.

Notes

1 Bob Dylan, *Chronicles Volume One* (London: Simon & Schuster, 2004), p. 122.
2 Ibid., p. 123.
3 Cited in Bob Spitz, *Dylan: A Biography* (New York and London: Norton, 1991), p. 395.
4 John Hughes, *Invisible Now: Bob Dylan in the 1960s* (Farnham: Ashgate, 2013), p. 190.
5 Bob Dylan quoted in Cameron Crowe, liner notes for *Biograph* (Special Rider Music/Columbia Records, 1985).
6 Robert Shelton, *No Direction Home: The Life and Music of Bob Dylan*, rev. and updated edn., ed. Elizabeth Thomson and Patrick Humphries (London: Omnibus, 2011), p. 276.
7 Michael Gray, *Song and Dance Man III: The Art of Bob Dylan* (London: Continuum, 2000), p. 6.
8 Ibid.
9 Cited in Andy Gill, *Bob Dylan: The Stories behind the Songs 1962–1969* (London: Carlton Books, 2011), p. 196.
10 Bob Dylan, interview with Jonathan Cott, *Rolling Stone*, November 16, 1978; reprinted in Jonathan Cott (ed.), *Dylan on Dylan: The Essential Interviews* (London: Hodder & Stoughton, 2006), p. 260. On *Nashville Skyline*, see Gill, op. cit., pp. 195–204; Tim Riley, *Hard Rain: A Dylan Commentary* (New York: Da Capo Press, 1999), pp. 185–190; Nigel Williamson, *The Dead Straight Guide to Bob Dylan* (London: Red Planet, 2015), pp. 189–190; Brian Hinton, *Bob Dylan Album File and Complete Discography* (London: Cassell Illustrated, 2006), pp. 70–75.
11 Graham Nash, *Wild Tales: A Rock & Roll Life* (London: Viking/Penguin, 2014), p. 156. For Bob Dylan's own recollection of that occasion, see Dylan, op. cit., pp. 101–102.
12 Dylan, ibid., p. 122.
13 Riley, op. cit., p. 190.
14 Bob Dylan, interview with Kurt Loder, *Rolling Stone*, June 21, 1984; reprinted in Cott (ed.), op. cit., pp. 300–301.

15 Jonathon Green, *All Dressed Up: The Sixties and the Counterculture* (London: Pimlico, 1999), p. 436.

16 Howard Sounes, *Down the Highway: The Life of Bob Dylan*, rev. and updated edn. (London: Doubleday, 2011), p. 252; 'Wavy Gravy' (Hugh Romney) quoted in ibid.

17 Bob Dylan, interview with Kurt Loder, in Cott (ed.), op. cit., p. 301.

18 Dylan, op. cit., p. 109.

19 Ibid., p. 115.

20 Ibid., p. 120.

21 Ibid., p. 124.

22 Bob Dylan quoted in Crowe, op. cit., p. 16.

23 Hughes, op. cit., p. 48.

24 Riley, op. cit., p. 157.

25 See Ray Foulk with Caroline Foulk, *Stealing Dylan from Woodstock* (Surbiton: Medium Publishing, 2015), p. 136. For a detailed and vivid first-hand account of the 1969 Isle of Wight Festival of Music, see ibid., passim. For another first-hand account, see Shelton op. cit., pp. 276–279. See, too, Clinton Heylin, *Behind the Shades: 20th Anniversary Edition* (London: Faber & Faber, 2011), pp. 306–309. On the 1968, 1969, and 1970 Isle of Wight Festivals of Music, see Green, op. cit., pp. 437–442.

26 Bob Dylan quoted in Shelton, op. cit., p. 277.

27 Foulk, op. cit., p. 207.

28 On The Band's performance, see ibid., pp. 211–215.

29 Sounes, op. cit., p. 255; Stephen Scobie, *Alias Bob Dylan* (Alberta, Canada: Red Deer College Press, 1991), p. 39; Donald Brown, *Bob Dylan: American Troubadour* (Plymouth, UK: Rowman & Littlefield, 2014), p. 89.

30 Bob Dylan, at a television press conference, KQED (San Francisco), December 3, 1965; reprinted in Cott (ed.), op. cit., p. 65. See, too, Ch.5 above, n. 64.

31 Foulk, op. cit., pp. 217, 235–236.

32 On press coverage of the 1969 Isle of Wight Festival, see ibid., pp. 238–244.

33 Cited in Shelton, op. cit., p. 279.

34 George Harrison to the *Daily Express*; cited in Foulk, op. cit., p. 244, and in Shelton, ibid.

35 Eric Clapton, interview with Roger Gibbons for *The Telegraph*, May 1987; reprinted in John Bauldie, *Wanted Man: In Search of Bob Dylan* (London: Black Spring Press, 1990), p. 150.

36 Al Aronowitz, 'The Isle of Wight Papers', first published in *Isis*, 96, May 2001; reprinted in Derek Barker (ed.), *Isis: A Bob Dylan Anthology*, rev. edn. (London: Helter Skelter, 2004), p. 168.

37 See Foulk, op. cit., pp. 143–144. For further confirmation of this point, see, too, Pattie Boyd quoted in Graeme Thomson, *George Harrison: Behind the Locked Door* (London: Omnibus, 2013), p. 200.

38 Foulk, op. cit., p. 144.

39 Thomson, op. cit., p. 160.

40 Foulk, op. cit., p. 143.

41 Al Aronowitz quoted in Foulk, op. cit., pp. 143–144.

42 Bob Dylan quoted in Shelton, op. cit., p. 279.

43 Shelton, ibid.

44 Ibid.

45 For Dylan's own reactions to his performance at the Isle of Wight and to the responses to it, see Foulk, op. cit., pp. 241–242, 248.

46 Bob Dylan, interview with Don Short, *Melody Maker*, August 13, 1969; cited in Foulk, op. cit., p. 253.

47 Shelton, op. cit., p. 279.

48 For a concise summary of interpretations of Dylan's motives in releasing *Self-Portrait*, see Willliamson, op. cit., pp. 93–95, 190–191.

49 See note 10 above.

50 Bob Dylan, interview with Jonathan Cott, in Cott (ed.), op. cit., pp. 259–260.

51 Heylin, op. cit., p. 295.

52 Cott (ed.), op. cit., p. 260.

53 Bob Dylan, interview with Ron Rosenbaum, *Playboy*, March 1978; reprinted in Cott (ed.), op. cit., pp. 221–222.

54 On this point, see Williamson, op. cit., pp. 95–96; Heylin, op. cit., pp. 368–369.

55 Foulk, op. cit., p. 217.

56 Shelton, op. cit., p. 279.

57 See Heylin, op. cit., p. 309.

58 All the songs from Dylan's Isle of Wight live performance were included on disc three of the de luxe edition of *Bob Dylan: The Bootleg Series Vol. 10: Another Self-Portrait* (2013).

59 See Foulk, op. cit., pp. 257, 258.

10
CONCLUSION

Bob Dylan's influence on songwriting in modern British popular music during the 1960s was, as we have seen, profound and far-reaching. The effect of his influence was felt on three main levels: first, in widening the range of subjects and themes that could be addressed in the lyrics of modern popular music; second, in conveying the notion that such lyrics could have something reflective and significant to say about contemporary society, human relationships, or even the existential realities of the human condition; and third, in fostering a more personal and emotionally direct mode of address.

In Britain the influence of Dylan's songwriting was particularly evident during the 1960s in the case of The Beatles, and John Lennon and George Harrison especially. Mark Donnelly has noted that in the early period of The Beatles' musical development before Dylan had exerted his influence, the lyrics of all 49 of their songs copyrighted between 1963 and 1964 were about boy–girl romance.[1] That was indeed also the case with the vast majority of British (and American) pop-music lyrics in the post-1945 era. With regard to The Beatles' later development, in 1970, the year they broke up as a group, in January, the British jazz singer and writer George Melly observed:

> I now suspect it was the influence of Bob Dylan which secured their release from the prison of commercial pop. This is not to diminish the use to which they put their freedom... The Beatles simply followed his example in trusting their own memories and feelings as the source for their music.[2]

Bob Dylan himself, in a 1978 interview, later referred favourably, without in anyway implying his own influence, to the highly personal nature of John Lennon's songwriting when he stated that:

John has taken poetics pretty far in popular music. A lot of his work is overlooked, but if you examine it, you'll find key expressions that have never been said before to push across his point of view. Things that are symbolic of some inner reality and probably will never be said again.[3]

As for George Harrison, the other Beatle most influenced in his songwriting by Dylan, his widow Olivia Harrison later underlined the spiritual and reflective quality of her late husband's songwriting, while acknowledging his lyrical debt to Dylan, when she stated that:

> I believe they stand the test of time because they are written about man's eternal quest, dilemmas, joys and sorrows. George's lyrics were, in my opinion, the most spiritually conscious of our time, although George, in turn, usually referred to the lyrics of Bob Dylan when trying to make a point or elucidate his own feelings of isolation and frustration brought about by things in and beyond this life.[4]

Ian MacDonald, writing 25 years after The Beatles broke up, largely concurred with that judgement when he maintained that: 'Of the songwriting Beatles, Harrison was the one with the most coherent belief system and the one most likely to think his lyrics through.' Moreover, in terms of both the philosophical content of Harrison's songwriting and his wider popular influence, he was also, MacDonald added, 'arguably more responsible than any other individual for popularising oriental, and particularly Hindu, thought in the west'.[5] Referring more broadly to Bob Dylan's overall influence on the songwriting of contemporary popular music, John Peel, the British music broadcaster who had promoted and encouraged much of alternative rock music during the late 1960s and 1970s, simply stated that: 'Dylan was the single most important force in maturing our popular music.'[6]

The impact of Dylan's songwriting during the 1960s even thereby posed a challenge at the time to the dominant influence of leading American songwriters, largely based at the Brill Building in New York City. Gerry Goffin and Carole King, for example, authors of songs of the quality of the Shirelles' 'Will You Still Love Me Tomorrow?', The Drifters' 'Up on the Roof', and many others, were affected and impressed by the nature of Dylan's achievement. As Gerry Goffin later pointed out: 'Dylan managed to do something that not one of us was able to do: put poetry in rock 'n' roll, and just stand up like a mensch and sing it.'[7] Indeed, after hearing Dylan's songs, Goffin became convinced, as Bob Stanley has noted, that 'everything he'd ever written was shallow and worthless', consequently even 'trashing his old tapes and acetates, to the horror of his friends'. Nevertheless, in 'trying to get close to Dylan's muse', Goffin in the process 'wrote "Going Back" for Dusty Springfield and the Byrds "Wasn't Born to Follow", two philosophical songs you could build your life around'.[8]

Goffin's distinguished songwriting partner Carole King later recalled, too, more broadly of that period that:

> There was a cultural phenomenon that had nothing to do with songwriting. So it was: Wait a minute. What's happening, what's going on? Things are changing. How do we write this stuff? How do we fit in?[9]

Bob Dylan's wider influence on British popular music during the 1960s, a central part of that cultural phenomenon, not merely in terms of songwriting, was equal to that of The Beatles and The Rolling Stones. In Dylan's case it was part of what has been noted as a process of Anglo-American cross-fertilisation, of mutual musical influence. That had first developed during his initial, four-week visit to London in the winter of 1962–63 when he had learned from Martin Carthy the melodies of traditional English, Scottish, and Irish folk songs and ballads, and had adapted them to his early topical, 'finger-pointing' songs, his so-called 'protest songs' that appeared on his second and third studio albums, *The Freewheelin' Bob Dylan* and *The Times They Are A-Changin'*. In spite of charges of plagiarism unjustly levelled at him by some folk-music traditionalists and purists, Dylan nonetheless thereby appeared in tune with the adaptive and transformative traditions of troubadours, minstrels, and country blues singers of the past.

During the early to mid-1960s that process of transatlantic cross-fertilisation had continued, with Dylan's musical influence in Britain exerted not only on The Beatles but also on what were to become other leading British rock musicians, such as The Animals, Pete Townshend of The Who, Van Morrison, and others. Dylan in turn, highly impressed by the re-energised rock 'n' roll of The Beatles and The Animals, had from 1965 taken the step of moving towards electric music, labelled to his distaste as 'folk-rock', a fusion of electric, often blues-based, rock 'n' roll music with more poetic, reflective, and significant lyrical themes.

By the second half of the 1960s Dylan's influence on British popular music was further apparent in cover versions of his songs recorded, to his approval, by Manfred Mann and Jimi Hendrix, as well as in the work of contemporary acoustic musicians such as Al Stewart and others, and later in the music of the leading British electric-folk groups Fairport Convention and Steeleye Span. The extent of his influence on popular music during the 1960s, in Britain, the United States, and worldwide, was well understood by Dylan himself when he told his friend Robert Shelton in New York City in early 1971, 18 months after performing at the Isle of Wight in the late summer of 1969:

> Changing the face of pop music is not necessarily changing its metabolism. I didn't change the metabolism; all I did was just open up a whole lot of doors. But, you have to admit, the influence – *my* influence – is there, all over, even in country music. Now you can hear the street sound in pop music almost anywhere. The influence is there.[10]

By the time the British Sixties had run their course, Dylan's longstanding influence on rock musicians in Britain was secured well into the 1970s. Rod Stewart included a sensitive interpretation of 'A Man of Constant Sorrow', recorded on Dylan's first, at the time underrated, eponymous album of 1962, on Stewart's own 1969 debut album *An Old Raincoat Won't Ever Let You Down*. Later Stewart added his own version of Dylan's highly personal and poignant, yet less well known, 'Tomorrow Is a Long Time' on his 1971 album *Every Picture Tells a Story*, as well as his version of 'Girl from the North Country' on *Smiler* (1974).[11]

As a more directly personal tribute, David Bowie on his fourth album, *Hunky Dory* (1971), recorded his 'Song for Bob Dylan', in which he wrote and sang in words evocative of that era:

> I wrote a song for you
> About a strange man called Dylan
> With a voice like sand and glue.
> …Gave your heart to every bedsit room,
> At least a picture on my wall.
> …Now hear this Robert Zimmerman,
> Though I don't suppose we'll meet,
> Ask your friend Dylan
> If he'd gaze a while down the old street.

Those words in some ways conveyed the nature and extent of Dylan's appeal to many young people in Britain during the 1960s, exemplified by the size of his audience at the Isle of Wight in late August 1969. By that time, and in the wake of Dylan's eight studio album released earlier that year, *Nashville Skyline*, Mike Marqusee has maintained, in his predominantly political study of Dylan's work:

> The impetus that had taken him from his first album through to *John Wesley Harding* had come to an end; there would never again be the sense that his albums comprised an unfolding succession of artistic-philosophical visions and revisions. The thread that had bound Dylan to his era and his audience – even when he was castigating both severely – had snapped.[12]

Those successive 'visions and revisions' revealed in Dylan's various stages of musical development throughout the 1960s, in his prolific songwriting, in his studio albums, and in his live concert performances, exerted an appeal to his British audiences during that decade that was more deep-rooted than one that merely sprang from their youthful idealism, their optimistic belief in social and political progress, characteristic as those factors were, in many respects, of the 1960s. Rather, for those idealistic, generally well-educated, and often intellectually or artistically inclined young people in Britain, Dylan's music at that time appealed, too, in Jonathan Gould's words, to 'their maturity, their sensitivity, their morality, and their verbal sophistication'.[13] Such responses were in themselves closely related to the pervasive spirit of individuality and individual freedom, of sceptical release from illusions and self-deception of various kinds, which animated Bob Dylan's music and lyrics, as well as the mood and attitude underlying them. For all, then, the ambiguities, inconsistencies, fantasies, and pretensions of that decade, those individualistic qualities, inherent in Dylan's music, were also, in many ways, distinctive features of the transient yet memorable British Sixties.

Notes

1 Mark Donnelly, *Sixties Britain: Culture, Society and Politics* (Harlow: Pearson Longman, 2005), p. 45. I would add a possible qualification to that statement by citing the example of John Lennon's highly introspective early song 'There's a Place' on The Beatles' first studio album, *Please Please Me* (1963). On this point, see above Ch. 5. John Robertson in 1994 described 'There's a Place', recorded in February 1963, as Lennon's 'first piece of self-analysis', and added the interesting if questionable comment that: 'No one – not even Bob Dylan – was writing songs like that in 1963.' See John Robertson, *The Complete Guide to the Music of the Beatles* (London: Omnibus, 1994, p. 7. Some 17 years later Lennon himself, in his last major interview before his death, merely stated that 'There's a Place' 'was my attempt at a sort of Motown, black thing. It says the usual Lennon things. "In my mind there's no sorrow." It's all in your mind.' John Lennon quoted in David Sheff, *Last Interview: All We Are Saying. John Lennon and Yoko Ono* (London: Pan Books, 2001), p. 193.

2 George Melly, *Revolt into Style: The Pop Arts* (Oxford: Oxford University Press, 1989 [first published 1970]), p. 85.

3 Bob Dylan, interview with Ron Rosenbaum, *Playboy*, March 1978; republished in Jonathan Cott (ed.), *Dylan on Dylan: The Essential Interviews* (London: Hodder & Stoughton, 2006), p. 213.

4 Olivia Harrison, introduction to republished edn. of George Harrison, *I Me Mine* (London: Weidenfeld & Nicolson, 2002), p. 3.

5 Ian MacDonald, *Revolution in the Head: The Beatles' Records and the Sixties* (London: Pimlico, 1995), p. xiii.

6 Cited in Derek Barker (ed.), *Isis: A Bob Dylan Anthology*, rev. edn. (London: Helter Skelter, 2004), p. 334.

7 Gerry Goffin, speaking in 2001, cited in Greil Marcus, *Like a Rolling Stone: Bob Dylan at the Crossroads* (London: Faber & Faber, 2005), p. 138.

8 Bob Stanley, *Yeah Yeah Yeah: The Story of Modern Pop* (London: Faber & Faber, 2014), pp. 166, 172–173.

9 Carole King, speaking in 2001, cited in Marcus, op. cit., p. 138.

10 Bob Dylan in conversation with Robert Shelton at the Henry Hudson Hotel in Manhattan, New York City, early 1971; quoted in Robert Shelton, *No Direction Home: The Life and Music of Bob Dylan*, rev. and updated edn., ed. Elizabeth Thomson and Patrick Humphries (London: Omnibus, 2011), p. 20.

11 On Rod Stewart's admiration for Bob Dylan, see Roy Coleman, *Rod Stewart: The Biography* (London: Pavilion Books, 1994), pp. 66, 97–98, 146, 208, 221.

12 Mike Marqusee, *Chimes of Freedom: The Politics of Bob Dylan's Art* (New York and London: The New Press, 2003), p. 270.

13 Jonathan Gould, *Can't Buy Me Love: The Beatles, Britain and America* (London: Portrait, 2007), p. 253. See above Ch. 7.

BIBLIOGRAPHY

Primary sources

Joan Baez, *And a Voice to Sing With: A Memoir* (London: Century, 1988)

Joe Boyd, *White Bicycles: Making Music in the 1960s* (London: Serpents Tail, 2006)

Ray Davies, *X-Ray* (London: Penguin, 1995)

Bob Dylan, *Chronicles Volume One* (London: Simon & Schuster, 2004)

Marianne Faithfull with David Dalton, *Faithfull* (London: Michael Joseph, 1994)

Ray Foulk with Caroline Foulk, *Stealing Dylan from Woodstock* (Surbiton: Medium Publishing, 2015)

George Harrison, with introduction by Olivia Harrison, *I Me Mine* (London: Weidenfeld & Nicolson, 2002)

Levon Helm with Stephen Davis, *This Wheel's on Fire: Levon Helm and the Story of the Band* (London: Plexus, 1994)

Mick Jagger, Keith Richards, Charlie Watts, and Ronnie Wood, *According to the Rolling Stones* (San Francisco, CA: Chronicle Books, 2003)

Roy Jenkins, *The Labour Case* (London: Penguin, 1959)

Donovan Leitch, *The Hurdy Gurdy Man* (London: Random House, 2005)

Ewan MacColl, *Journeyman: An Autobiography*, re-ed. with an introduction by Peggy Seeger (Manchester: Manchester University Press, 2009)

Chas McDevitt, *Skiffle: The Definitive Inside Story* (London: Robson Books, 1997)

Melody Maker, London, 1966–1969

Graham Nash, *Wild Tales: A Rock & Roll Life* (London: Viking/Penguin, 2013)

Keith Richards with James Fox, *Life* (London: Weidenfeld & Nicolson, 2010)

Robbie Robertson, *Testimony* (London: William Heinemann, 2016)

Suze Rotolo, *A Freewheelin' Time: A Memoir of Greenwich Village in the Sixties* (London: Aurum Press, 2009)

Pete Townshend, *Who I Am* (London: HarperCollins, 2012)

Dave Van Ronk with Elijah Wald, *The Mayor of MacDougal Street* (Cambridge, MA: Da Capo Press, 2005)

Bill Wyman with Ray Coleman, *Stone Alone: The Story of a Rock 'n' Roll Band* (London: Viking, 1990)

Secondary sources

Derek Barker (ed.), *Isis: A Bob Dylan Anthology*, rev. edn. (London: Helter Skelter, 2004)

Richard Barnes, *The Who: Maximum R&B* (London: Plexus, 1982)

Keith Batman, *The Beatles off the Record* (London: Omnibus, 2000)

John Bauldie, *Wanted Man: In Search of Bob Dylan* (London: Black Spring Press, 1990)

J.P. Bean, *Singing from the Floor: A History of British Folk Clubs* (London: Faber & Faber, 2014)

Carl Benson (ed.), *The Bob Dylan Companion: Four Decades of Commentary* (New York: Schirmer Books, 1998)

Mark Blake (ed.), *Dylan: Visions, Portraits and Back Pages* (London: DK/Mojo, 2005)

David Boucher and Gary Browning (eds.), *The Political Art of Bob Dylan*, 2nd edn. (Exeter: Imprint Academic, 2009)

Georgina Boyes, *The Imagined Village: Culture, Ideology and the English Folk Festival* (Manchester: Manchester University Press, 1993)

Michael Brocken, *The British Folk Revival 1944–2002* (Aldershot: Ashgate, 2003)

Donald Brown, *Bob Dylan: American Troubadour* (Plymouth, UK: Rowman and Littlefield, 2014)

Paul Cable, 'A Savage Gift on a Wayward Bus: The Influence of Bob Dylan on Popular Music', in Elizabeth M. Thomson (ed.), *Conclusions on the Wall: New Essays on Bob Dylan* (Manchester: Thin Man, 1980)

John Campbell, *Roy Jenkins: A Well-Rounded Life* (London: Jonathan Cape, 2014)

Robert Cantwell, *When We Were Good: The Folk Revival* (Cambridge, MA: Harvard University Press, 1996)

Ronald D. Cohen, *Folk Music: The Basics* (London: Routledge, 2006)

Ray Coleman, *Lennon: The Definitive Biography* (London: Pan Books, 2000)

Ray Coleman, *McCartney: Yesterday and Today* (London: Boxtree, 1995)

Ray Coleman, *Rod Stewart: The Biography* (London: Pavilion Books, 1994)

Andrea Cossu, *It Ain't Me Babe: Bob Dylan and the Performance of Authenticity* (Boulder, CO: Paradigm Publishers, 2012)

Jonathan Cott (ed.), *Dylan on Dylan: The Essential Interviews* (London: Hodder & Stoughton, 2006)

Cameron Crowe, liner notes for *Biograph* (Special Rider Music/Columbia Records, 1985)

David Dalton, *Who Is That Man? In Search of the Real Bob Dylan* (London: Omnibus, 2012)

Anthony De Curtis and James Henke (eds.), *The Rolling Stone Illustrated History of Rock and Roll* (London: Plexus, 1992)

Robin Denselow, *When the Music's Over: The Story of Political Pop* (London: Faber & Faber, 1989)

Gerard DeGroot, *The 60s Unplugged: A Kaleidoscopic History of a Disorderly Decade* (Basingstoke: Palgrave Macmillan, 2014)

Kevin J.H. Dettmar (ed.), *The Cambridge Companion to Bob Dylan* (Cambridge: Cambridge University Press, 2009)

Jenny Diski, *The Sixties* (London: Profile Books, 2009)

Peter Doggett, *Are You Ready for the Country? Elvis, Dylan, Parsons and the Roots of Country Rock* (London: Viking, 2000)

Mark Donnelly, *Sixties Britain: Culture, Society and Politics* (Harlow: Pearson Longman, 2005)

Paul Du Noyer, *In the City: A Celebration of London Music* (London: Virgin Books, 2009)

Sean Egan, *Animal Tracks: The Story of the Animals: Newcastle's Rising Suns* (London: Helter Skelter, 2001)

Sean Egan (ed.), *Keith Richards on Keith Richards: Interviews and Encounters* (London: Omnibus, 2013)

Sean Egan (ed.), *The Mammoth Book of Bob Dylan* (London: Constable & Robinson, 2011)

Daniel Mark Epstein, *The Ballad of Bob Dylan: A Portrait* (London: Souvenir Press, 2011)

Anthony Farrell, Vivienne Guiness, and Julian Lloyd (eds.), *Rock 'n' Roll Remembered: An Imperfect History* (Dublin: The Lilliput Press, 1996)

Bill Flanagan, *Written in My Soul: Candid Interviews with Rock's Great Songwriters* (London: Omnibus, 1990)

Simon Frith and Howard Horne, *Art into Pop* (London: Methuen, 1987)

Andy Gill, *Bob Dylan: The Stories behind the Songs 1962–1969* (London: Carlton, 2011)

Charlie Gillett, *The Sound of the City*, rev. edn. (London: Souvenir, 1983)

Jonathan Gould, *Can't Buy Me Love: The Beatles, Britain and America* (London: Portrait, 2007)

Michael Gray, *The Bob Dylan Encyclopedia* (London: Continuum, 2006)

Michael Gray, *Song and Dance Man III: The Art of Bob Dylan* (London: Continuum, 2000)

Jonathon Green, *All Dressed Up: The Sixties and the Counterculture* (London: Pimlico, 1999)

David Hajdu, *Positively Fourth Street: The Lives and Times of Bob Dylan, Joan Baez, Mimi Baez Farina and Richard Farina* (London: Bloomsbury, 2001)

Colin Harper, *Dazzling Stranger: Bert Jansch and the British Folk and Blues Revival* (London: Bloomsbury, 2000)

Trevor Harris and Monica O'Brien Castro (eds.), *Preserving the Sixties: Britain and the 'Decade of Protest'* (Basingstoke: Palgrave Macmillan, 2014)

Nick Hasted, *The Story of the Kinks: You Really Got Me*, rev. edn. (London: Omnibus, 2013)

Clinton Heylin, *Behind the Shades: The 20th Anniversary Edition* (London: Faber & Faber, 2011)

Clinton Heylin, *Can You Feel the Silence? Van Morrison: A New Biography* (London: Viking, 2002)

Clinton Heylin, *Revolution in the Air: The Songs of Bob Dylan Vol. I 1957–73* (London: Constable, 2009)

Brian Hinton, *Bob Dylan: Album File and Complete Discography* (London: Cassell Illustrated, 2006)

Brian Hinton and Geoff Wall, *Ashley Hutchings: The Guvnor and the Rise of Folk-Rock* (London: Helter Skelter, 2002)

John Hughes, *Invisible Now: Bob Dylan in the 1960s* (Farnham: Ashgate, 2013)

Patrick Humphries, *Meet on the Ledge. Fairport Convention: The Classic Years* (London: Virgin Books, 1997)

Ian Inglis (ed.), *Performance and Popular Music: History, Place and Time* (Aldershot: Ashgate, 2006)

Ian Inglis, 'Synergies and Reciprocities: The Dynamics of Musical and Professional Interaction between the Beatles and Bob Dylan', *Popular Music and Society*, 20 (4), 1996

Colin Irwin, *Bob Dylan: Highway 61 Revisited* (London: Flame Tree Publishing, 2008)

Neville Judd, *Al Stewart: The True Life Adventures of a Folk Troubadour* (London: Helter Skelter, 2005)

C.P. Lee, *Like the Night: Bob Dylan and the Road to the Manchester Free Trade Hall* (London: Helter Skelter, 1998)

Ian MacDonald, *The People's Music* (London: Pimlico, 2003)

Ian MacDonald, *Revolution in the Head: The Beatles' Records and the Sixties* (London: Pimlico, 1995)

Greil Marcus, *Invisible Republic: Bob Dylan's Basement Tapes* (London: Picador, 1997)

Greil Marcus, *Like a Rolling Stone: Bob Dylan at the Crossroads* (London: Faber & Faber, 2005)

Mike Marqusee, *Chimes of Freedom: The Politics of Bob Dylan's Art* (New York and London: The New Press, 2003)

Lee Marshall, 'Bob Dylan: Newport Folk Festival, July 25, 1965', in Ian Inglis (ed.), *Performance and Popular Music: History, Place and Time* (Aldershot: Ashgate, 2006)

Lee Marshall, *The Never Ending Star* (Cambridge: Polity, 2007)

Arthur Marwick, *Culture in Britain since 1945* (Oxford: Basil Blackwell, 1991)

Arthur Marwick, *The Sixties: Cultural Revolution in Britain, France, Italy and the United States, c.1958–c.1974* (Oxford: Oxford University Press, 1998)

George Melly, *Revolt into Style: The Pop Arts* (Oxford: Oxford University Press, 1989) [first published 1970]

Barry Miles, *London Calling: A Countercultural History of London since 1945* (London: Atlantic Books, 2011)

Barry Miles, *Paul McCartney: Many Years from Now* (London: Secker & Warburg, 1997)

Keith Negus, *Bob Dylan* (London: Equinox, 2008)

Philip Norman, *Lennon: The Life* (New York: Ecco, 2009)

Philip Norman, *Mick Jagger* (London: Harper Collins, 2013)

Philip Norman, *Shout! The True Story of the Beatles*, rev. and updated edn. (London: Sidgwick & Jackson, 2003)

Philip Norman, *The Stones*, updated edn. (London: Sidgwick & Jackson, 2001)

John Platt, *London's Rock Routes* (London: Fourth Estate, 1985)

Tim Riley, *Hard Rain: A Dylan Commentary* (New York: Da Capo Press, 1999)

John Robertson, *The Complete Guide to the Music of the Beatles* (London: Omnibus, 1994)

Theodore Roszack, *The Making of a Counter-Culture: Reflections on the Technocratic Society and Its Youthful Opposition* (New York: Doubleday, 1969)

Dominic Sandbrook, *White Heat: A History of Britain in the Swinging Sixties* (London: Little, Brown, 2006)

Jon Savage, *1966: The Year the Decade Exploded* (London: Faber & Faber, 2015)

Anthony Scaduto, *Bob Dylan* (London: Helter Skelter, 2001) [first published 1971]

Michael Schumacher, *Eric Clapton* (London: Sphere, 2008)

Stephen Scobie, *Alias Bob Dylan* (Alberta, Canada: Red Deer College Press, 1991)

Harry Shapiro, *Alexis Korner: The Biography* (London: Bloomsbury, 1996)

David Sheff, *Last Interview: All We Are Saying. John Lennon and Yoko Ono* (London: Pan Books, 2001)

Robert Shelton, *No Direction Home: The Life and Music of Bob Dylan*, rev. and updated edn., ed. Elizabeth Thomson and Patrick Humphries (London: Omnibus, 2011)

Howard Sounes, *Down the Highway: The Life of Bob Dylan*, rev. and updated edn. (London: Doubleday, 2011)

Bob Spitz, *Dylan: A Biography* (New York and London: W.W. Norton & Co., 1991)

Bob Stanley, *Yeah Yeah Yeah: The Story of Modern Pop* (London: Faber & Faber, 2014)

Derek Taylor, *It Was Twenty Years Ago Today* (London: Bantam Press, 1987)

Gordon Thompson, *Please Please Me: Sixties British Pop, Inside Out* (Oxford: Oxford University Press, 2008)

Elizabeth M. Thomson (ed.), *Conclusions on the Wall: New Essays on Bob Dylan* (Manchester: Thin Man, 1980)

Elizabeth Thomson and David Gutman (eds.), *The Dylan Companion* (London: Macmillan, 1990)

Graeme Thomson, *George Harrison: Behind the Locked Door* (London: Omnibus, 2013)

Elijah Wald, *Dylan Goes Electric: Newport, Seeger, Dylan and the Night That Split the Sixties* (New York: Harper Collins, 2015)

Dick Weissman, *The Blues: The Basics* (New York and London: Routledge, 2005)

Paul Williams, *Bob Dylan Performing Artist 1960–1973: The Early Years* (London: Omnibus, 2004) [first published 1990]

Sean Wilentz, *Bob Dylan in American* (London: Vintage, 2011)

Nigel Williamson, *The Dead Straight Guide to Bob Dylan* (London: Red Planet, 2015)

INDEX

Procol Harum 121
'Prodigal Son' 120
production 119
protest songs 19, 57, 137, 146; 1964 in
    London 40–1, 43–4, 46–7; 1966 tour
    106, 109; going electric 72–4
psychedelia 115–16, 119–20, 134
'Purple Haze' 123

The Quarrymen 26
'Quinn the Eskimo' 115, 136, 141

R&B *see* rhythm and blues
radio 32
Radio Caroline 32
Radio One 32, 104
Raeben, Norman 140
Ready Steady Go! 31, 60, 80
Redding, Noel 123
Rediffusion 31
Redlands 124, 127
Rees-Mogg, William 124–5
Reid, Keith 121
relationships 46, 51, 82
Relf, Keith 26, 29
'Restless Farewell' 44
revivalists 13–14
Revolver (Beatles) 94, 98, 106
rhythm and blues 25–9, 33–4, 97, 110; 1964
    in London 48–9; 1965 tour 55–6, 65,
    see also blues
Richards, Keith 26, 29, 79, 136; 1965–66
    revisited 94, 97–8; roots turns 55–6,
    119–20; trial 123–6
Richmond 97
Riley, Tim 61, 111, 116, 118, 133
'Rising Sun Blues' 34
Ritchie, Jean 16
Robertson, Robbie 89–90, 101–5, 107–8,
    114–15, 118
rock 5, 68, 71, 74–5, 81–3, 118; 1965 tour
    62–4; 1965–66 revisited 87, 94, 97;
    transatlantic influences 27–9, *see also*
    folk-rock
'Rock Island Line' 25
'Rock and Roll Music' 52
rock'n'roll 15, 57, 82, 110; 1964 in
    London 49, 52; transatlantic influences
    24–8, 30, 33
Rolling Stone magazine 132
The Rolling Stones 48, 79, 131, 146; 1965
    Dylan tour 60, 62; 1965–66 revisited
    93–4, 96–7; 1966 Dylan tour 107, 110;
    Isle of Wight 136–7; roots turns 55–6,

118–20; transatlantic influences 25–6,
    28–9, 31–3; trial 123–7
romance 47, 51, 57, 144, *see also* love songs
Rome 18
Romney, Hugh 133
roots 56, 75, 115, 118–19, 137
Roszack, Theodore 92
Rothschild, Paul 71
Rotolo, Suze 9–10, 15, 43–4
Roundhouse 26, 45
Royal Albert Hall 11, 59–61, 64, 91, 105–10
Royal Festival Hall 19, 36, 45
Royal Shakespeare Company 11
Rubber Soul (Beatles) 36, 78, 82–3, 91, 94

'Sad-Eyed Lady of the Lowlands' 97
San Francisco 63, 73, 75
Sandbrook, Dominic 29, 31, 33, 93–4
Sandison, David 103
Sartre, Jean-Paul 58, 76
Savage, Jon 7, 94–5, 97
Saville, Philip 9, 11
Savoy Hotel 56, 60–2
Scaduto, Anthony 46–7, 70, 74, 82, 111
'Scarborough Fair' 16, 18, 43
Scobie, Stephen 136
Scorsese, Martin 57
Scotch of St James' Club 107
Scotland 104
Scottish music 16, 40–1
The Searchers 27
'Searchin' 27
'See Emily Play' 121
Seeger, Charlie 17
Seeger, Peggy 12, 15
Seeger, Pete 11, 13–14, 18, 41, 57
Self-Portrait 139, 141
Sergeant Pepper's Lonely Hearts Club Band
    (Beatles) 94, 118–19
Shaftel, Ann 121
'Shapes of Things' 97
Shapiro, Harry 29
'She Belongs to Me' 57, 141
'She Loves You' 23
Sheff, David 50
Sheffield 103
Shelton, Robert 131, 146; 1962–63 winter
    9–10, 12, 17; 1965 Dylan tour 56, 58;
    1965–66 revisited 88, 91, 94; 1966 Dylan
    tour 102–3, 111; going electric 70, 74,
    81–2; Isle of Wight 138–9
The Shirelles 27, 145
Short, Don 138
Shuel, Brian 12